Migration, Displacement and Identity in Post-Soviet Russia

Upon the collapse of the Soviet Union, around 25 million ethnic Russians found themselves politically and culturally displaced, forming a new 'Russian minority' in each of the newly independent states. Since then, around 3 million Russians have either chosen or been forced to return to Russia. The process of 'going home' has been far from smooth for returnees and receiving population alike.

Using completely new empirical data drawn from in-depth interviews with almost 200 forced migrants and refugees, Hilary Pilkington's extensively researched study explores the experience of reintegration from the perspective of those displaced. She asks how the experience of these self-confessed 'other' Russians informs an understanding of contemporary Russian society and, in particular, the problematic reconstruction of a post-Soviet *Russian* identity. The study also places the experience of Russian returnees in the context of the wider political significance of the Russian 'diaspora' question. In so doing it develops a critical appraisal of current Russian Federation and regional migration policy.

Hilary Pilkington's book employs the example of post-Soviet Russia to illuminate wider debates surrounding migration, displacement and identity of significance to the global community.

Hilary Pilkington is Senior Lecturer, Centre for Russian and East European Studies at the University of Birmingham.

For Tony
and our daughter Eleanor

Migration, Displacement and Identity in Post-Soviet Russia

Hilary Pilkington

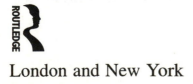

London and New York

JV
8190
.P55
1998

First published 1998
by Routledge
11 New Fetter Lane, London EC4P 4EE

Simultaneously published in the USA and Canada
by Routledge
29 West 35th Street, New York, NY 10001

Typeset in Times by Keystroke, Jacaranda Lodge, Wolverhampton
Printed and bound in Great Britain by Creative Print and Design
(Wales), Ebbw Vale

British Library Cataloguing in Publication Data
A catalogue record for this book is available from the British Library

Library of Congress Cataloging in Publication Data
Pilkington, Hilary.
    Migration, displacement and identity in post-Soviet Russia /
Hilary Pilkington.
    Includes bibliographical references and index.
    1. Russia (Federation) – Emigration and immigration. 2. Russians – Former
Soviet republics – Migrations. 3. Russia (Federation) – Emigration and
immigration – Government policy. 4. Former Soviet republics – Ethnic relations.
I. Title.
JV8190.P55   1998
304.8′347 – dc21   97–20608

ISBN 0–415–15824–9 (hbk)
ISBN 0–415–15825–7 (pbk)

Contents

Part I Policy and practice: The formation of the Russian migration regime

Part II Going home? Social and cultural adaptation of refugees and forced migrants

Figures

Tables

Acknowledgements

The research for this book was funded by the Economic and Social Research Council under the Research Grant scheme (Award R000221306 'Going Home: A socio-cultural study of Russian-speaking forced migrants', June 1994–August 1995) and would have been impossible without its financial support. I am grateful also to my colleagues at the Centre for Russian and East European Studies at the University of Birmingham for their support especially in covering teaching and administrative work during the period of fieldwork in Russia. Thanks, in particular, go to Mike Berry for alerting me to relevant Russian-language literature and to Marea Arries and Tricia Carr for their technical assistance.

This research was highly exploratory and marked a new direction in my work, so I am particularly grateful for the comments of colleagues which I have received. Papers based on the research findings were presented at the Fifth World Congress for Central and East European Studies, Warsaw, 1995, the BASEES Annual Conference, Fitzwilliam College, Cambridge, 30 March–2 April 1996, the ERCOMER Conference, Utrecht, 18–20 April 1996 and the 'Displacement, Migration and Ethnic Relations in Countries of the Former Soviet Union' Conference at the Berlin Institute of Comparative Sociological Research, 4 December 1995 as well as at the universities of Odense, Göteborg, Essex and Birmingham. I would like to thank the organizers of and participants in these conferences and seminars, in particular John Russell and Kees Groenendijk, for their extremely helpful comments and suggestions and Helma Lutz, Khalid Koser and Mary Buckley for their helpful editorial suggestions on related publications. Annie Phizacklea, Effie Voutira, Thomas Schwarz and Christiano Codagnone have fuelled my imagination with their shared thoughts and have encouraged me to believe that the Russian experience can be studied in a way which speaks to migration studies more widely.

The fieldwork for this research was carried out in some of the most difficult circumstances I have encountered in Russia – materially, professionally and administratively. Its successful completion would not have been possible without the knowledge, skill, support and endurance of Elena Omel'chenko, Guzel' Sabirova and Ul'iana Bliudina in Ul'ianovsk, and of Natal'ia Kosmarskaia and Tat'iana Sheikina in Orel. My deepest thanks to them and to the team of sociologists at the Centre 'Region' at Ul'ianovsk State University for their invaluable contribution to the project. In Moscow Vladimir Mukomel' and Lidiia Grafova gave me invaluable insights into the complexities of working to improve the understanding of migrant issues and I thank them for sharing information and opinions with me. I am indebted also to Nikolai Semenovich, the director of the farm in Orel region where I conducted most of the interviewing, who sadly died earlier this year. The fieldwork itself would not have been possible without the selfless help and interest shown by a number of families in Orel region and Ul'ianovsk whose assistance made the work run more smoothly than I could have anticipated and whose kindness, hospitality, support and friendship will remain the strongest memories of those months. In particular my deepest thanks to Valentina Leonidovna and Gennadii Ivanovich, Arta and Kostya, Svetlana Grigor'evna, Aleksandr Nikolaevich and Natasha, Faina and Rafael and Boris Petrovich.

Finally, my thanks to my family who continue to tolerate my absences and to my friends in Russia without whom I might lose the will to see all that is positive in contemporary Russian life.

Hilary Pilkington
Birmingham, July 1997

Note on transliteration

Works cited in the text in Russian are transliterated according to the Library of Congress system except where names of individuals or places have become widely known in a different form (e.g. Yeltsin). Bibliographical references to works in English by Russian authors are cited in the form in which they have been published and where these publications are referred to in the text, that form is used.

Part I

Policy and practice: The formation of the Russian migration regime

1 Did they jump or were they pushed?

Empirical and conceptual issues in post-Soviet migration

This book does not provide a history of migration studies in the former Soviet Union[1] or an exhaustive account of current migrational movements in the former Soviet space.[2] It focuses on a particular social phenomenon: the movement of the Russian-speaking populations[3] in the former republics of the Soviet Union to the Russian Federation during and following the collapse of the USSR. It charts the experience of those displaced by this political upheaval and asks how that experience informs an understanding of the relationship between migration, displacement and identity in post-Soviet Russia. By way of introduction, this chapter outlines the empirical and theoretical obstacles which must be negotiated in order to address this question. It argues that traditional divisions between macro- and micro-level studies and existing categories of migration studies, based on a differentiation between economic (voluntary) and political (involuntary) migrants, may have to be unfixed in order to conceptualize successfully current migrational flows in the former Soviet space.

NUMBERS AND NAMES: MEASURING MIGRATIONAL FLOWS IN THE FORMER SOVIET UNION

By 1992, the world counted 17 million officially registered refugees and asylum-seekers, 4 million people in 'refugee-like situations', and an estimated 23 million people 'internally displaced' (Overbeek 1995: 17). By the beginning of the 1990s, in the public mind 'international migration' was no longer associated – as it had been in the 1960s and 1970s – with primary and, subsequently, secondary labour migration but had become synonymous with the term 'refugee crisis' (Salt 1989: 432). In a world already deeply troubled by mass population movements, the collapse of the Soviet Union was, without doubt, unwelcome; it created a host of new international borders and potential refugees to cross them. Moreover, the collapse of the Soviet Union did not solve ethnic conflict in the region or the flight across borders which it had provoked. The process of decolonization and nation-state building in the newly independent states only encouraged further population displacement in the region. Consequently, in the last decade the former Soviet Union has been transformed from a country whose population was surprisingly reluctant to migrate, especially over long distances, into a region whose very stability is threatened, according to the United Nations High Commissioner for Refugees (UNHCR), by current migration trends.[4]

In these migrational flows, it is Russia which has proved the net recipient; since 1993 Russia has had a positive migrational exchange with all of the former Soviet republics. Table 1.1 indicates net migration rates between Russia and the former Soviet republics in 1994.[5] Using official data broken down by nationality on the numbers entering and leaving Russia from each of the former Soviet republics, this table illustrates three important trends. First, the positive total balances ('all nationalities') show that Russia today is a recipient, not a donor nation, in terms of migration within the post-Soviet space. Second, the data show that, with the exception of the war-torn Transcaucasian states, it is ethnic Russians[6] who make up the majority of the net in-migration, ranging from 85 per cent from Belarus to 62 per cent from Tajikistan. Finally, the data show that many non-Russians choose to migrate to Russia, including, in the case of the Transcaucasian states and

Table 1.1 Net migration between the Russian Federation and the former Soviet republics, 1994

Country	Russians	All nationalities	Titular nationality
Azerbaijan	18,982	43,371	9,685
Armenia	4,555	44,574	36,542
Belarus	13,274	15,632	–40
Estonia	8,223	10,192	104
Georgia	24,224	62,176	11,792
Kazakstan	234,323	304,499	703
Kyrgyzstan	42,901	56,542	–3
Latvia	19,340	25,031	328
Lithuania	5,389	6,931	332
Moldova	7,553	11,978	4,866
Tajikistan	25,841	41,969	2,057
Turkmenistan	13,036	17,369	417
Uzbekistan	93,481	135,352	3,783
Ukraine	101,256	138,981	27,576
Total	612,378	914,597	–

Source: Goskomstat 1995: 424–7

Ukraine, large numbers of the former republics' titular nationalities;[7] 82 per cent of net in-migration from Armenia consisted of ethnic Armenians, for example.

Given the concern in government circles about the prospects for future natural population growth in Russia – due to rising mortality but falling birth rates – one might expect a favourable response to what are quantitatively moderate rises in in-migration. Indeed, as Figure 1.1 shows, total in-migration from republics of the former Soviet Union has fallen for two years in succession and the figure for 1996 – 700,000 – is actually less than the in-migration to Russia in 1980 (876,000) (Goskomstat 1995: 400). However, it is not the annual in-migration figures which concern the Russian authorities so much as the manner in which these people arrive – since they have significant social welfare needs – and, above all, the ethnic character of the migration which indicates a potential for mass inward flows in the future. There were 25.3 million ethnic Russians living in Soviet republics other than the Russian Federation according to the last Soviet census of 1989. In addition there were approximately 11 million members of other ethnic groups living outside their titular republic whose primary cultural affinity is to Russia and who are often subsumed into the 'Russian' diaspora as 'russophones' or the 'Russian-speaking' population and considered potential returnees to Russia.

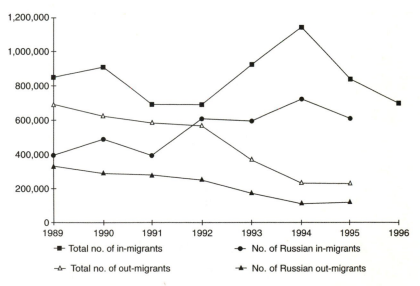

Figure 1.1 In-migration to and out-migration from the Russian Federation from and to the former Soviet republics, 1989–96
Source: Goskomstat 1995: 422–3

Since July 1992, the Federal Migration Service of the Russian Federation has been monitoring migrational flows from the former republics and registering those arrivees who were forced to leave their former place of residence as a result of persecution. Of the 3 million people having moved from the former republics to Russia since then, just over a million have been registered as forced migrants or refugees.[8] Figure 1.2 shows the number of forced migrants and refugees registered annually since data collection began. These figures represent registered forced migrants and refugees only and, although the procedures for gathering data have been significantly improved since 1992, none the less there are considerable problems in using these data as a reliable indicator of total numbers of 'involuntary' migrants from the former republics.[9] The most recent problem is that of the peculiar status being given to those displaced as a result of military conflict in Chechnia. Although currrent Russian legislation does provide for the granting of 'forced migrant' status to those displaced within the Russian Federation (see Chapter 2), the authorities have been increasingly reluctant to register those fleeing Chechnia as refugees or forced migrants. The Russian Federal Migration Service registered a total of 117,000 refugees or forced migrants from Chechnia in the period 1992–5 (Codagnone forthcoming). Thus it is estimated that less than 9 per cent of those who fled Chechnia after December 1994 obtained such status and that there are currently almost 500,000 displaced people from this region who have not been registered and granted appropriate status in the normal way (Mukomel 1996: 143).

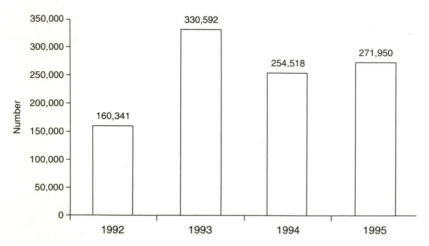

Figure 1.2 Number of refugees and forced migrants registered by the Federal Migration Service, 1992–5
Source: Federal Migration Service data cited in Codagnone (forthcoming)

From these data, the Federal Migration Service seeks above all to determine the size and direction of future migrational flows. Figure 1.3 shows the change in the region of origin of refugees and forced migrants over time. It clearly indicates the replacement of the Transcaucasian[10] states by Central Asia[11] and Kazakstan as chief sources of out-migration from 1994. Of course, these data require contextualization. The fact that half a million Russians have left Kazakstan since 1990, for example, does not necessarily indicate a mass exodus; it actually constitutes only 8 per cent of the Russian population in Kazakstan (which numbered over 6 million in 1989) (Codagnone forthcoming). On the other hand, the very size of the Russian population suggests that there is potential for even greater numbers to return to Russia in the future. Russian government estimates are that a further 2 million to 5 million forced migrants will move to Russia from the former republics over the next ten years (Dmitriev 1995b; Lemon 1995a).[12] Figure 1.4 shows the percentage of the Russian populations in the former republics having out-migrated in the period 1990–4 and indicates that it is in only a few former republics – specifically Tajikistan and the three Transcaucasian republics – that the movement of the mobile Russian population is almost exhausted. Indeed, the Federal Migration Service has already recorded a rise in the number of forced migrants and refugees registered in 1995 over 1994 ('Migratsionnii prirost uvelichilsia pochti v dva raza' 1995; Dmitriev 1995b), even without including those displaced following the military intervention in Chechnia. The source of this increase is equally clear: 73 per cent of refugees and forced migrants registered in 1995 arrived from Central Asia and Kazakstan.[13]

Predictions regarding the region of origin of future returnees suggest the largest inflow will continue to come from the states of Central Asia and Kazakstan. The head of the Federal Migration Service, Tat'iana Regent, has estimated that Russia will receive 3 million returnees from that region alone (Slater 1994: 41) while academic analyses suggest that 30–50 per cent of the Russian-speaking population from the region will migrate (Levanov 1993: 26).[14] However, estimates of the number of Russians likely to leave other areas are being revised down. Regent's prediction in 1993 that 500,000 would return from the Baltic states[15] now appears high. The Russian Ministry of Labour currently expects no more than 300,000; a figure in agreement with Levanov's estimate of 18–20 per cent of the Russian-speaking population in the Baltic states (Levanov 1993: 36). The migration of Russians from those former republics which are culturally close to Russia – Belarus and Ukraine – appears more likely to take the form of labour migration than permanent out-migration in the majority of cases. This is supported by the data in Table 1.1 and Figures 1.3 and 1.4;

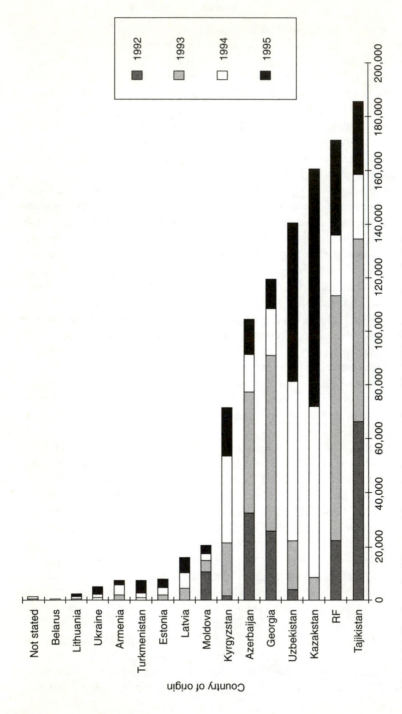

Figure 1.3 Number of refugees and forced migrants registered in 1992–5, by region of origin
Source: Federal Migration Service data cited in Codagnone (forthcoming)

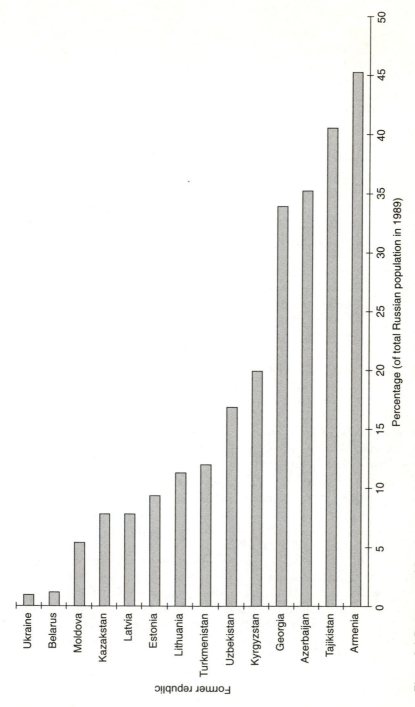

Figure 1.4 Percentage of Russian populations in the former republics having out-migrated, 1990–4
Source: Codagnone (forthcoming)

the former showing high in-migration from Ukraine, for example, the latter indicating that this constitutes only a very small proportion of the Russian population and that this inward migration is not 'forced'.

Federal Migration Service data confirm the indication in Goskomstat (State Statistics Committee) statistics that the majority of those entering Russia are ethnic Russians. Russians have consistently constituted the majority of inward migrants from the former republics as a whole (54 per cent in 1990, 66 per cent in 1992 and 63 per cent in 1994 (Goskomstat 1995: 422)) as well as of officially registered refugees and forced migrants (76 per cent in 1993, 67 per cent in 1994 and 77 per cent in 1995 (Komitet po delam SNG i sviaziam s sootechestvennikami 1996; *Informatsionno-analiticheskii Biulleten'* 1995: 21)). The balance is constituted primarily by members of the titular nationalities arriving from their own countries afflicted by civil war, economic crisis and political instability. Table 1.1 indicates that Armenians, Azerbaijanis and Georgians are most likely to move from their own states to Russia. In contrast Belarusians and Kyrgyz are more likely to *leave* Russia for their own countries.

As is discussed in detail in Chapter 2, these data are so coloured by the politics of the migration debate that it is difficult to construct any 'true' picture; they can be read either as showing a sharp increase in the proportion of non-Russian immigrants in 1994 (Russian Independent Institute for Social and Nationality-based Problems 1994) or as indicating an overall increase in the proportion of Russians over the period 1990–4 (Trubin 1996). What is probably indisputable is that the figures suggest that a significant number of those migrating to Russia at the current time are labour migrants. Indeed, during the first half of 1996, 222,000 foreign citizens from 116 countries were officially employed in Russia, which is 30 per cent more than during the corresponding period of 1995. Of these over half had come from countries of the Commonwealth of Independent States and labour migration almost certainly accounts for the surprisingly high in-migration noted in Table 1.1 from Ukraine; over a third of the total number of registered foreign workers are currently citizens of Ukraine ('Labour immigrants in Russia' 1996).

A new flow of citizens of countries from beyond the former Soviet Union (the 'far abroad') into Russia is causing the Russian government increasingly to distinguish between these people (often referred to as 'asylum-seekers') and refugees from the former republics (the 'near abroad').[16] According to UNHCR data, by 1 July 1996 almost 19,000 families (70,000 people in total) from the 'far abroad' had submitted applications for asylum. Most were fleeing Afghanistan (63 per cent), Iraq (mainly Kurds) (10 per cent) and Somalia (9 per cent) (*Vynuzhdennie Pereselentsy v Rossii* 1995: 54; Michugina and Rakhmaninova 1996: 48).

The Moscow office of the International Organization for Migration estimates the current number of such asylum-seekers at 120,000. As in other
countries of Europe, in government thinking the issue of asylum-seekers
is inextricably bound to that of illegal or undocumented migrants. In
Russia this concern is new but very real; there are claims that hundreds of
thousands of illegal immigrants have entered Russia due to poor security
along the external borders of Russia and other CIS states (Rutland 1995).
The head of the Federal Migration Service stated that there were 500,000
'illegals' in Russia at the end of 1995 and suggested that this number
would grow by 100,000 annually. More extreme estimates are that illegal
immigration may be running at more than 500,000 people a year (Russian
Independent Institute for Social and Nationality-based Problems 1994).
Some of these are economic migrants (mainly Chinese and Vietnamese),
others are so-called 'transits': asylum-seekers and undocumented migrants
– mainly from Ethiopia, Somalia, Sri Lanka and Iraq – using Russia as a
staging post to Scandinavia, Western Europe and North America.

A final migrational flow causing concern is the outflow from the former
Soviet Union of its most active and educated population to the west. Fears
were raised by the rapid growth in emigration following the enactment of
legislation allowing free exit from the Soviet Union; whereas up to the
mid-1980s an average of around 3,000 people emigrated abroad from
Russia annually, by 1990 the annual total had reached 104,000 (Michugina
and Rakhmaninova 1996: 47). Initial alarm about emigration to the west
has largely abated, however, as predictions of its acceleration – ranging
from 2.5 million to 25 million (Segbers 1991: 6) – have not been realized.
These estimates were constructed from public-opinion data and sociological surveys which clearly captured aspiration rather than real intention
and are cited now primarily for political effect (see Salt 1992: 66; Chesnais
1992: 37; Grecic 1993: 145).

Although the issue of out-migration from Russia to the west lies beyond
the scope of this book, there are points of intersection with migrational
flows from the former republics to the Russian Federation, with which this
book is concerned. First, emigration from Russia to the 'far abroad' has
stabilized in the 1990s; just 110,000 people emigrated from the Russian
Federation in 1995 compared to the 104,000 in 1990 noted above. Second,
emigration out of Russia to the west has been low in comparison to
emigration from other former Soviet republics. Emigration from Russia has
constituted around 30 per cent of total migration out of the former Soviet
Union when the population of Russia constituted 51 per cent of the Soviet
population (Michugina and Rakhmaninova 1996: 47). Likewise, ethnic
Russians have constituted only 26 per cent of those emigrating (ibid.). This
is explained by the fact that the initial wave of east–west emigrants largely

consisted of members of smaller ethnic groups who had 'ethnic homelands' or established diasporas in the west, primarily Armenians, Jews,
Germans, Poles and Greeks (Terekhov 1994; Shevtsova 1992). Indeed,
52 per cent of those having emigrated abroad from Russia are ethnic
Germans (Michugina and Rakhmaninova 1996: 47). Thus Michugina and
Rakhmaninova suggest that as few as 140,000 Russians have emigrated
between 1989 and 1995 and these primarily due to mixed marriages with
other ethnic groups more prone to emigration. Fears in the west of mass
economic migration from Russia to Western Europe thus have not been
realized; emigration continues to bear an ethnic character consisting
primarily of Germans, Jews and Greeks emigrating to Germany, Israel, the
USA and Greece; these countries received between 95 and 97 per cent of
emigrants from Russia between 1989 and 1994 (Goskomstat 1995: 402).

FRAMING THE THEORETICAL ISSUES: GOODBYE TO THE 'PUSH' AND 'PULL'?

Since naming these migrational flows constitutes the first step in conceptualizing them, it might be considered expedient to draw up a typology or
classification of types of migrant in the former Soviet space for further
study. Indeed, in the course of the above discussion a number of *de facto*
(administratively defined) 'types' of migrant have already emerged: the
'forced migrant'; the 'refugee'; the 'asylum-seeker'; the 'transit migrant';
the 'undocumented' or 'illegal' migrant; the (internally) 'displaced person';
and the 'labour migrant' ('guest-worker'). In addition there is a broad group
of incoming migrants from the former Soviet republics who are not registered by the Federal Migration Service and thus not 'named'. By default the
latter become viewed as 'voluntary' migrants – sometimes referred to as
'repatriates' or 'returnees' – to be considered separately from 'involuntary'
or 'forced' migrants.

The split between 'voluntary' and 'involuntary' migrants is the first
dichotomy which has traditionally shaped migration studies. The distinction is grounded in a deeper theoretical division between explanations
of migratory movements either as a result of a combination of 'push' and
'pull' factors (voluntary migration) or as the product of structural, global
inequalities and the violence associated with nationalism and independence
movements (forced migration and refugees) (Richmond 1993: 7–8).
Although in academic studies typologies are now highly sophisticated and
most will recognize grey areas between voluntary and involuntary migration, the fundamental dichotomy between refugees and economic migrants
has been persistently reinforced by the migration regimes of recipient
countries and thus remains the dominant discourse. Post-Soviet Russia

provides an excellent example of such a migration regime in formation and this forms the subject of the first part of the book. It traces the changing political agenda of the recipient state and the impact of this upon the migration regime which has increasingly drawn on the distinction between economic (voluntary) and political (involuntary) migrants which underlies theoretical migration models and state practice in the west.

The second dichotomy obscuring the theorization of current migratory processes is the distinction between 'structure' and 'agency' in explaining migratory movements (Richmond 1994). Classic models of migration are grounded in an assumption that the movement of populations is driven by rational choices borne of economic hardship. 'International migrations' are in this sense merely extensions of long-established rural to urban migration processes which arise due to the economic underdevelopment of the home country and the attraction of economic prosperity elsewhere. Migration is driven by 'push' and 'pull' factors acting on the individuals who move either because social and economic forces in the place of origin impel them to do so or because they are attracted to places of destination by one or more social and economic factors (Boyd 1989: 640). The approach assumes that individuals make rational decisions on the basis of available knowledge of objective conditions (Goss and Lindquist 1995: 320).

The alternative to this voluntarist approach is the adoption of a structuralist framework. The structuralist approach to labour migration focuses on the macro-economic processes that produce socio-spatial inequalities and constrain the life chances of individuals as members of specific social groups in particular places. Migration is seen not as the aggregate consequence of individuals exercising rational choice but as the result of socio-spatial inequalities systematically reproduced within global and national economies. International migration, in this understanding, far from reducing spatial inequalities and leading to equilibrium, intensifies inequalities and perpetuates underdevelopment as human capital is lost abroad (ibid.: 322). Even in structuralist theories which do not rely on the concept of direct 'exploitation of the periphery' via colonialism (as does dependency theory), the global market economy nevertheless is seen to establish flows of capital and commodities and create the ideological conditions that produce potential migrants (ibid.: 323).

The third dichotomy concerns the level of analysis of migrational processes which is conducted *either* at the macro *or* at the micro level (Richmond 1993: 10). It is the macro level of analysis which has dominated the literature to date on post-Soviet migration between states of the former Soviet Union. This literature seeks to identify actual and potential migration flows by describing the socio-economic, demographic and ethnic characteristics of the 'Russian diaspora' and their position in the successor states of the Soviet Union – the length of time resident in the former republic, degree of integration into the host community and position within the political structure of the new republics (Bremmer 1994; Kolstoe 1995; Melvin 1994 and 1995; Shlapentokh, Sendich and Payin (eds) 1994; Chinn and Kaiser 1996). Macro-level studies of immigrant adaptation (economic, social and cultural integration) have not been so numerous, although a number of Russian studies exist (Cherviakov, Shapiro and Sheregi 1991; Vitkovskaia 1993; Boikov and Levanov 1993b; Efimova 1994; Kozlov 1994). Micro-level studies concerned primarily with socio-psychological or socio-cultural components of migration decisions and experience are virtually absent in the literature on migration in the former Soviet space.[17] Micro-level studies of migration in western literature often focus on motivation for migration weighing up the 'push' and 'pull' factors involved, and this is repeated in what literature there is in Russian.

These three dichotomies have implicitly, if not explicitly, governed conceptualizations of Soviet and post-Soviet migration. This has led to fundamentally opposed explanations of the phenomenon of the in-migration of Russians from the former Soviet republics in the post-Soviet period and these explanations are outlined below. What is argued is that in fact all three of these dichotomies must be abandoned in order both to describe and conceptualize current migration from the former Soviet periphery to Russia. The chapter concludes with the elaboration of an alternative framework within which to approach the phenomenon of post-Soviet migration; it is this framework which structures the subsequent chapters of the book.

HOMO SOVIETICUS AS 'RATIONAL MAN'? STRUCTURE AND AGENCY IN POST-SOVIET MIGRATION

In western Sovietology, political compulsion was seen to govern most aspects of Soviet life. Surprisingly, therefore, patterns of migration in the Soviet Union were most often interpreted using classic migration models rooted in modernization theory. Classic studies such as that by Lewis and Rowland (1979) explain long-term trends in migration in the USSR as adjustments by a population to changing economic conditions and the structure of production and consumption, which occur with economic development. People were seen to move in response to job opportunities and migration to act to equalize the supply of and demand for labour on a regional basis (Lewis and Rowland 1979: 5–10). Inter-republican migration was interpreted as a continuation of inter-regional migration in that it extended the normal rural to urban migration patterns driven by individual rational choice.

Despite widespread images of organized population movement and strict social control, therefore, Lewis and Rowland argue that, in fact, most migration in the USSR occurred as a result of individual volition. Migration, they suggest, was primarily voluntary and also largely unorganized (Lewis and Rowland 1979: 15–19); rapid industrialization led to a fundamental redistribution of the Soviet population largely as a result of free migration while wars, famines and collectivization produced mass migrations not envisaged by government plans. Thus, while the Soviet government had some influence on migration, population movement in the USSR during the Soviet period was predominantly unfettered (ibid.: 27).

Lewis and Rowland do recognize the existence of compulsory political and criminal migration as well as that of army draftees in the Soviet period; however, they clearly err towards agency over structure in their conceptualization of Soviet migration. Indeed, despite the apparent displacement crisis in the region in the post-Soviet period, Rowland remains reluctant to throw out his original theses. Explaining the rise of in-migration into Russia primarily from former republics of the southern tier of the USSR in the late 1980s and 1990s, he points to the rise in educational levels among the Muslim nationalities, who are now better able to provide more educated and skilled labour, reducing the need for Russians (Rowland 1993: 171–2). Indeed Rowland and Lewis had anticipated an in-migration into Russia in this period, although they had expected it to come from titular nationalities of the southern Soviet republics rather than from ethnic Russians.

Mitchneck and Plane also prioritize agency over structure in their explanations of current migration trends in the former Soviet Union. They note four important shifts in migrational processes in the period 1989–92: increased relative mobility for the older – but still working – population; the increasing importance of urban-to-rural flows; the reconcentration of ethnic groups into their respective homelands within the former Soviet Union via an increase in inter-republican migration; and a shift towards female migration among non-Russian ethnic groups (Mitchneck and Plane 1995: 28). However, they describe these trends not as mass displacement due to structural constraints acting upon distinct communities but as individual reactions to 'economic shock' in the region. Explicitly rejecting forced migration and repatriation theories, they argue that the structure of the migration system in the former Soviet Union is predictable using an analysis of historical trends and standard approaches (ibid.: 27–8).

The attraction of the modernizationists' approach is that it clearly links current migration to the process of return to Russia by ethnic Russians which began well before ethnic conflict became a prime political and social mover in the mid-1980s. As early as the 1960s there was evidence of out-migration from the Transcaucasian republics of Azerbaijan and Georgia and by the 1970s there was considerable out-migration from Central Asia and Kazakstan. Moreover, these interpretations successfully capture the role of migration in personal mobility strategies rather than viewing the Soviet state as the only real social agent. Indeed, the push and pull perspective more clearly focuses on micro-economic processes, particularly the decision-making behaviour of individuals, who respond to real or perceived inequalities in the distribution of economic opportunity by migration to another place (Goss and Lindquist 1995: 317; Richmond 1993: 10). Given the political and economic instability of the former Soviet space, Russia appears from the former Soviet periphery as relatively stable and prosperous while the newly independent states are perceived to be discriminating against their new Russian minorities. Together this would seem to make a powerful combination of 'push' and 'pull' capable of provoking a significant flow of returnees to Russia.

Perhaps most importantly, the attention paid to individual and household survival strategy helps counter constricting structuralist explanations and break down rigid distinctions between economic (voluntary) and political (forced) migrations. Structural factors such as the politically institution-alized ethnic dominance (via language and citizenship laws) over new minority groups are intertwined with individuals' concerns about future employment, social and political status and ethnic comfort in the motivational structure of out-migrants from the former republics. The significance of this welding of economic and political motivations is explored on the basis of empirical data in Chapter 6.

The use of a classic 'push and pull' model to illuminate Soviet migration processes tends, however, towards selective historical blindness, resting, as it does, on an assumption that individuals acted as rational economic agents in a relatively free market place. As migration in the Soviet period is re-examined, however, Russian researchers talk of a history of forced migrations in the region beginning with the emigration for political reasons during and after the 1917 revolutions through the forced migrations of whole social strata in the 1930s and whole ethnic groups prior to and during Russia's participation in the Second World War and ending with forced migration from ecological disasters and the mass relocation of military personnel in the late and post-Soviet period. Re-reading migration in the Soviet Union, therefore, Oberg and Boubnova argue that forced migration was a widespread phenomenon; of those born in the western part of the former Soviet Union between 1880 and 1920, 5–10 per cent became forced migrants because of their social origin, ideological position or ethnic belonging (Oberg and Boubnova 1995: 241; Kotov 1994).

The existence of forced migrations does not deny the parallel process of voluntary migrations for economic reasons such as the movement of skilled workers and professionals to the former republics where their social mobility would be enhanced by urban – even capital city – residence and social status. Even this process was largely state managed, however, via the system of allocating graduates to specific positions (*raspredelenie*). While many original migrations are thus objectively 'voluntary' (in that they are not flights from violence) and are held to be personally beneficial by outsiders, subjectively they are perceived by those now returning as having been moves not for personal gain but out of duty to the 'motherland'. The implications of this for the integration of Russians currently returning are explored in the second part of this book.

A second problem with the employment of an undiluted voluntarist approach is that it tends towards the overemphasis of continuity between the migration system before and after the collapse of the Soviet system. Such an approach is not supported by leading Russian migration experts who argue that migrational flows in the post-1989 period on the territory of the former Soviet Union constitute a major divergence from patterns prior to the break up of the Soviet Union and that underpinning this massive redistribution of population are ethnic sentiments (Zayonchkovskaya, Kocharyan and Vitkovskaya 1993: 207). Grounding this interpretation theoretically, the authors clearly err towards a structuralist position, arguing that post-Soviet migration patterns are explained by a set of constraints and structures which have acted to force out certain *ethnic* communities and encourage a trend towards return to traditional homeland and national isolation (ibid.). The structural explanation is linked clearly to a characterization of migration as forced: Soviet migration flows are becoming refugee flows in the post-Soviet space according to Zayonchkovskaya *et al.*

While western migration experts may have held fast to push–pull models, political scientists and historians looking more widely at the implications of the collapse of the Soviet Union have tended towards the employment of structural explanations of population movements in the post-Soviet space. Such explanations adapt traditional structuralist frameworks which have focused on *economic* structures compelling people to move, replacing them with *political* structures. The evidence for this approach rests on the apparent disruption of past migration patterns; even Rowland – whose belief in the explanatory power of the modernization model to explain Soviet migrational processes is outlined above – concedes that the south to north migration which he had predicted for the 1980s and 1990s had in fact been realized not as a result of labour redistribution but as a result of *Russians* returning to Russia (Rowland 1993). Western historians and political scientists are inclined to interpret this process within a collapse of empire paradigm, suggesting that the structural relations between Russia and the former Soviet republics explain the flow of people first out to the colonies and then back to metropole upon the collapse of empire.

The problem with such interpretations is that they often work only at a macro level, tend to falsely homogenize the Russian 'diaspora' in the former republics and fail to provide any real insight into migration decisions at the individual, family or community levels.

FUSING THE MACRO AND MICRO: DESIGNING THE EMPIRICAL PROJECT

Given the nature of published literature to date, it would seem that in order to enrich the study of post-Soviet migratory processes any future study must be conceived within an explanatory framework which: allows for different types of migration and does not prejudge the nature of that migration; acknowledges the importance of the migration regime of the receiver society as well as the links between it and the migrants arriving;[18] and allows movement between macro and micro levels on the empirical front.

The empirical design of the project which forms the basis of this book was elaborated with specific reference to the first of these criteria. The methodological details of the project are outlined in the introduction to Part II of the book; here it is necessary only to note the rationale of respondent selection. Two principal criteria were employed to determine research subjects:

- those who had moved to Russia from any part of the former Soviet Union (including other parts of the Russian Federation) between 1988 and 1994, regardless of ethnicity or citizenship and who expected that move to be long term or permanent;
- those who considered themselves to have moved *involuntarily*, regardless of whether they had directly experienced persecution. 'Involuntarily' was interpreted widely to mean that the respondent would not have migrated at that time 'in normal circumstances'.[19]

Thus, in line with a growing body of thought in migration studies, the project design did not recognize any clear distinction between economic and political migrants since political violence and ethnic conflict are increasingly triggered by worsening social and economic conditions while economic hardship often results from the exercise of repressive political power (Jessen-Petersen 1994: 3; Overbeek 1995: 15; Salt 1989: 432). Nor did the project recognize the main criterion for registration as a forced migrant or refugee by the Federal Migration Service in Russia, although respondents were asked whether they had registered. A total of 195 respondents were involved in the project – conducted between July and December 1994 – the majority of whom gave one or more in-depth interviews.

The decision to focus on the experience of migrants after resettlement rather than in the former republics before migration was determined by the desire to study actual migratory behaviour rather than wish or 'intention' to migrate. It was also driven by the aim of linking the micro-empirical project to a macro-level analysis not via a final prediction of future flows of migrants but by analysing the possible implications of displacement for both incoming migrants and the society to which they had moved. Despite widely held assumptions that the shared ethnicity and language of Russian-speaking forced migrants would ensure problem-free reintegration into Russian society, this process is deeply problematic both for the migrants themselves (who undergo a massive social-status drop and a cultural shock on confronting their 'historic homeland' often for the first time) and for receiver communities, who are struggling with their own severe socio-economic difficulties and often appear ambivalent, if not openly hostile, to outsiders. The process of coming to terms with social, economic and cultural shock forms the basis of Chapters 7 to 9.

The second criterion – the significance of the migration regime for migrant experience – is met in the research design by a thorough examination of the development of the migration regime in the post-Soviet period. The results of this study – which included not only an examination of the legislative and institutional frameworks shaping the migration regime in post-Soviet Russia but also a discussion of the media and academic construction of the debate on refugees and forced migrants – are outlined in Chapters 2 to 5. This part of the book traces the formation and re-formation of the migration regime over the period 1991–6. It argues that an initially liberal and humanitarian approach to refugees and forced migrants on the part of Russia was rooted in a Russian agenda of keeping the borders between the newly independent states and Russia 'soft'. In other words, with the tacit agreement of the international community which had an interest in encouraging Russia to manage those displaced 'internally' in the post-Soviet space, Russia was allowed to treat the borders between former Soviet republics as less than full international borders marking independent states.[20]

Over the period under study, however, the migration regime re-formed dramatically. This has culminated in the securitization of migration issues which is grounded in a significant redrafting of Russian foreign policy agendas as the Russian government has bowed to domestic pressure to prioritize the securing of its own territorial borders over appeasement of the international community. This is not necessarily a victory of the hawks over the doves; in many ways it has been the result of the retention of power of those who do not support the re-establishment of either the Russian or the Soviet empire. However, it is also the result of concrete threats to Russia's state integrity emanating most dramatically from Chechnia. In terms of the migration regime these wider debates have led to legislative amendments which seek to reduce Russia's responsibility for Russian returnees as well as the reorientation of the Federal Migration Service away from universal aid programmes towards immigration control and policing functions. The dubbing of immigrants as a 'security' threat has furthermore allowed regional authorities to approach migrants as suits the needs of the local situation, closing and opening doors in relation to specific regional agendas. How this is manifest in individual regions is outlined in Chapter 5.

Thus, the migration regime in post-Soviet Russia is a dynamic entity which has evolved in close connection with the reconfiguration of Russian national identity and self-esteem.[21] However, the migration regime of Russia is not seen solely as a constraining force on would-be migrants; as Goss and Lindquist suggest, the structures of the migration regime should be seen not only as forces constraining or directing migrants but as rules and resources which are used *by* migrants (Goss and Lindquist 1995: 332). In at least one fundamental way, the migration regime has acted as an enabler of inward migration in that Russia has remained essentially open to immigration by former Soviet citizens. Moreover, in the post-Soviet case it is clear that inward migrants not only make decisions about their level of involvement with structures of the migration regime, choosing their level of incorporation and interaction, but also use those structures to their own advantage where possible. The ways in which this is manifest are discussed in Chapters 5, 6 and 7. Particularly important to the empirical project was the way in which definitions of refugees and forced migrants by the migration regime and in the receiver community have shaped migrants' own perceptions and memories of their pre-migration lives and affected their integration into their new home (Chapters 6 and 8).

The study of the migration regime of receiver countries is essential to understanding migrational flows which make up a migration system (Fawcett 1989: 672). Part I of the book does not simply provide a macro context for the micro empirical work described in Part II, therefore, but establishes the link between structural and voluntarist explanatory models and indicates the interaction between global and national migration regimes, migrant flows and individual migration decisions. In the same way it allows movement between the macro and micro levels by showing the way in which emergent migration discourses shape migrant experience while the latter's narratives may impact on the wider discourse.

CONCLUSION

This book makes no claims to offer a new 'model' of migration that resolves the problems of the false dichotomies which have developed between structure- and agency-based theorizations, between typologies of forced and voluntary migrants and between the narrowly macro or micro levels of study which often accompany such initial conceptualizations. Above all, the project was an empirical one aiming to capture the experience of migrants into Russia from the former Soviet republics. In unravelling the intertwined structural (consequences of modernization) and conjunctural (exclusionary nationalist sentiments in the process of nation-state formation) forces in activating migration, however, the post-Soviet experience clearly speaks to some of the wider theoretical and empirical problems in migration studies more generally. In particular it recognizes the role of the migration regime – at both international and national levels – in perpetuating a by now defunct dichotomy between the economic (voluntary) and political (involuntary) migrant and seeks to show a migration regime in formation which illustrates this vividly. It tends towards replacing this dichotomy with what Richmond refers to as a continuum between the rational choice behaviour of proactive migrants, who seek the best for themselves and their families but often make these decisions *in anticipation* of impending political or economic conflict or hardship, and reactive migrants who react not only to direct persecution or violence towards them but to war, famine, economic collapse and ecological catastrophe (Richmond 1993: 10–11). It does not make any claim to refining these definitions, however; it provides only some concrete examples of the way in which these divisions must be problematized.

Based as it was on a small-scale and highly exploratory research project, the book claims no more than to have shifted the focus of study away from the Russian 'diaspora' as the sorry objects of empire fall-out who are of interest, above all, in terms of their strategic importance for Russian foreign policy. Instead the project highlights the experience of those members of the Russian communities in the 'near abroad' who have resettled permanently in Russia and who constitute a distinct socio-cultural group in post-Soviet Russian society. The distinctiveness of this group of 'other' Russians is explored via an analysis of both the 'objective' – socioeconomic – obstacles to integration of these incomers and the 'subjective' – cultural – barriers to their return 'home'. On the basis of a concrete example from a region often ignored by migration experts, some tentative questions are raised about the relationship between migration, displacement and identity in the contemporary world.

2 Redrawing a nation's borders

The politics of the migration debate in Russia

In this chapter a broad-brush picture of the press debate on current migratory processes in Russia is presented in order to provide the peculiar context of this issue in the post-Soviet environment. It will be suggested that the media debate on the issue of refugees and forced migrants constitutes a central component of the discussion on post-Soviet Russian foreign policy and on the identity of post-Soviet Russia *per se*. This discussion differs significantly from debates in other Western European societies which focus on immigration policy, human rights issues or the welfare burden refugees place on the receiver state. In contrast, coverage of forced migration and refugee issues in contemporary Russia takes place within the wider debate about the relationship between Russia and her 'near abroad' as seen through the prism of the rights of the Russian diaspora. The period of the press review described in this chapter – June to November 1994 – epitomizes this approach as it was in this period that the Russian government began to 'talk tough' on the defence of the Russian-speaking population in the 'near abroad' (Zevelev 1996).

This dominant discourse on forced migrants and refugees is balanced by human-interest stories – mainly located in the local press – concerned with the individual plight of refugee and forced-migrant families. There is also a more critical counter-current in the debate in the central press which emphasizes the potential value to the new Russian state of the returnees and criticizes attempts by the government to manipulate the position of the Russian diaspora for its own ends.

Tracing how these dominant themes emerge, and where and by whom they are promoted, helps to identify key constituents of the migration regime in Russia and their priorities. The overall frame of the debate is outlined below before the dominant and subordinate strands of its content are drawn out. The analysis is based on an ongoing review of press and academic material from 1991 to 1996 and a formal content analysis of selected central and local press over a five-month period from June to November 1994.[1]

FRAMING THE DEBATE: THE POLITICS OF MIGRATION

Migrational exchange between the former republics of the Soviet Union is viewed as a highly sensitive political issue in contemporary Russia as reflected in Russian press coverage. The content analysis of central and local press conducted in 1994 revealed that the absolute majority of articles considered the issue of refugees and forced migrants primarily from a political angle (57 per cent of articles). In contrast only one in five articles (21 per cent) focused on the legal context of current migratory processes while even fewer treated the issue primarily from an economic standpoint (less than 7 per cent) or as a social ('inter-personal') question (6 per cent). Although local papers were more likely to discuss the issue in its social or human context, such papers were less likely to discuss the issue in the first place; only 4 per cent of articles discussing forced migrants and refugees were located in the local press.[2]

Monitoring of the press over the whole post-Soviet period suggests that it focuses on the scale and geopolitics of migration. This is articulated via three recurrent questions which underlie media discussion of current migratory practice:

- How many refugees and forced migrants are there already and how many more intend to come to Russia?
- Which are the key refugee-producing areas and where are forced migrants and refugees most likely to come from in the future?
- What causes people to migrate: ethnic conflict, ecological disaster, unemployment or exclusionary political and economic reform?

The framing of the debate by these questions is significant in that it establishes the scene as 'there'. In this way the problem becomes the situation in the former Soviet republics and the Russian agenda one of finding ways to alter that situation. A discussion of the situation in the former republics which had led to the decision to migrate, for example, was discussed in 85 per cent of the articles – 325 in total – analysed in 1994. This focus suggests the Russian mandate is one of control and management rather than support and provision; a political rather than social agenda. The process of adaptation of new migrants – a central issue for welfare or social-policy discourses – is, for example, found to be relatively low on the press agenda: 25 per cent of articles mentioned this.

It would, of course, be wrong to suggest that the contemporary Russian press speaks with one voice. As will be indicated in more detail below, the circumstances of forced migrants and refugees in Russia are discussed. Indeed, some reports, many written by refugees themselves[3] or those involved with NGOs concerned with forced migrants, are highly critical of both policy and reporting on the issue. The academic community has also been critical of media reporting of migration issues, claiming that journalists and politicians tend towards articulating alarmist opinions about the imminent swamping of Russia with refugees (Kozlov 1994). But these commentators dominate the reporting: 59 per cent of articles were written by journalists and almost 10 per cent by politicians (the two largest single categories) while sociologists (who, Kozlov suggests, are more likely to see current migratory processes in their historical context) wrote just 0.5 per cent of such articles. This reflects perhaps a wider failure of the Russian academic community to input effectively into discussion and policy-making in relation to the Russian diaspora (Kolstoe 1995: 279). Historians have paid significant attention to the complexities of the situation in each individual former republic in order to provide a better picture of likely rather than simply potential migratory intention, and a number of sociological studies have tried to include issues of reception and adaptation of migrants in Russia alongside questions concerning migrational intention (Cherviakov, Shapiro and Sheregi 1991; Vitkovskaia 1993; Susokolov 1994). However, academic studies have been generally either devoid of policy recommendations or, in the case of the Fund for the Foreign Policy of Russia, consciously oriented towards toughening Russian policy in the protection of Russians abroad (Kolstoe 1995: 279).

At the most general level of analysis, therefore, it must be concluded that the issue of forced migration and refugees in Russia since 1991 has been reflected in the press as a political as opposed to a social, economic, legal or 'human' issue. The nature of the exact political agendas into which the discussion has been slotted is discussed below.

THE 'RIGHT TO STAY': A COINCIDENCE OF INTERESTS?

The first of these agendas is characterized by concern over the degree to which Russia is asserting the kind of influence over the newly independent states in the 'near abroad' commensurate to her great-power status. The expression of concern over the protection of Russians beyond the borders of the Russian Federation effectively redraws the borders of post-Soviet Russia according to the geographical location of the Russian ethnos rather than the current administrative borders of the Russian state and thus might be labelled a neo-imperialist or ethno-nationalist agenda. This discourse is clearly flagged by two markers: the labelling of the subjects of action (those migrating); and the siting of the location of action.

The content analysis in 1994 revealed fifteen terms used to describe the subject of migratory processes (see Figure 2.1). Most frequently authors of articles use terms such as 'the Russian-speaking population' (*russkoiazychnoe naselenie*), 'Russian-speakers' (*russkoiazychnie*),

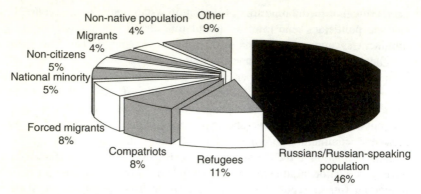

Figure 2.1 Labelling of the subjects of forced migration in the Russian press

'Russians' (*russkie*) or 'ethnic Russians' (*etnicheskie russkie*); one or more of these terms were used in 46 per cent of articles. While only two of these terms can be described as ethnically exclusive, they all securely establish the connection of these people through ethnicity or linguistic and cultural proximity to Russia proper and establish the location of action as 'there'. In this way the interest of Russia in their fate is also indicated. Although 'ethnic Russians' and 'the Russian-speaking population' are not co-terminous, most authors other than academics use the terms inter-changeably.

The increasingly popular term 'compatriots' (*sootechestvenniki*) – mentioned in 8 per cent of articles – is also highly inclusive and un-differentiated. Indeed, it incorporates a potentially unlimited section of the population in the 'near abroad' since it sets criteria of neither ethnicity nor citizenship for membership of the group. The term is employed in government circles to denote: Russian citizens living in the 'near abroad', stateless persons in the former Soviet Union (that is those former Soviet citizens not holding citizenship of their state of residence), and former Soviet citizens who had gained such citizenship but who sought to retain their links with Russia (Zevelev 1996: 273). The endorsement of the term in official circles marked a wider strategic development in policy towards the 'near abroad' which is discussed in Chapter 4.

Such terms as 'national minority' (5 per cent), 'non-citizens' (*negrazh-dane*) (5 per cent) and 'non-native population' (4 per cent), all of which place the subjects clearly under the jurisdiction of the newly independent states, in contrast, are employed infrequently.

A second means of establishing the issue as one of the Russians abroad is achieved via a silencing of other issues. Although 17.4 per cent of Russians live outside Russia at the moment, other nationalities have equally significant diaspora populations; 15.3 per cent of Ukrainians live outside Ukraine, 21 per cent of Belarusians live outside Belarus and 33.4 per cent of Armenians live outside Armenia, for example (Shevtsova 1992: 249). Issues surrounding their situation and return to their native land are rarely raised, however.

The siting of the location of action is probably the most significant means by which the neo-imperialist agenda is set, however. The siting of migration stories 'there' does not confine the issue to the foreign news pages. On the contrary, as Melvin notes, forced migration is as much a domestic political issue for Russia as it is a foreign policy one (Melvin 1994: 27). The situation of Russians abroad is seen as an indicator of Russia's general standing and their plight is symbolic of the collapse of Russia internally.

This agenda is particularly evident from an analysis of the areas of the 'near abroad' most frequently referred to in press reports; attention to the plight of the Russian population – with the exception of Tajikistan – appears to be inversely proportionate to its migratory intention (see Figure 2.2). There has been relatively little discussion of the mass exodus of Russians from the Transcaucasus (see Figure 1.3). In contrast, the situation of Russians in the Baltic republics, specifically Latvia and Estonia, where the Russian population is generally oriented towards integration, dominated the debate in all of the central papers included in the content analysis. The media focus on the Baltic states is particularly striking given that in 1994, when the content analysis was conducted, the vast majority of forced

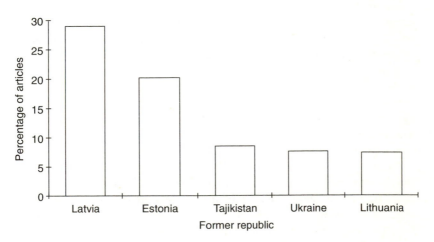

Figure 2.2 The geopolitical location of the discussion of migration in the Russian press

migrants were actually leaving Central Asia and Kazakstan (accounting for 71.7 per cent of the total number of registered forced migrants and refugees) rather than the Baltic states (3.9 per cent of the total) (*Vynuzhdennie Pereselentsy v Rossii* 1995: 26).[4]

The unwarranted concentration of debate on the Baltic region means that there is an unrepresentative reporting of *political* factors in motivating migration. 'The political situation' is the most commonly cited reason influencing migration (cited in almost two-thirds of articles), and this is explored through the discussion of attitudes of the Russian-speaking population which, in 63 per cent of cases, are assessed as 'negative'. In particular there is heavy criticism of local authorities in the newly independent states who are said to view the Russian-speaking population negatively in 81 per cent of articles.[5] This is reflected in the discussion of the rights accruing to the Russian minorities and the degree to which these rights are observed. Discussion in the press covers overt political rights (such as the right to citizenship and residency, the right to elect and be elected) (Veretennikov 1994; Grudinina 1994) and politically controlled rights in the social and cultural sphere (such as the right of use of Russian language and access to the Russian media) (Prikhodko 1994). Where such rights are discussed, it is their absence or restriction which is noted in 71 per cent of cases.

In discussing attitudes and policy towards the Russian-speaking population in the 'near abroad' a very clear picture emerges: while the policy of Russia is evaluated positively (being defined as 'a policy of co-operation' directed towards the support of compatriots abroad and the active participation in the resolution of their problems), the opposite picture is painted of the governments of the Baltic states. The latter's policy is portrayed as a 'policy of confrontation' characterized by measures designed to push out the Russian-speaking population and a lack of will to seek compromises in the resolution of their problems. The recent coining of the term 'stateless persons' (*apatridy*) (used in 1.4 per cent of articles) to refer specifically to Russians in Estonia and Latvia is indicative of the view of the Russian government that Russians in the Baltic states have been denied full political and civic status in the new states and turned into 'second-class citizens'.

The situation in Central Asia and Kazakstan is reported quite differently.[6] Although criticisms are made (especially of language laws and the dislodging of Russians from senior professional posts), when discussing the situation of Russians in Central Asia and Kazakstan much emphasis is laid on the growing recognition in the newly independent states of the damage done to their economies by the exodus of Russians (through the loss of Russian specialists). Retreats from national language policies and positive moves on citizenship rights by the newly independent states are praised, however, as are cooperative initiatives (on economic and diplomatic fronts) to slow down the outflow (Denisenko 1994; Dotsuk 1993; Savin 1994; Tishkov, Rotar' and Tsilevich 1994). The economic cost to Russia of having to reabsorb migrants from Central Asia and Kazakstan and of reconstructing the southern borders of Russia is also noted (Safarov 1994). The tone of natural superiority here significantly contrasts with the resentment and humiliation evident in the discussion of the treatment of Russians by the new administrations in the Baltic republics.

As will be argued in Chapters 3 and 4, the *Realpolitik* behind concern for the Russians abroad is a growing consensus that state interests are best served by the continued presence of Russian minorities in the 'near abroad'. Thus, when politicians articulate in the press concerns over the Russian population in the 'near abroad', there is often a crude equation between their interests and the interests of the Russian state (see, for example, Parshutkin 1994; Abdulatipov 1994: 41). This is epitomized by the suggestion of Sergei Shakhrai (former deputy prime minister)[7] that, while Russia's real interest is in letting the diaspora remain *in situ* with protection from the Russian state, those who do return should be settled in areas important for Russia's security such as the Far East (Nekrasova 1994b).[8]

This reflects a significant sea change in attitudes at government level, as Koshchueva notes with a certain irony:

> If we compare how papers wrote about the Russian-speaking population in the 'near abroad' five years ago and today, there is a massive difference; earlier we were uniformly called migrants, occupiers and even *'mankurty'* ...[9] Now, however, the tone has changed. Those same papers simply ooze sympathy for the former 'occupiers'.
>
> (Koshchueva 1994)

'Democratic' thinking in power had turned out to be rather different to how it had been in opposition; Russians in the 'near abroad' had come to be seen as the stepping stone to raising Russia's profile in the determination of CIS politics – and, indeed, the internal politics of the newly independent states – and, thereby, reasserting Russia's 'big brother' status (see Chapter 4).

THE REALITY WITHOUT THE POLITICS?
COUNTER-CURRENTS FROM BELOW

Although the issue of forced migration is predominantly approached from the point of view of its significance for Russian statehood and Russian foreign policy in its 'near abroad', the experience of refugees and forced migrants themselves is not completely ignored.[10] One in four articles mentioned adaptation problems of Russian-speaking migrants on return to Russia and in local papers the issue of adaptation actually received more attention than the reasons for migration (the former being discussed in 69 per cent of articles, the latter in 62 per cent).[11]

The discussion of adaptation shows concern for the social and economic difficulties faced by forced migrants such as employment, housing, children's school and nursery places. The press appears less ready to discuss other problems, however: the 'psychological' problems of adaptation[12] were raised in just 10 per cent of articles while problems of cultural adaptation were not raised in any of the articles falling within the delimited content analysis in 1994.[13] As will be argued in Chapters 8 and 9, the absence of the latter is especially significant since, at least in the case of Russian-speaking forced migrants, the admission of problems of cultural integration would challenge the 'Russianness' of the Russian diaspora and thus break the link of one nation divided by pseudo-borders.

Even attention to the question of the socio-economic difficulties of forced migrants and refugees has a political subtext, however. What concerns policy makers about adaptation processes among migrants is the degree to which such problems might impact upon migrants' political integration. There is great concern that migrants might form the base of a conservative backlash to reform within Russia, or even be rapidly absorbed into extremist nationalist groups. There thus appears a widespread characterization of forced migrants as: 'prone towards the support of nationalist forces and nationalist organizations' (Toshchenko 1994); a 'fifth column' ready to overthrow the government (Rotar' 1993); 'potential sources of authoritarian trends, nationalism or chauvinism' (Shevtsova 1992: 250); and an embittered and humiliated mass of people who 'might easily fill the ranks of all sorts of national-extremist organizations' (Safarov 1994). Explanations of this leaning include: poor housing and unemployment faced on arrival (Abdulatipov 1994); alienation from the current Russian regime and its unfamiliar (capitalist) economic institutions (Mukomel' 1995a); the momentous drop in social status (loss of specialist jobs, secure housing and lifestyle) (Safarov 1994);[14] frustrated expectations following Yeltsin's declaration that Russia would welcome all Russians wanting to return to Russia from former republics (Grafova 1995a); disillusionment with Yeltsin as a result of the democrats' blind support of the anti-communist national-liberation movements in the former republics (Rotar' 1993); and the colonization by Communists of the defence of rights of the Russian-speaking minority in the former republics (ibid.).

It is also feared that the influx of refugees (especially of Transcaucasian origin) may provide an excuse for violent behaviour by parties on the far right who would exploit increased competition for housing and jobs experienced in receiver communities (Marnie and Slater 1993: 51). This is exacerbated by the new settlers' desire to live comfortably and tastefully and by their superiority complex *vis-à-vis* the local population, both of which antagonize local rural populations (Rotar' 1993). Both within Russia and in other former Soviet republics, it is suggested, an influx of refugees (often the victims themselves of ethnic conflicts) into one area may result in increased competition for housing and jobs and thus a new ethnically based violence (Morozova 1993). Those less sympathetic to the needs of refugees suggest that they heighten the potential for ethnic conflict in Russia since they tend to move into employment in the service sphere, trade and intermediary business ventures where their activities sometimes acquire a 'criminal character' (Kotov 1994). As evidence of the dangers ahead the author cites figures of the Moscow independent association of sociologists suggesting that 70 per cent of murders in Moscow and more than 90 per cent of armed extortion, 80 per cent of assaults ending in death and up to 65 per cent of rapes in large Russian cities are committed by those originating in the Caucasus and Central Asia (ibid.).

While, on the one hand, it is important that the real problems faced by migrants should be reflected in the press, critics of the government's attempts to encourage the Russian population to resist migration options warn that a consistently negative picture of migrant experience may be being painted in order to deter potential migrants (Pavlov 1996). This 'democratic opposition' has presented a consistent critique of government policy which will be discussed in greater detail in Chapter 4. Here it is worth noting that this undercurrent in the press debate tends towards the labelling of its subject by the legally accurate, but socially laden, terms of 'refugees' (used by 11 per cent of authors) and 'forced migrants' (8 per cent) which are politically unpalatable in official circles. Sergei Shakhrai, in admitting his dislike for the terms, for example, indicates the sense of the failure of Russian foreign policy with which the terms are associated (Nekrasova 1994b). Since refugees can only cross international borders, the very word reinforces the collapse of the Russian/Soviet empire as well as conjuring up images of poverty, hunger and disease unfitting to the general tone of the debate.

The increasing adoption of the term 'repatriates' (*repatrianty*) in the press (used in 1 per cent of articles) is the most striking evidence of a small but significant undercurrent in the migration discourse.[15] The term clearly indicates the democrats' interpretation of the causes of forced migration as the natural fall-out of empire for which the present Russian government should take responsibility. This is a line most clearly associated with the newspaper *Literaturnaia Gazeta* and the non-governmental organization headed by one of their columnists, Lidiia Grafova. While retaining a highly critical stance on the abuse of the rights of ethnic minorities in Estonia and Latvia, Grafova blames the situation on the Russian government's failure to address the issue while consciously conducting a policy of keeping the 'Russian-speakers' in the former republics and of subordinating their welfare to what they define as Russia's 'geopolitical interest' (Grafova in Sokolov 1994: 5–6). With time *Literaturnaia Gazeta*'s battle has increasingly been conducted as a direct attack on the Federal Migration Service and in particular its head, Tat'iana Regent; most recently the paper has directly accused the government of treating the Russians abroad as 'hostages of the imperialist policy of Russia' (Pavlov 1996).

From a less involved position, an effective attack on any kind of neo-imperialism by Russia today is advanced through historical analysis by Vishnevskii who explains the current Russian diaspora as the end result of the policy of the expansion of her defensive and offensive borders which Russia has undertaken since the fourteenth century (Vishnevskii 1994: 178).[16] Moreover, Vishnevskii is sympathetic to perceptions of Russians in the newly independent states as a fifth column of 'big brother'; Russia is too near, the ties are too strong and the memory of the imperial past is still too much alive for successful integration of Russians into their new states (ibid: 180). Vishnevskii, like Grafova, suggests that current migratory flows are not threatening but a natural end result of the collapse of empire, and cites the post-war rise of Germany to suggest that the return of Russians from the 'near abroad' – if met with the right policies – could strengthen and enrich Russia (ibid: 184–5). Arguing along similar lines, Fadin labels those returning 'repatriates' (*repatrianty*) and argues that Russia simply has to face up to her future and *choose* between an anachronistic desire to restore the empire and the possibility of a decisive modernization of her defence system and realization of her national interests (Fadin 1994).

Okulov takes the argument one step further by suggesting that the very people who now accuse the Russians in the near abroad of aligning with the red-brown camp had driven them there by failing to defend their rights (Okulov 1994).[17] The key not only to neutralizing potential nationalist opposition, but to providing a positive force for reform from among the ranks of the Russians abroad, he argues, is the guarantee of their legal and civic rights which will allow them to integrate fully into Russian society and use their initiative and energies successfully (ibid.).

Finally, there are even oases of rational thought countering the widespread scapegoating of refugees for the ills of contemporary Russia. Warning bells have been sounded about the dangers of spreading myths about the ethnic roots of crime (Vladimirov 1994) while others celebrate the potential enrichment of Russia from the cultural diversity immigrants bring with them (Kobishchanov 1995).

CONCLUSION

The question of the discursive construction of forced migrants is not one of biased reporting; it is one of uncovering agendas which frame the migration debate. In terms of open authorial agendas, the content analysis revealed that authors of articles generally try to present either a neutral or balanced view of the incidents or facts they are reporting and only a handful of articles revealed clear national or nationalist bias in reporting.[18]

The content analysis undertaken as part of this research suggests that forced migration is constructed in the press as a problem of the maltreatment of the Russian population in the 'near abroad' – focusing on the situation in the Baltic states – and that this reflects an agenda of hurt Russian national pride rather than the real questions facing returnees. However, claims by the democratic opposition – reflected as an undercurrent in the media debate – that there is an exclusively negative portrayal of the experience of migrants upon return is not confirmed. Although overall evaluations provided by authors of migrational processes were more frequently negative rather than positive, many authors, 42 per cent, try to retain a neutral position.[19] Articles discussing migrants' experience gave both positive and negative indications of the housing and employment possibilities for migrants and of attitudes to the migrants by both the local population and state authorities.

The positions represented in the press debate to some extent reflect journalistic and academic agendas but are largely rooted in different institutions of the migration regime (see Chapter 4). Given the increasing activity and successful networking of non-governmental agencies supporting forced migrants and refugees, we should expect this arm of the migration regime to appear more widely reflected in the media debate in the future. Indeed, NGOs have persistently raised the question of biased media reporting of the forced-migrant issue and called for a more positive attitude in the media to the resettlement of compatriots. The need consciously to promote television programmes and special columns in the press devoted not only to the problems of forced migrants and their resettlement in Russia but to the contribution they make to the development of regions and depopulated territories was included in the final document from the parliamentary debate on forced migrants and refugees held in April 1996.[20] To what extent this will change the overall reporting of forced migrant issues, however, will depend on ongoing policy development *vis-à-vis* the 'near abroad', domestic economic success or failure and the relative weight of related discourses such as Russia's nationhood, security and demographic vitality.

3 The legislative framework
When is a refugee not a refugee?

By definition a refugee is an individual who seeks refuge from persecution from *outside* their own country.[1] It is the physical crossing of international borders which differentiates refugees from other kinds of 'displaced persons' since the latter might adequately describe anyone who has been forced to leave his or her home through actual or potential threat of violence or persecution (Schwartz 1993: 240; Susokolov 1994: 187). Thus, when the press first began to talk of 'refugees' in the Soviet Union at the end of the 1980s the term was doubly problematic. Ideologically the concept of a 'Soviet refugee' in a country which had prided itself on the establishment of an historically new community of peoples appeared nonsensical and, since the first refugees appeared before the collapse of the Soviet Union and moved only within the Soviet single space and before the USSR had adopted any law on refugees, or indeed on immigration (ibid.), they did not strictly conform to the international definition of refugees either.[2] As a result, when towards the end of the 1980s significant numbers of displaced persons appeared on Soviet territory, *ad hoc* executive government resolutions rather than comprehensive legislation defined the rights of refugees and other 'involuntary' migrants while, in practice, the actual granting of status was left to those on the front line – the police.

The collapse of the Soviet Union complicated the situation further. The borders between the former republics of the Soviet Union did not coincide with the physical location of discrete nations in their territorial homelands and by 1989 a migratory trend towards 'national isolation' was clearly discernible (Zayonchkovskaya, Kocharyan and Vitkovskaya 1993: 203) as ethnic groups returned to their titular homelands. Overnight, on 1 January 1992, these movements became international migration flows including refugee movements.

The adoption of legislation to manage these flows was an urgent but complex task. The protection of those displaced was a delicate operation of determining the new relationship between nationality, citizenship, territory and state responsibility. Russia had assumed the rights and obligations of the defunct Soviet Union but to grant anyone displaced across the territory of the former Soviet Union not only the right to resettle in Russia but also special welfare provision would have been to commit the state to accepting responsibility for the welfare of potentially tens of millions of people. On the other hand, to grant no exceptional status to those former Soviet citizens leaving the republics to settle in Russia, or to restrict entry to ethnic Russians, would have been tantamount to accepting Russians in the near abroad as colonizers returning home after the collapse of empire and to ethnicize further the process of state-building in the former USSR.

The identified legislative resolution was the creation of a dual category of displaced person entitled to refuge and assistance upon entry to Russia: the refugee and 'the forced migrant'.[3] Russia appeared to be acting in a humane and 'liberal' manner since subsequent legislation covering refugees and forced migrants effectively permitted the settlement in Russia of all displaced people on former USSR territory as well as refugees from the 'far abroad' in accordance with the 1951 UN Convention to which Russia became a signatory in December 1992. Indeed, as will be suggested in Chapter 4, there is a growing feeling in government circles that, having acted in haste in drawing up legislation, Russia is now entering a phase of repenting at leisure as the full economic implications of the initial 'liberalism' are gradually realized.[4] From another perspective, however, the all-encompassing nature of the legislation is another indication of Russia's imperial heritage; as Peter Gatrell notes, the Russian imperial state took a similar expansive responsibility *vis-à-vis* refugees during the First World War (Gatrell 1996: 5). At the same time the legislation – through its distinction between 'refugees' and 'forced migrants' – effectively created a notion of special ties between Russia and the Russian diaspora in the 'near abroad', reflecting a clear political agenda for Russia as a post-imperial state.

LEGISLATING THE FALL-OUT OF EMPIRE: GOOD INTENTIONS

There are three laws which provide the basic legal framework for the treatment of displaced persons in the Russian Federation: 'The Law on Refugees' passed on 19 February 1993; 'The Law on Forced Migrants' also passed on 19 February 1993 and amended on 22 December 1995; and 'The Law on Citizenship' which came into effect on 6 February 1992 and was amended on 17 June 1993 and 18 January 1995.

The laws on refugees and forced migrants came into effect on 20 March 1993 after their publication (for full texts of the laws see *Vedomosti S"ezda*

Narodnikh Deputatov RF i Verkhovnogo Soveta RF 1993: 714–20, 721–7 and for the amended law *Sobranie Zakonodatel'stva*, no. 52, 25 December 1995: 9317–27). The essential difference between a legally defined 'refugee' and 'forced migrant' is that eligibility for the latter status (to which both more rights and more benefits accrue, at least in terms of long-term settlement in Russia) is Russian citizenship. Those who are not citizens of the Russian Federation, whether they be from the 'near' or the 'far' abroad, may apply for refugee status only:

> A refugee is an individual who does not have citizenship of the Russian Federation and who has, or wants to, come to the Russian Federation and who has been forced to leave, or who has the intention of leaving, his or her place of residence on the territory of another state as a result of violence or other form of persecution towards him or herself, or who is under real threat of being subjected to such on the grounds of his or her race, nationality, religion, language, affiliation to a particular social group or political conviction.
>
> ('O bezhentsakh' 1993: 714)

> A forced migrant is an individual who has citizenship of the Russian Federation and who has left, or intends to leave, his or her place of residence on the territory of another state or on the territory of the Russian Federation as a result of violence or other form of persecution towards him or herself or members of his or her family, or who is under real threat of being subjected to persecution on the grounds of his or her race, nationality, religion, language, affiliation to a particular social group or political conviction in connection with the conducting of hostile campaigns towards individuals or groups of individuals, mass violations of public order or other circumstances significantly restricting human rights.
>
> ('O vynuzhdennikh pereselentsakh' 1993: 721)[5]

Since citizenship is the key criterion for determining status, the third piece of legislation essential to interpreting provision for refugees and forced migrants in contemporary Russia is 'The Law on Citizenship'. This law came into effect on 6 February 1992 and grants Russian Federation citizenship to all those permanently resident in the Russian Federation before that date. In addition Article 18 of the law allows all those who held USSR citizenship on that date and were resident in a former Soviet republic prior to that date to receive Russian citizenship if they applied within three years of the law's promulgation and were not already citizens of another republic. Amendments to the law on 18 January 1995 extended this three-year period for application to 31 December 2000. Foreign citizens and stateless persons must fulfil a five-year residence requirement to qualify for citizenship (reduced to two and a half years for refugees). Thus the 25.3 million Russians in the near abroad had a guaranteed right to Russian citizenship (Marnie and Slater 1993: 47). Also important for refugees and forced migrants was the addition to this law passed on 17 June 1993 which abolished the requirement for 'permanent residence' and documental proof of refusal of any former citizenship (Sokolov 1994: 8).

Enjoying her rehabilitation into the global community, Russia not only enacted ostensibly liberal domestic legislation but also acceded to the humanitarian international refugee regime. At the end of 1992 Russia signed the 1951 United Nations convention and the 1967 protocol on the status of refugees and this international legislation came into force on Russian territory from 4 May 1993.[6] As well as committing Russia to upholding international agreements on the rights of displaced persons, this meant that as a 'country of first resort' Russia had to make provision for the care of foreigners fleeing their countries outside the former Soviet Union and seeking refuge in Russia (Marnie and Slater 1993: 47).

It is widely accepted that the federal Russian laws largely conform to international standards and international bodies have not felt the need to challenge the principles of Russian legislation. Moreover, the laws clearly lay down the rights of refugees and forced migrants and thus have gone a considerable way towards alleviating the kinds of problem encountered by refugees before the adoption of legislation. Previously, refugees had found that, outside officially designated resettlement places, they were denied normal citizenship rights such as the purchase of housing or provision of medical assistance (Livshin 1991). The status of refugees and forced migrants also entitles its bearers to a number of benefits, including a one-off payment to the most socially vulnerable categories of refugees and forced migrants (see Chapter 4).

The actual workings of this legislation in the context of the overall provision for refugees and forced migrants in contemporary Russia are discussed in Chapter 4. This chapter raises only a number of general problems which have arisen with the legislation and the attempts made to rectify the situation.[7]

Reinterpretation and local re-reading

Lack of clarity in the legislation and thus the possibility of reinterpretation and re-reading of its provisions in practice has proved to be the greatest difficulty with the legislation passed in 1993.

Although in theory the distinction between refugee and forced-migrant status entitlement is clear, in practice people with similar fates often have different status while people leaving very different circumstances have the same legal status. This has come about primarily as a result of the procedure for acquiring Russian citizenship. Although all citizens of the former USSR whose reason for changing place of residence conforms to those stipulated in the law on forced migrants are entitled to forced-migrant status, providing they have Russian Federation citizenship, for citizens of the former USSR who arrived in the Russian Federation *before* 6 February 1992 the procedure for acquiring that citizenship is complicated. It effectively requires their return to the state which they were forced to leave (Kovalev 1994: 3). The result is that many opt to take refugee status instead which puts them on a par in terms of legal status and rights with refugees from the 'far abroad' who have never been Soviet citizens. Ironically, it was this distinction (between citizens of a previously unitary state and foreign refugees) which the creation of 'forced-migrant' status was meant to ensure (Sokolov 1994: 10).

A second problem concerns the eligibility for status of those arriving from the 'near abroad'. As noted above, the 1993 laws stipulate that the status of refugee or forced migrant can only be granted to those people who have left their former place of residence on the grounds of violence, persecution or the threat of such. In global practice eligibility is determined in very different ways; while in most western countries, and especially in Western Europe, cases are reviewed individually, in Africa the practice has been to accept refugee movements – defined as including those forced to leave their country due to external aggression, occupation or domination and internal conflict – *en masse* (Black 1993: 7). In Russia the eligibility for status has been accorded primarily on a bureaucratic basis. Although the wording of legislation suggests that status depends on the nature of each individual case, in practice who qualified for status was pre-defined by the Federal Migration Service. The latter circulated a list – which was periodically amended – stating which parts of the former Soviet Union were considered to be refugee-producing regions.[8] Individuals who claimed persecution (and thus status) from outside such regions had their cases heard by the local migration service commission. In practice this gave considerable leeway to local migration services whose own regional policies often determined whether to grant status; as is evident from the case-studies described in Chapter 5, this meant significant regional variation in the granting of status.

Finally, the application of legislation has revealed a number of abuses of the rights of forced migrants and refugees. Former head of the Presidential Human Rights Commission and member of the Presidential Council, Sergei Kovalev,[9] notes that refugees and forced migrants are required to state their nationality when applying for forced-migrant status despite the right not to do so provided for by Article 26 of the Russian Federation Constitution and that files on forced migrants generated by the registration procedure contain personal details for which confidentiality or limitation of access is not guaranteed (Kovalev 1994: 3).

Thus while, in theory, Russian legislation conforms to international standards, indeed – some would argue – surpasses those standards, in practice it has created anomalies in the granting of status, allowed significant localized variation in application of the law and contradicted constitutionally embedded human rights for this section of the population.

Contradictory laws: the *propiska* is dead, long live the *propiska*

The legislative environment into which the laws on refugees and forced migrants have been inserted has inhibited the working of refugee legislation as other laws and normative regulations at federal and regional levels have restricted or skewed its implementation.

One of the rights of forced migrants stated in the legislation is that to freedom of choice of place of residence, including the right to live with relatives or other individuals (with their agreement) *regardless of the size of their housing* ('O vynuzhdennikh pereselentsakh' 1993: 723).[10] Since the publication of these laws, the right to freedom of movement for all citizens of the Russian Federation has been further strengthened by Article 27 of the new Russian Federation Constitution (which came into force immediately after the December 1993 elections) and the abolition of one of the most universally detested Soviet institutions, the residence permit (*propiska*), which was officially abolished as of 1 October 1993. From this date individuals' residency was to be simply registered, not granted, thus effectively ending the use of the *propiska* as a mechanism to control population movement. A constitutional court decision in April 1995 marked a further step towards the complete eradication of the residence permit from the lives of Russian citizens; finding for an individual citizen who complained that she had not been given housing because she did not have a residence permit. The consequence is the removal of the last trace of mention of the residence permit in federal legislation (in the housing code) (Zhukov 1995).

While its abolition is extremely popular with the public at large, many in both central and local bureaucracies remain committed to the role of the residence permit in controlling migration. Tat'iana Regent (head of the Federal Migration Service) herself has suggested that its abolition was likely to 'provoke a new, powerful wave of illegal migration' which, in turn, would send the crime rate in large cities soaring (Regent 1993). This stance from above has encouraged local authorities to continue to use the residence permit to resist the registration of refugees and forced migrants. They are able to do this since current law fails to draw on any normative act setting procedures for establishing residence and thus local authorities have been able to introduce their own procedures, effectively retaining the *propiska* (Zhukov 1995). Moreover, the December 1993 'Statute on forced migrants', which details the procedures for the registration of forced migrants, contains a clause subordinating the authority of the Federal Migration Service and the regulations on forced migrants to local legislation in any area of the Russian Federation that restricts immigration and the right to residence. The Federal Migration Service is thereby empowered to introduce specific local procedures and regulations for would-be immigrants in line with this local legislation (Slater 1994: 43).

Without doubt the greatest violations of the right to choose one's place of residence have occurred in Moscow. The Moscow authorities have exploited widespread belief in Moscow's 'refugee problem' to violate the laws on refugees and forced migrants directly (see Chapter 5). Refugees also fall victim to controls on foreign visitors to the capital. New regulations demand that visitors to the city from nations for which visas are not required must register with the police within twenty-four hours and pay a fee of 10 per cent of the minimum monthly wage. Refugees – especially those of a Transcaucasian appearance – find themselves repeatedly stopped by Moscow city police and may be fined and expelled from the city, even if they have refugee status for Moscow region (Gannushkina 1996c).

Moscow has acted as a lead for other cities. The former mayor of St Petersburg – Anatolii Sobchak – went further still by introducing a requirement that not only foreigners but all citizens of Russia visiting the city who were not permanent residents must register with the police.[11] During 1994 similar rules and regulations were adopted in Iakutiia, Krasnodar territory and Rostov region and, in 1995, Iaroslavl' region. The thrust of all these provisions is that visitors who are not citizens of Russia must register their presence, pay a registration fee, and seek permission to extend their stay (ibid.). In March 1995 Voronezh region went one step further in drawing up its own legislation designed to regulate migration into the region. The law requires all newcomers to register within twenty-four hours and the maximum period of temporary residence in the region is limited to forty-five days. Those wishing to purchase housing in the region are liable to a tax of up to 100 times the minimum (monthly) wage (for Russian citizens) and up to 300 times the minimum wage (for foreigners and stateless persons) (Mikhailov 1995). Although refugees and forced migrants are exempt from this tax, the appendix to the law lays down a quota for the admission of migrants of 0.5 per cent of the total population (Gannushkina 1996c).

The Voronezh case suggests that although Moscow, St Petersburg and tourist cities of the south where residence permits were always difficult to obtain are severe cases, refugees and forced migrants are likely to face increasing administrative obstacles to their settlement across the country. Indeed, they are already refused registration frequently on the grounds that they have no place of residence or have no official de-registration document from their former place of residence.[12] An expert survey to determine procedures for handling registration of refugees and forced migrants in the city of Ul'ianovsk conducted in 1994[13] revealed that those responsible for registering forced migrants and refugees considered the residence permit (*propiska*) to be the single most essential document in beginning the registration procedure. This provision is used effectively to implement a local policy of accepting forced migrants and refugees only if they have relatives in the region and have been guaranteed somewhere to live by them (see Chapter 5).

Absence of subsidiary legislation to enable implementation

Finally, the *ad hoc* and non-uniform nature of implementation of the legislation on forced migrants and refugees can be at least partially attributed to the fact that although the main acts were passed in early 1993, the crucial sub-legislation required to implement the working of the laws was not passed until much later. This subsidiary legislation consists of regulations and instructions on how to implement the law and, in the case of forced migrants, the necessary acts were taken only in December 1993 (Sokolov 1994: 8) while the procedures on working with foreign citizens (required to implement the law 'On refugees') were not passed by the government until 8 September 1994. In the meantime temporary, departmental procedures for handling refugees' affairs had to suffice.

THE LEGISLATIVE AMENDMENTS OF 1995: FACILITATION OR BACKTRACKING?

In response to the recognized failings of the legislation, amendments to both the Law on Refugees and the Law on Forced Migrants have been drafted. Amendments to the latter were passed by parliament on 22 November 1995 and signed by the President a month later while the draft amendments to the Law on Refugees passed their first reading in July 1995 but remain under discussion. It has been widely recognized by independent observers and NGOs active in the field that the amendments to the Law on Forced Migrants, at least, have gone some way towards providing clearer guidelines on the rights of, and provisions for, forced migrants. In analysing the process of the adoption of these amendments, however, it would appear that the clarificatory aspect of the amendments was a positive side-effect of the process whose chief momentum lay rather in the need to tackle the problem of the mismatch between the scale of the migration and the resources made available to the Federal Migration Service to manage it.

Low funding allocation, non-fulfilment of budget target and a series of new crises (such as the Chechen War and the Kurile earthquake) have meant that federal programmes have failed to be met and the regions have had to rely largely on funding from the regional budget (see Chapter 4). Meanwhile, the flow of migrants continues to grow and most commentators are in agreement that, in its present economic state, Russia cannot meet the obligations currently set out in its legislation. It is the concerns of the government and its agencies which were expressed in the draft amendments to the laws on refugees and forced migrants rather than those of refugees and migrants themselves, or of the independent bodies defending their rights.

As in other parts of the world this top-down legislative initiative essentially seeks to tighten the definition of who constitutes a 'refugee' and 'forced migrant' in order to direct the meagre resources available more effectively. The amendments, now adopted, appear to do this in three ways: by making a clear distinction between economic and political migrants; by delimiting the period for which status is granted; and by strengthening the rights of the migration service at the cost of those of its clients.

Redefining the forced migrant

The explicit aim of the amendments to the Law on Forced Migrants enunciated at the discussion on 22 May 1995 in the upper chamber of parliament – the Council of the Federation – was 'the need to more clearly determine the legal status of forced migrants taking into account new realities' (Sergeev 1995). This does not mean the abandonment of the category of 'forced migrant' as unworkable *per se*. What it means is the strengthening of the requirement (for which proof may be demanded of applicants) that forced-migrant status be granted only to those having experienced 'violence or persecution on racial, national or other social grounds (religious, language, political conviction)'. Thus the amended law emerged with the inclusion of a distinct new article explicitly stating who is not eligible for forced-migrant status. These are: those convicted of serious crimes;[14] those not applying for forced-migrant status within twelve months of leaving their place of residence or within a month of losing refugee status after receiving Russian citizenship; and – most significantly – those leaving their former place of residence 'for economic reasons or as a result of famine, epidemics or natural or man-made (technological) disasters' ('O vnesenii izmenenii i dopolnenii v Zakon Rossiiskoi Federatsii "O vynuzh-dennikh pereselentsakh"' 1995: 9318). A time period – twelve months from arrival – has now been stipulated within which applications must be made.[15]

The second significant change in the amended law is its rendering of forced-migrant status as temporary. Whereas previously this status was permanent once granted, it is now valid for a period of five years, extended only in exceptional circumstances, and forced migrants must re-register with their territorial migration service annually.[16] Moreover, this law is effectively back-dated; those who received forced-migrant status before the amendments were adopted nevertheless have their period of status counted from the day it was granted.

Finally, it would appear that the law tends towards the strengthening of the rights of the migration service while limiting its obligations. Article 7 of the amended law no longer talks about the 'obligations' of the authorities *vis-à-vis* forced migrants but about their 'powers'. Article 10, meanwhile, clearly makes conditional the duty of the Federal Migration Service to help forced migrants find housing and employment by adding the clause 'within its powers'. Indeed, the thrust of specific articles on help with housing and employment is now towards helping the migrants help themselves (by means of offering loans for building housing rather than preferential treatment on housing lists, for example). In its official response to the draft law on forced migrants, the Coordinating Committee for Aid to Forced Migrants and Refugees suggests an even more sinister inter-pretation of the redefinition of the role of the Federal Migration Service. If adopted, the committee stated, the amendments would effectively make forced migrants wholly dependent on the Federal Migration Service and thus enhance the departmental status of the organization. In particular, the removal of the article on the 'fund' to help forced migrants from the current law and the introduction of a temporary system of residence in special housing is described as evidence of the attempt by the Federal Migration Service to monopolize the right to dispose of money directed towards the help of forced migrants (Sokolov 1995).

Redefining the refugee

For some time it has been clear that, in practice at least, refugees are treated as second-class immigrants. Despite the statement in the current Law on Refugees that refugees have all the basic rights of Russian citizens, in fact they have significantly fewer rights than forced migrants (who are, by definition, Russian citizens). Refugees only have the same rights to property ownership as do foreigners, not Russian citizens. Refugees are not entitled to priority housing as are forced migrants or to interest-free loans for housing construction or purchase. Refugees are not given grants during training or retraining for employment and they are not entitled to benefits accruing to Russian citizens for relocation to rural areas from cities (Sokolov 1994: 11, 60).

The distinction between 'ours' and 'not ours', moreover, is one which has been clearly instilled in the minds of those working with refugees and forced migrants. One local migration worker implied that it was specifically stated in legislation that the migration service should assist only the Russian-speaking population. The amendments to the Law on Refugees which are still under parliamentary discussion do nothing to redress this balance but seek to rewrite the law radically in a way that will significantly restrict the granting of refugee status. According to Tat'iana Regent, the need to tighten the law has arisen from the 'unforeseen economic implications' of the increase in numbers of refugees from the 'far abroad' (especially Somalis, Kurds from Iraq and Afghans) in addition to the increasing inflow of refugees (of titular nationalities) from the 'near abroad' as the result of conflict (Regent 1993).

The underlying agenda for the rewriting of refugee legislation, however, is the disillusionment of the Russian government with the international community. A member of the presidential apparatus was unambiguous on this point in his statement that the new law's stricter limitation of the status of refugees, the period of status and the right to receive aid had been necessitated by the fact that Russia's unconditional accession to the 1951 UN Convention had placed an increasing burden on the state (Mukomel' 1995a). A second indication is in the issuing of a presidential decree in July 1995 outlining a procedure for the granting of 'asylum' to foreigners facing a 'threat of falling victim to persecution in their country of citizenship or in their country of permanent residence for public and political activities and convictions in compliance with principles recognized by the international community' (Open Society Institute 1995d). This decree clearly mirrors tough asylum laws in Europe and sits uneasily alongside the relatively liberal refugee law; nowhere is the relationship between the two set out. Despite the intention for the asylum procedure to be used in rare, high-profile cases, it appears that some FMS officials are presenting it as an additional step that all asylum-seekers alleging political persecution must take before a regular status determination under the Law on Refuges can be accessed. This is significant since the decree falls short of international standards and the norms of the Law on Refugees by providing that political asylum is denied if a person has been charged with any crime in the Russian Federation or if the applicant has arrived from a third country where they 'have not been threatened with persecution' regardless of whether they could have stayed in that country or were afforded protection there (Korkeakivi 1996: 8–9). Moreover, there is no established procedure for an applicant to apply for political asylum under the 1995 decree and the task of processing applications has been entrusted to the Presidential Commission on Citizenship which has neither the experience nor the personnel to carry out this function. Consequently, not a single case in which asylum has been granted under the decree has been reported and the whole political-asylum procedure seems only to have added to an already confused legal picture (ibid.: 17–18).

As with the Law on Forced Migrants, the Law on Refugees is ostensibly liberal – indeed more so than that of many other European countries – but in practice has been restricted by violations and the application of local or departmental instructions which contradict the provisions of the federal law. The American-based Lawyers Committee for Human Rights has registered particular concern about the treatment of refugees from outside the former Soviet Union who are often expelled without being granted the opportunity to apply for refugee status and are even returned to the country of flight in contradiction of international norms of non-*refoulement* (ibid.: 11–12). The amendments to the law which passed their first reading in July 1995, however, appear to lower standards set in the law not only to the minimum required by the 1951 Convention, but in some cases to well below these norms. The amendments contain a long list of exclusion clauses,[17] limit refugee status to three years and propose a quota for asylum-seekers. As Korkeakivi suggests, these amendments imply significant backtracking from the norms of the 1951 Convention.

CONCLUSION: THE LEGISLATIVE FRAMEWORK – FROM BENEVOLENCE TO BELLIGERENCE?

Post-Soviet legislation with regard to refugees and forced migrants began by taking an expansive and liberal position *vis-à-vis* entrants to Russia which not only formally met, but often exceeded, the standards set by international law enshrined in the 1951 UN Convention and the 1967 Protocol. Recent amendments to Russian legislation of 1993, however, suggest a growing belligerence borne not only of economic constraints but also a resentment of the apparent hypocrisy of the west in requiring that Russia sign up to the 1951 Convention while at the same time operating a fortress-Europe policy against Russian immigrants. Learning from western experience, therefore, federal legislative initiative is currently concentrated on controlling migrational flows, including for the first time an immigration policy designed to deter incomers. At the same time the federal authorities turn a blind eye to confusions and loopholes in the legislative framework which allow a tightening of the refugee regime by local authorities or institutions of government.

The indications are not wholly negative, however. The amendments made at the end of 1995 to the Law on Forced Migrants were significantly more migrant-friendly than those originally proposed by the Federal Migration Service. Svetlana Gannushkina, co-chair of the Civil Assistance Committee,[18] claims that more than 80 per cent of changes to the amendments proposed by NGOs were adopted following their participation in a parliamentary committee working on the draft law between its first and second readings (Gannushkina 1996b).[19] In its final form, Gannushkina argues, the new law includes provisions which should strengthen the right to freedom of movement of forced migrants and, by standardizing forced-migrant identity cards across regions and establishing a five-year registration period, protect the forced migrant from the arbitrary behaviour of local bureaucracies (Gannushkina 1996a). Thus, despite harsh criticism of the original amendments by NGOs (Grafova 1995a), there now appears to be a general consensus that the amendments to this law have an essentially clarificatory function. The Coordinating Council for Aid to Refugees and Forced Migrants notes that for the first time the amended law positively encourages cooperation with associations of forced migrants in building housing and creating an engineering and social infrastructure in places of their compact settlement (Sokolov 1995). It is also apparent that relations with international organizations (such as UNHCR, the International Organization for Migration and the International Labour Organization) have developed and are treated in an increasingly positive way.

Legislative initiative appears to remain in the hands of the Federal Migration Service. However, NGOs and outside bodies such as the Lawyers Committee for Human Rights continue to lobby for legislative change which conforms to the highest standards of protection of the rights of displaced persons. The experience of the passage of the bill on amendments to the Law on Forced Migrants, moreover, suggests the growing ability of NGOs and independent experts to influence legislation; these amendments were revised at least six times before being passed in a form largely acceptable to independent observers (Gannushkina 1996d). Their agenda is currently headed by the struggle to alter the draft amendments to the Law on Refugees in order to: ensure it provides for the freedom of movement of refugees; prevent the limitation of the period of status of refugee to three years regardless of whether the threat of persecution remains; remove the possibility of deportation in contravention of the UN Convention on the voluntary nature of repatriation; and ensure adequate funding of assistance to refugees. The provision in the presidential decree on asylum for the denial of asylum on grounds of national security is also causing great concern.

There is set to be further activity in the sphere of legislating migration in 1997. NGOs are promoting a series of legislative amendments which would exempt refugees from the fees and taxes levied on foreigners for residence in the most popular cities and which would ensure medical help to all migrants (Gannushkina 1996b). They are also calling for a law 'On migration policy', 'On communal settlement and the status of migrant organizations' as well as 'On tax concessions for the construction of housing' which would strengthen the legal status of migrant organizations and ease the application for tax concessions.

Perhaps the most intriguing battle will concern the potential introduction of a new judicial status, that of 'repatriate'. NGOs have been seeking such a law for some considerable time and have drawn up their own draft which would override the requirement of those wishing to return to Russia from the former Soviet republics to prove discrimination against them which, according to NGOs, indicates the government's actual desire to maintain the Russian diaspora in the former republics. However, the parliamentary Committee on CIS Affairs and Relations with Compatriots has drawn up a bill which incorporates the status of 'repatriate' into broader legislation 'On support for the Russian diaspora, protection of Russian compatriots and repatriation'. This bill considers repatriation to be the voluntary permanent resettlement in Russia of Russian citizens or Russian compatriots currently permanently resident outside Russia, and thus envisages a more formal status of 'Russian compatriot' for members of the Russian diaspora without Russian citizenship but who declare their spiritual or cultural connection to the Russian Federation.

In its current form, however, the bill appears to do little to facilitate the process of resettlement for Russians in the 'near abroad'. The process of applying for approval of repatriation appears no less bureaucratic than an application for forced-migrant status and potentially envisages the possibility of a new executive body to handle matters concerning repatriation. The competing agendas of supporters and opponents of the bill will emerge, no doubt, as the bill proceeds through parliament. At this early stage, however, it already appears that the bill is fundamentally misconceived. If the new legislation is to work it must free up the resettlement process in such a way as to give returnees greater ability to re-establish themselves as citizens who can make a significant contribution to society. The current bill, however, seeks to retain bureaucratic control of the process of repatriation and short-term financial savings. Article 41 of the bill, for example, suggests that potential repatriates will be offered a choice of just three possible places of resettlement if they have not already been able to secure approval for their resettlement in a particular area. For reasons outlined in the following chapter this is likely to be used to promote state interests in the resettlement process as well as potentially constituting a contravention of the right to the freedom of movement enshrined in the Constitution of the Russian Federation. Thus, rather than facilitating resettlement, the bill appears to have as its main objective the curtailment of state assistance to returnees; Article 38 promises to prioritize the consideration of applications from those who have the right to apply for forced migrant status but choose instead to apply only for repatriation. The context of the introduction of the notion of 'repatriation' in this bill – which establishes the legal status, rights and mechanisms of support of Russian compatriots – thus suggests a very different agenda to the migrant-centred draft proposed by the NGOs. It must be hoped, therefore, that the latter can exert as much influence over the content of this draft legislation as it appeared to do over amendments to the Law on Forced Migration in 1995.

4 The institutional framework
Securitizing migration

Chapters 2 and 3 outlined the discursive and legislative frameworks within which government policy on refugees and forced migrants is conceived and enacted. This chapter turns its attention to the roles of federal-level parliamentary, governmental, and non-governmental bodies and international organizations in the formulation and implementation of such policy. It identifies the key institutional actors in the formation and implementation of migration policy, maps areas of influence, cooperation and potential conflict and seeks to determine overall patterns of policy and institutional development.

The government body entrusted with the implementation of policy towards refugees and migrants is the Federal Migration Service, and this body provides the focus of this chapter. However, the Federal Migration Service operates within a wider institutional environment consisting of: myriad other governmental bodies – both legislative and executive – which take the issue of forced migrants within their purview; a growing number of non-governmental organizations; and key international organizations.

Figure 4.1 attempts to delineate bodies of the presidential, parliamentary and governmental arms of state active in the spheres of policy-making and implementation on refugees and forced migrants.[1] Inevitably this visual representation gives a false impression of discreteness; in fact there are numerous areas of overlap, competition and conflict. The Federal Migration Service, for example, is primarily an executive body of government whose role it is to implement policy agreed upon by parliament and president. However, as was clear from the discussion of the process by which amendments to existing legislation have been introduced (see Chapter 3), the Federal Migration Service does enjoy rights of legislative initiative and thus enters a potential area of conflict with both parliamentary and presidential branches. Government ministers – appointed by the president – may also lead policy in a direction opposed by parliamentary committees and, in the area of foreign policy and relations with the 'near abroad', parliament and government have had fundamental disagreements. The tendency,

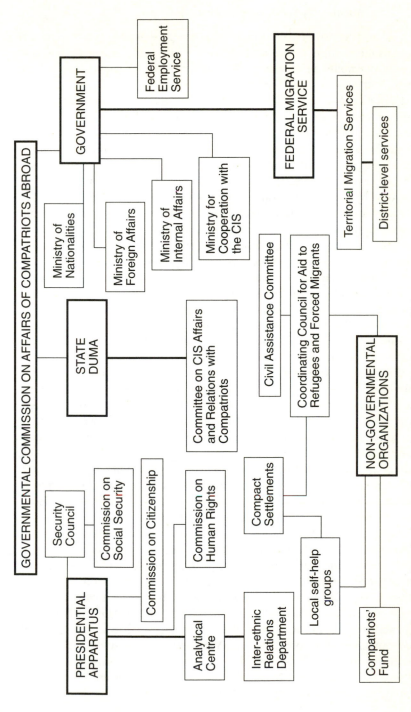

Figure 4.1 Refugee and forced-migrant policy: the institutional framework, 1994

typical of post-Soviet societies, towards the genesis of non-governmental organizations from above also creates a grey area between state and NGOs, exemplified by the Fund 'Compatriots' whose relationship to state organizations is discussed below.

Institutional overlap and conflict in the sphere of migration policy-making and implementation, however, was initially minimized by the post-Soviet Russian government as a result of the formation of two distinct 'battlefields': concern with policy towards 'compatriots abroad'; and issues relating to the resettlement of refugees and forced migrants in Russia. The latter were largely relegated to the status of a 'social problem' to be resolved by local social-support agencies (including the regional branches of the Federal Migration Service). Even the Federal Migration Service has increasingly distanced itself from these issues, seeking rather a greater role in policy-making and macro-level monitoring and regulation of migration. Conflict over resourcing priorities and migration policy, therefore, has often been shifted both vertically – to the regional level – and horizontally to the sphere of government–NGO relations.

In contrast the presidential and parliamentary bodies featured in Figure 4.1 were concerned primarily with coordinating policy in relation to Russian 'compatriots' in the 'near abroad', which constitutes the main context of debate about forced migration in post-Soviet Russia. While the Federal Migration Service might be expected to have come into conflict with president and parliament – given the wholly inadequate funding for its activities – in practice it has been a loyal government agent. Indeed, it appears to have viewed the shift in government policy towards discouraging migration to Russia and tightening definitions of 'forced migrants' and 'refugees' as commensurate with its own interests; the fewer arrivees, the lighter the resource burden on the Federal Migration Service.

Potential for conflict between parliament and presidential/government bodies is clearly much greater and is discussed in more detail below. However, as was argued in Chapter 2, there has been a growing consensus – in rhetoric at least – about the role of Russia in protecting Russian minorities abroad (Kolstoe 1995: 263) and it would appear that disagreements are as likely to be within one branch of the apparatus or even within one ministry as between different branches. Thus, the Presidential Commission on Human Rights,[2] headed, until January 1996, by Sergei Kovalev, persistently sought to protect refugee and migrant rights while the Security Council has played on fears of the 'swamping' of Russia especially by economic migrants from China and Vietnam, Africa and the Middle East, despite both being firmly rooted in the presidential apparatus. Likewise, different sections of the Ministry of Foreign Affairs and Ministry of Internal Affairs may pursue very different lines (Fadin 1994).

The politics of migration in post-Soviet Russia goes beyond institutional conflict, therefore. It centres on the relationship between policy towards the Russian diaspora in the 'near abroad', actual migratory activity and Russia's interpretation of her moral obligation to, and provision for, those Russians returning as refugees or forced migrants. As was suggested in Chapter 3, government policy has moved in an increasingly exclusive direction. This has already had some institutional impact as, in line with more fundamental shifts in foreign policy in relation to the 'near abroad', the Federal Migration Service in Russia has undergone a reorientation from its original role of developing universal aid programmes for refugees and forced migrants and towards immigration-control functions. This has meant the increasing exclusion of 'forced migrants' from the category of citizens requiring special state support and a concomitant reliance on ill-equipped non-governmental organizations to provide practical assistance. The latter have, in turn, increasingly criticized the government's policy of encouraging the majority of Russians abroad to remain *in situ* – a policy conducted more by the failure to provide any real assistance to returnees than by any incentive to stay – and have begun to network increasingly effectively to lobby both parliament and government on behalf of the forced migrant and refugee community. In this way, these organizations have successfully retied the knot between policy towards the Russian diaspora and questions of social provision for returning Russians creating a single battlefield upon which strange alliances are emerging.

THE PARLIAMENTARY AGENDA: A NEO-IMPERIALIST CONSOLIDATION?

Since the early days of post-Soviet Russia it has been the State Duma – the lower house of the Russian parliament – which has taken a proactive line with regard to the 'near abroad' and the Russian communities residing there. The Duma's apparent neo-imperialist stance appeared a stark contrast to that of the government in the image of Russian foreign minister, and would-be 'westernizer', Andrei Kozyrev. The Russian parliament consistently called for the resignation of Kozyrev and pressed for a tougher line by the Russian government with regard to Russian minorities policy. Institutionally this pressure was exerted by the parliamentary Committee on CIS Affairs and Relations with Compatriots which was chaired by Konstantin Zatulin until the December 1995 elections.[3] The parliament frequently expressed its concern over the violation of rights of ethnic Russians in the 'near abroad' and Kazakstan increasingly joined the Baltic republics as chief villain of the piece.[4]

The concern with Russians abroad shown by the parliament was in stark contrast to the apparent indifference of the government and thus, despite sometimes very different political motivations, it was with parliament that NGOs representing forced migrants and refugees increasingly interacted. Good cooperation with individual members of parliament such as Viacheslav Igrunov (of the democratic grouping Yabloko) was institutionalized in spring 1995 when a parliamentary commission 'On refugee and forced migrant affairs' was created under the chair of parliamentary deputy Zhanna Lozinskaia. This commission comprised parliamentary deputies and their aides, presidential apparatus workers, Federation Council members, representatives of social organizations and independent experts as well as Federal Migration staff and it effectively redrafted the amendments to the Law on Forced Migrants. A more informal, analytical–consultative body, the Council of Compatriots, was created in June 1995 in order to provide the parliament with its own information and monitoring channel to help promote the case for tougher action in support of the compatriots abroad (Parrish 1995a; Zevelev 1996). In December 1995 the outgoing parliament made a final declaration 'On support by the Russian Federation of the Russian diaspora and protection of Russian compatriots' setting out the rights of compatriots upon return to Russia as well as Russia's concern to promote equal rights for Russians who chose to remain in their current place of residence.

Electoral campaigning in the run up to the December 1995 parliamentary elections and, subsequently, for presidential elections in June 1996, however, significantly raised the profile of debate about 'compatriots abroad'. The parliamentary electoral campaign pushed the debate far beyond the 'potential fifth-column' concerns voiced by the press in 1994 (see Chapter 2) to a more wide-ranging debate about Russia's obligations to Russian citizens and ethnic Russian and Russian-speaking populations beyond Russia's borders, and the latter's role in Russian domestic politics.

The intensification of the debate was precipitated by the emergence into top-flight politics of more serious pretenders to the role of 'defenders of Russians abroad' than had been constituted by Vladimir Zhirinovskii and the Liberal Democratic Party in the December 1993 elections. In particular the Congress of Russian Communities (CRC) – founded in March 1993 with the explicit aim of representing the interests of ethnic Russians living in the 'near abroad' (Belin and Orttung 1995: 49) – emerged, in the course of 1995, as a major political grouping. On the eve of the December 1995 parliamentary elections it claimed eighty Russian regional branches, forty-three branches in the non-Russian republics with a membership of 460,000 and, arguably, the most dynamic leadership of any bloc registered for the 1995 parliamentary elections: a triumvirate of Iurii Skokov, Aleksandr Lebed' and Sergei Glazev.[5]

The CRC was widely tipped for significant electoral success and threatened to become the focus of a powerful, concentrated lobby from within parliament intent on promoting the interests of Russians in the 'near abroad' and encouraging the active political participation in Russian politics of the Russian minorities themselves. However, the CRC polled a surprisingly low 4.3 per cent and thus had no seats allocated from the party lists; but it did manage to gain representation in parliament via the election of five members to single-member seats (for which it had fielded ninety candidates). Relatively poor regional organization may have been responsible for the failure of the Congress of Russian Communities to clear the 5 per cent floor to gain entrance to parliament in December. However, Mukomel' also points to declining interest in the fate of Russians abroad among the Russian electorate as a whole as well as a growing isolationist mood, reducing the appeal of those setting out to defend compatriots abroad (Mukomel' 1995b).

The poor showing of the CRC does not mean parliament will abandon its mission to defend the Russian communities in the 'near abroad'.[6] In March 1996 the Duma symbolically voted to repeal the December 1991 Belovezhskaia agreement which had disbanded the USSR. More significantly the balance of opinion in the new parliament is towards an emphasis of the defence of the rights of compatriots abroad rather than their right to return,[7] and the new parliament has already recommended that a Nationalities Council be created consisting of state officials and members of public organizations which would work on legislation to help safeguard the civil rights of Russian citizens living in other countries of the former Soviet Union (Paretskaya 1996). Moreover, the initial signs are that the interest in the issue of refugees and forced migrants in both houses of parliament,[8] as well as at the highest levels of the executive apparatus, will encourage institutional cooperation and foster an awareness of the problems facing returnees. On 23 April 1996, parliament held a debate on cooperation between legislative, government and social organizations in the resettlement of refugees and forced migrants. The debate marked the end of a two-day forum of migrant organizations arranged by a leading NGO but attended by government agencies, members of parliament and international organizations as well as by migrant associations and their non-governmental representatives. The debate effectively constitutes the first real attention paid to issues of forced-migrant and refugee settlement – as opposed to the plight of 'compatriots' abroad – by parliament and potentially marks a new stage in cooperation between all bodies concerned. If this potential is to be realized, however, it is essential that the inter-departmental commission on refugee and forced-migrant affairs which proved so effective in the redrafting of the amendments to the Law on Forced Migrants in 1995 is reconstituted in the new parliament to provide an ongoing forum for exchange of opinion and institutional cooperation.

THE GOVERNMENT AGENDA: PREVENTING 'COMPATRIOTS' BECOMING 'REPATRIATES'

Government policy on the Russian populations in the 'near abroad' has its roots in the complex process of the disintegration of the USSR. The pre-independence RSFSR government under Yeltsin actively supported the national democratic movements in the former Soviet republics on the (correct) assumption that this would help accelerate the collapse of the Soviet Union from within. Moreover, in the immediate post-independence period, Russia appeared to downplay her own 'interests' in the former republics, leaving them free to form as separate nations, while concentrating Russia's foreign policy on swift acceptance into the global community. However, new policy priorities rapidly rose to the top of post-Soviet political agendas and increased pressure on the Russian government to recognize the 'near abroad' as a key 'sphere of vital interests' (Migranian 1994), and, consequently, to protect Russians in the newly independent states as the human embodiment of these interests. Migranian suggests that despite initial criticism by the democratic press and sections of the Foreign Ministry, by the summer of 1992, his notion that the entire geopolitical space of the former Soviet Union was a sphere of Russia's vital interests had come to prevail in political and public circles (ibid.).

Movement by both Yeltsin and Kozyrev towards this position was not just a victory for Migranian in the battle of ideas, however; there were real policy issues in the post-independence period which forced the question of the Russian diaspora to be reconsidered. The conflict in the Dniestr region of Moldova, the dispute with Ukraine over Crimea and the introduction of anti-Russian citizenship laws in Latvia and Estonia put increasing pressure on the Russian government, and the Foreign Ministry in particular, to take a tougher line on the protection of the interests of Russians abroad (Kolstoe 1995: 280).[9] This pressure intensified following the December 1993 elections to parliament as criticism began to flow from the parliamentary committees on geopolitics, security and international affairs (Karpov 1994). The result was a shift in rhetoric on the part of both the President and the Minister of Foreign Affairs. Yeltsin and Kozyrev expressed their concern about the status of Russian speakers in the 'near abroad' (Mihalka 1995). Kozyrev, moreover, appeared to have adopted the language of his opponents in acknowledging that the 'countries of the CIS and the Baltics are a region where Russia's primary vital interests are concentrated' ('Kozyrev favors military presence in neighboring states' 1994) and that the protection of Russians' rights in the other former Soviet republics must be one of the main strategic issues of Russian foreign policy (ibid.).

While it would be hard to deny that vacillations in foreign policy indicate a steady but sure move towards a more interventionist approach to the 'near abroad', the Yeltsin government has only once (in Moldova) given in to pressures to protect the Russian population abroad militarily.[10] Kozyrev, although renowned for his 'scare tactics' *vis-à-vis* the west, also persistently pursued a line of pressurizing the newly independent states by appeal to international organizations and western political structures (Kolstoe 1995: 269), and raising issues of discrimination against ethnic Russians (Parrish 1995a). Thus, while making concessions to the nationalists, Kozyrev persistently emphasized that Russia's interests in the 'near abroad' should be protected 'through partnership not confrontation' and that 'compatriots' in the 'near abroad' should be protected not by guns but by the implementation of 'internationally recognized standards in the field of human rights and the rights of national minorities' secured by bilateral and multilateral agreements with CIS partners and the involvement of the international community (Kozyrev 1994).

The context of government policy-making in the sphere of the 'near abroad' has, of course, been redrawn following parliamentary and presidential elections in 1995 and 1996. The resignation of Kozyrev on 5 January 1996 – ostensibly to take up his parliamentary seat won in December 1995 – marked Yeltsin's surrender to constant calls to replace Kozyrev with a more hard-line figure, while the – albeit brief – appointment of Lebed' as national security adviser shows a willingness to be drawn in a more belligerent direction. However, as Zevelev (1996) rightly notes, the increasingly tough rhetoric from the government failed to be supported by any assertive policy in practice. This may well be testament to the important role of advisory bodies from within the presidential apparatus which have consistently argued that mass forced migration is best prevented by providing guarantees of the protection of minority rights at a CIS level.

THE GOVERNMENT'S DUAL POLICY TOWARDS RUSSIANS ABROAD

In specific relation to migration policy, the pressure for firmer action *vis-à-vis* the 'near abroad' led to the emergence of a set of clearer government priorities in the course of 1994. In August of that year the 'Basic conception of a programme to help compatriots' was adopted,[11] and a governmental Commission on the Affairs of Compatriots headed by Sergei Shakhrai was established. The commission included representatives of the Russian government, the presidential administration, the Federation Council and social organizations and was designed to coordinate the efforts of a range of ministries and departments in the fulfilment of the outlined policy directions. These policy directions clearly reflect the dual approach to the 'near abroad' described above. They are underpinned by a two-pronged policy: to aid the integration of compatriots in the newly independent states while simultaneously providing a formal commitment by Russia to accept refugees and forced migrants.

In principle this kind of two-pronged policy is not only politically pragmatic, but also culturally sensitive and realistic; it reflects the real need for considerable flexibility in approach. The policy guidelines emphasized the need for the conclusion of bilateral agreements on migration,[12] including those on dual citizenship, alongside the improvement of existing cooperative agreements at the CIS level,[13] and the promotion of new ones such as a CIS agreement on ethnic minority rights which Russia has been promoting. However, since there is not one but many Russian minority communities in countries of the former Soviet Union the dual policy promoted by the government contains an implicit recognition that blanket approaches will not work; although dual citizenship agreements, for example, may suit the interests of Russia and thus be pursued as a desirable principle, it is accepted that they are realistic only in those states where there is a small Russian population such as Turkmenistan (with whom such an agreement does indeed exist) and, as the Russian community diminishes rapidly, possibly Armenia. In contrast, such agreements are virtually impossible in states such as Ukraine or Kazakstan, where they would effectively mean vast areas of the country being inhabited by citizens of another state (Mukomel' 1995a).[14]

In practice, however, the policy has become increasingly skewed towards integration rather than reception. Integration is defined in political, economic and socio-cultural terms and is understood as the provision of a secure home for Russians in the newly independent states while facilitating their retention of Russian cultural identity. On the political front this was to be achieved via dual citizenship, where possible, and the provision of information about measures taken by the Russian government to protect the rights of compatriots. Economic integration was to be promoted through: greater links between, or the buying out of, enterprises in the 'near abroad' with a predominantly Russian workforce; the use of economic sanctions against those states violating the rights of compatriots; and the condition that 20–30 per cent of credit given to states of the former USSR be used for the needs of the Russian diaspora. Socio-cultural integration would be furthered by a series of measures designed to ensure adequate access to Russian-language media and education in Russia and the support of Russian and Slavic cultural initiatives.

The unbalanced nature of the twin-track policy is at least partially due to the inability to implement reception programmes fully as a result of a lack of finances (in 1995 only 10 billion[15] roubles were allocated within the framework of this programme) (Mukomel' 1995a). Above all, however, it is a reflection of the growing recognition throughout the government that Russia's own best interest lay in their 'compatriots' not becoming 'repatriates'. This judgement was made on economic grounds – the cost of mass resettlement would be high indeed – but also on social ones; there was a growing concern in government circles that the reception of refugees and forced migrants might provoke social tension in Russia itself as a result of increased competition for already scarce resources (Mukomel' 1995a).

This concern is apparent in the prioritization in resettlement programmes of the 'interests of the state' which meant channelling returnees away from the heavily populated European part of Russia and towards the sparsely populated Siberia, the Far East and the non-Black Earth zone (Nekrasova 1994b). This was reflected in the policy guidelines in the statement of the need to provide state support specifically to those migrants moving to regions which were 'particularly important for the development of Russia' and to promote voluntary settlement of the Central Russia, Southern Siberia and the Russian Far East regions through government investment in industry and infrastructure, the provision of farming land and building materials for the construction of housing and tax concessions to aid small-business development.[16] It is also evident in the growing input from internal security organs into migration policy; a resolution of the inter-departmental Commission on Social Security of the Security Council of the Russian Federation introduced a mechanism for limiting migrational flows into Russia (primarily via entry quotas) on the grounds that Russian-speaking refugees from the 'near abroad' arriving in Russia might prove to be a 'destabilizing factor' in Russia and as such could 'create a threat to her national interests' (Fadin 1994). The 'securitization' of the forced-migration issue is a line which continues to be actively pursued by the Security Council which has openly stated that Russia is unable to meet the government's declared intention to accommodate all members of the Russian diaspora wishing to return, knowing that this plays on government fears that the inability to provide incomers with adequate material assistance could encourage resurgent communist–nationalist sentiments (Dmitriev 1996b).[17]

The turn in government policy – interpreted by migrants as manipulation and exploitation of their position – may yet backfire, however. Not only does such a blatant failure to recognize the needs and rights of migrants themselves threaten to encourage a political backlash to the government, it is also an irrational use of the skills brought to the country by forced migrants. Given that it is success in economic integration into the country which is likely to determine whether Russian-speaking forced migrants line up as an anti-democratic 'fifth column' – since while cultural alienation may be borne individually, economic disadvantage is likely to find collective political expression – the government may find that securitizing the migration issue provokes the very backlash they fear.

THE FEDERAL MIGRATION SERVICE: FROM DEFENCE TO CONTROL

The Federal Migration Service (FMS) is the central state body of the Russian Federation responsible for developing and implementing policies relating to refugees and forced migrants. It was established as an independent body by presidential decree on 14 June 1992, taking over functions previously performed by the Committee for Migration within the Ministry of Labour, which had been established by presidential decree in early 1992 (Totskii 1996: 36; Marnie and Slater 1993: 49).[18] Subsequent government decrees had ordered the governments of all administrative units of the Russian Federation to set up 'migration services' under their labour and employment administrations and established the principle of their acting as a single migration service headed by the Committee on Migration Affairs (Komitet po delam migratsii naseleniia). This committee was chaired by Tat'iana Regent who went on to head the FMS. There are three subdivisions of the central FMS apparatus: executive departments (responsible for internal migration, reception of forced migrants, the organization of migration control, out-migration and international cooperation); functional departments (concerned with legal matters, the implementation of migration programmes, information services, relations with non-governmental organizations and the media, financial affairs, accounting and auditing); and departments serving the central apparatus and territorial branches (dealing with general administration, personnel, etc.) (Totskii 1996: 37).

By April 1996, the unitary Federal Migration Service had regional branches (Territorial Migration Services or TMS) in all the regions and republics of the Russian Federation employing a total of 3,697 people[19] responsible for implementing the Federal Migration Programme and thirty-five regional migration programmes (Regent 1996: 31). In theory the service has a strictly vertical structure – all territorial migration services being directly subordinate to Moscow where 243 officials work in the FMS structure. However, evidence from expert interviews of TMS workers in the city of Ul'ianovsk suggests that officials in the regions have dual loyalties.[20] As the head of the Ul'ianovsk region TMS, Vladimir Il'ich Svaev, put it: 'Ul'ianovsk TMS is subordinated to the FMS and the head of the administration of Ul'ianovsk region . . . we have a dual subordination. The district services also have a dual subordination.'[21] This situation is confirmed by Totskii who notes the variation in regional subordination: while in Moscow the migration service remains subordinate to the department of labour and employment, in Krasnodar territory it is subordinate directly to the head of administration (Totskii 1996: 38). The reason for this state of affairs is, of course, a deeply structural one and not peculiar to the migration service. The increasingly strong role of regional authorities in Russian politics, alongside the ongoing financial crisis in Moscow, often makes central bodies in the regions reliant on regional governments for the resourcing of activities. However, in the case of the migration service, the problem of dual subordination has been intensified by the imposition of the FMS structure over a largely *ad hoc* system of migration committees within the Ministry of Labour, and it has significant implications for the implementation of migration policy at the ground level. The problem is not so much one of dual power (*dvoevlastie*) in the sense that regional governments directly counter central edicts with their own instructions and documents. It is rather that the local administration and the migration service are interwoven at the day-to-day level which effectively means that the priorities and objectives of the district and regional administration are prominent, if not uppermost, in the minds of migration service workers. Since the implications of this for regional migration-policy implementation are discussed at length in the following chapter, the discussion here is confined to a number of general issues arising from the structural organization of the service.

The roots of the organization

The establishment of migration services as independent bodies is an ongoing process and, as yet, at regional level, there is a weak sense of the organization's specific goals. Although in Ul'ianovsk, the case-study being explored here, a Territorial Migration Service has been in existence since August 1992 (just two months after the founding of the FMS), in some regions of the country migration committees continued to handle migrational affairs through to 1996. Even in Ul'ianovsk, moreover, full independence for the TMS is a relatively recent event. District-level migration service workers dated this independence variously at August 1994 and June 1995 while one suggested that, in her district, migration service workers remained subordinate to the deputy head of that district administration and not the TMS. In the case of Ul'ianovsk, districts had first set up migration commissions within employment departments to deal with the first inflow of refugees from the Transcaucasus in 1990 (thus pre-dating the FMS) and their deep roots in these local administrations have proved hard to tear up.

These origins encourage a stronger identification with the local district or regional authority than the Moscow-based FMS. In daily practice crucial policy and implementation decisions about refugees and forced migrants are taken at the district and regional levels via a system of 'commissions' which meet monthly to approve the applications for registration put forward by the migration service worker, and resolve individual cases which are unusual or disputed. At the district level (where people are registered) this commission is made up primarily of representatives of the district administration. In Ul'ianovsk the norm was for the chair to be the deputy head of the district administration, the deputy chair to be the head of the Department of Employment and for other members to include representatives of the district Committee of Social Protection, the Passport Office, the Committee for the Protection of the Family, Children and Motherhood, the Housing Department and the District Social Security Department. Clearly there is a logic in having these people on the commission; they are the people whose cooperation is essential in solving the daily problems faced by migrants (obtaining residence rights, housing and welfare benefits). It is also easy to see, however, why such a commission often appears to refugees and forced migrants themselves as a closed mafia defending its own, rather than their, interests.

This problem is repeated at regional level. While officially the TMS is financed by, and subordinate to, Moscow, regional administration officials are also assigned specific briefs to work with the TMS (on social and housing issues) and pursuit of the federally defined migration programme is clearly negotiated with them. One migration service worker in Ul'ianovsk noted that the regional administration was particularly important in such regions as Ul'ianovsk since they were not included in the list of regions designated for reception of refugees and forced migrants. The latter are allocated greater federal resources for directly funded schemes and are thus subject to greater vertical integration.[22]

Therefore, while the staffing of the migration service is funded directly from Moscow, migration service workers claimed that much of the resourcing of actual programmes came from regional or city budgets rather than federal funds. This is not necessarily disruptive of federal programme aims, but it does clearly indicate who 'the real bosses' are for local migration workers. The weak sense of identity with the federal service for which they work, moreover, is reinforced among ground-level workers by: their isolation; their lack of contact with the centre; and their lack of specialist training. The Ul'ianovsk TMS had a core staff of nine with additional workers in each of the region's twenty-two district migration services. These ground-level workers essentially operate on their own,[23] with virtually no formal training structure.[24] Workers exhibited little sense of working in accordance with a clearly defined programme with measurable achievement objectives and the background of the majority of staff (as former party workers, teachers and middle managers) encourages regionalism over departmentalism. During interviews migration workers showed little awareness of wider migration policy; there was no knowledge of the draft amendments to legislation being discussed at the time in parliament or their potential implications, for example.

The FMS in action: aims and intentions

The policy objectives of the Federal Migration Service are set down in the federal programme 'Migration' of March 1993 (drawn up by the Committee on Migratory Affairs) (Boikov and Levanov 1993a: 37), and in amended and supplemented programmes drawn up by the FMS and approved by president and government on 9 August 1994 and 3 August 1996. These programmes have established four basic areas of work of the FMS:

1 The *protection of the interests* of citizens of the Russian Federation whether they live within the Russian Federation or beyond its borders. This includes the defence of the rights of migrants in accordance with the law and the preparation of suggestions for the improvement of legislation as deemed necessary. It also means the recognition, in accordance with legislation, of the legal status of individuals who have migrated or who intend to migrate to Russia and cooperation with international and foreign organizations on questions of migration.
2 The *regulation of migratory processes*. The broad brief assigned to the FMS of managing migrational processes in the country also includes responsibility for the formulation and implementation of policy relating to labour out-migration by Russian citizens and to foreign migrant workers coming to the Russian Federation.
3 The *provision of aid* to refugees and forced migrants.
4 The facilitation of the *socio-economic adaptation* of refugees and forced migrants.

The third and fourth areas of work overlap, differing in their short-term or long-term nature. Specific obligations pertaining to these aims include:

the formulation of drafts of federal and inter-regional migrational pro-grammes and responsibility for their implementation; the distribution and control of money allocated from the federal budget; and the organization of the reception and temporary housing of refugees and forced migrants in the Russian Federation as well as aiding settlement in permanent new places of residence (Sokolov 1994: 95–7).

What is attempted below is a brief survey of the actual work undertaken by the FMS in these stated areas and some indication of the changing priorities of the service and its likely future direction.[25]

The reception of refugees and forced migrants: the eyes and ears of the state

Registering and returning figures on the number of refugees and forced migrants arriving in Russia is the most basic task of the FMS and its regional branches.[26] Each district migration service collects data on forced migrants and refugees applying for registration on registration cards. Details of these are passed to the regional migration service (TMS) which collates them and passes them to Moscow. The data collated cover: cumulative totals of refugees and forced migrants registering with the FMS;[27] regions of origin of refugees and forced migrants and changes in this over time; the density of refugees and forced migrants in relation to the population as a whole for different regions of the Russian Federation and between rural and urban areas; the structure of resettlement by region and by urban/rural areas; numbers applying for status by region; number of applications rejected according to region of origin; and demographic data on forced migrants and refugees including sex, age, nationality, educational qualifications and source of income (before leaving). These data establish above all changes in flows of migrants from individual former republics, where they look to settle and whether in-migrants will be dependent on the state; the key data for establishing the likely burdens on the state, and individual regions, arising from forced migration.

The FMS also conducts an accounting of foreign citizens working in Russia including the kinds of job, and the region, in which they are employed. The service registers and administers authorizations for Russian citizens working abroad.

Aid and socio-economic integration: only the needy need apply . . .

The stated aim of the FMS is to help all refugees and forced migrants entering the country but budget allocations to the service have been persistently inadequate to meet this aim. In 1992 – the first year of the independent existence of the FMS – inflation rapidly devoured the budget of 3 billion roubles meaning it was only enough to build about 3,000 housing units (Schwartz 1993: 245). In 1993 110 billion roubles was allocated for the fulfilment of the federal migration programme (Baiduzhii 1993) but of this only 24 billion was received (ibid.; Schwartz 1993: 246; Regent 1993).[28] This constituted less than 15 per cent of the sum Regent said the service needed (Regent 1993) and emergency and local-government funding was necessitated.[29] In 1994 the budget allocation was 545 billion roubles but only 263 billion was received (*Vynuzhdennie Pereselentsy v Rossii* 1995: 63); this constitutes 48 per cent of the budget originally allocated.[30] An additional problem was the fact that 70 per cent of the money arrived in the second half of 1994 and thus was significantly devalued upon arrival. Moreover, in December 1994 the financing of a number of measures of the programme was stopped when money needed to be diverted urgently to cope with the refugee crisis arising from the military conflict in Chechnia. This swallowed almost 11 billion roubles and meant that thirty-four construction projects were not completed (*Informatsionno-analiticheskii Biulleten'* 1995: 16). In 1995 there was a double cutback. First the budget allocated was only a quarter of the calculated expenditure for the coming year ('Migratsiia v Rossiiu: Problemy ostaiutsia' 1995). But of this allocation only 42 per cent – just under 622 billion roubles – was actually received (Komitet po delam SNG i sviaziam s sootechestvennikami 1996).

To its credit, the FMS has handled this appalling state of affairs equitably; distributing cuts across the range of its activities in order to maintain its overall prioritization without axing any particular aspect of provision. In 1994, for example, the prioritization of housing was maintained – receiving 47.6 per cent of the budget – with an additional 20.9 per cent being used to provide families with interest-free loans to buy or build housing for themselves (*Vynuzhdennie Pereselentsy v Rossii* 1995: 65). Nevertheless, the money actually spent on housing refugees and forced migrants came to just 44 per cent of the original budget allocation. For 1996, the FMS requested 12 trillion roubles but was allocated by the Ministry of Finance just 2.2 trillion. Of this, 37 per cent is planned to be spent on new housing, with an additional 25 per cent being spent on refugee reception centres and 20 per cent on interest-free loans for refugees. However, the Ministry of Finance has earmarked 800 billion roubles of this money for compensation payments for loss of housing and property to refugees from Chechnia. This would devastate the FMS budget and the service is fighting to have these compensation payments paid out of the budget allocated for the reconstruction of Chechnia rather than the FMS budget (Regent 1996: 41; Glushko 1996).

The irregularity and insufficiency of financing means that the money received is used to deal with immediately essential measures while long-term programmes – such as permanent housing for forced migrants – become financed on a residual principle (*Informatsionno-analiticheskii Biulleten'* 1995: 16). In effect, instead of helping all, in practice only the most vulnerable groups of migrants receive help. Such groups are defined as single pensioners, disabled people, large families and single mothers and, together, they account for about 25 per cent of the total number of refugees and forced migrants (Baiduzhii 1993). Moreover, what help is given to individual refugees and forced migrants depends greatly on their own circumstances and on the policy and possibilities of the receiver region; evaluations of this by receivers and regional migration workers are analysed in Chapters 5 and 7. Below, the FMS perspective on the achievements and problems with the provision of help to refugees and forced migrants is outlined.

One-off payments

That one-off benefit payments cannot be universal is a state of affairs openly recognized by the FMS which defines benefit payments as 'a material benefit given to refugees (forced migrants), *in particular need* of help' (*Vynuzhdennie Pereselentsy v Rossii* 1995: 83). In the course of 1993, the FMS estimated that 150,000–170,000 people from particularly vulnerable sections of the refugee and forced-migrant population had received one-off cash benefits (Baiduzhii 1993; Kozlov 1994),[31] while in 1994 a total of 2.7 billion roubles (1 per cent of the total budget) was reported spent on such benefits (*Vynuzhdennie Pereselentsy v Rossii* 1995: 63), being received by a total of 120,000 people (*Informatsionno-analiticheskii Biulleten'* 1995: 17). In 1995, 4.5 billion was spent, accounting for 0.73 per cent of the total budget and significantly less than the 87 billion or 6 per cent of the planned budget (Komitet po delam SNG i sviaziam s sootechestvennikami 1996). The prioritization of the most needy was a policy adopted at regional level as well; in July 1995 local migration workers in Ul'ianovsk confirmed that one-off benefits (equivalent to the monthly minimum wage) were being given to the most needy forced migrants and refugees only.

Temporary housing

The improvement in provision of temporary reception centres and accommodation for refugees and forced migrants is a current FMS priority and there has been a steadily growing number of primary reception points

(*Punkt Pervichnogo Priema* or PPP) and temporary accommodation centres (*Tsentr Vremennogo Razmeshcheniia* or TsVR) to house temporarily
refugees and forced migrants who cannot be accommodated in any other
way. In 1993 fifteen temporary reception centres were operating in Russia,
offering places for 3,000 people (Baiduzhii 1993) and by 1 September
1994 the number had grown to twenty-eight with a further eight primary
reception points (Koshchueva 1994; Sokolov 1994: 33). If the TsVRs and
PPPs based in the troubled Northern Caucasus region are included, then
there are currently ninety in operation, able to receive 25,000 people,
according to the FMS ('Migratsiia v Rossiiu: Problemy ostaiutsia' 1995).
PPPs accommodate refugees and forced migrants until they have registered
their application for status, TsVRs until the decision on status is made and
permanent accommodation found. Accommodation is free and residents
may be given up to three free meals per day.[32]

Despite the progress made, the reality is that for 'ordinary' forced
migrants and refugees it is impossible to obtain temporary accommodation;
demand is far higher than the number of places available and the FMS does
not release information about these centres for fear of being swamped with
those seeking refuge. Places are allocated via territorial branches of the
migration service and preference is given to the most needy – single
pensioners, the most seriously disabled, single mothers with children under
3 years of age and large families with children under 18. It is now clear
that the current system of temporary accommodation has been overloaded
by the Chechen crisis; during 1994–5 65,000 of the 95,000 people who
passed through them were from Chechnia (*Informatsionno-analiticheskii
Biulleten'* 1995: 5). Moreover, due to the ongoing problems of finding permanent housing for refugees and forced migrants, the FMS admits that it
is currently unable to conform to the legal requirement of keeping refugees
and forced migrants in such temporary accommodation for no longer than
three months (ibid.)

Permanent housing

From the beginning of migration programmes and services in Russia,
there has been a highly pragmatic attitude towards the resolution of the
housing problem of migrants. Coinciding with the rejection of 'statist'
ideology, migration programmes have consistently stressed that best
practice is to help migrants to help themselves. But, as numbers of
migrants have increased while the construction of housing has virtually
collapsed, the government has made clear that it is now simply unwilling
to accept any commitment to provide migrants with housing (Regent 1993;
Illarionov in Baiduzhii 1993; Shakhrai in Nekrasova 1994b). Thus, the

1995 amendments to the Law on Forced Migrants make clear that the state is only obliged to register forced migrants on the general housing list; in stark contrast to the original provision in the 1993 law which obliged the state to provide the forced migrant with housing from a 'special housing fund designated for forced migrants' or to include them on a list of people who, according to Russian law, received priority in housing. The reasoning here is mainly economic – the state simply cannot afford it – but also political; housing is the single issue most likely to cause social tension in Russia and politicians are well aware that any sign that the government was prioritizing forced migrants (often perceived by the general public to be relatively well-off anyway) in provision of housing would be disastrous.

The migration programme thus envisages solving the permanent housing problem of forced migrants by providing incentives to build or purchase housing themselves. This is made possible through the availability of a ten-year interest-free loan.[33] The sum available depends on the size of the family and has been raised over the period of implementation (from 700,000 roubles when introduced to a current rate of 4.2 million for a family of up to four people). There are strict conditions set out for the receipt and repayment of the loan ('Poriadok predostavleniia vynuzh-dennim pereselentsam dolgovremennoi besprotsentnoi vozvratnoi ssudy na stroitel'stvo ili pokupku zhil'ia' 1993) which require: that forced migrants be officially registered as such with the FMS; that a residence permit for the region in which the loan is applied for be presented; and the provision of some guarantee of repayment (an individual guarantor or the use of the future home as security).

Estimates of the number of actual beneficiaries from the interest-free-loan scheme vary: figures for 1993 range from 9,700 families (Kozlov 1994) to 15,000 families (Baiduzhii 1993) while the FMS itself claims to have provided 20,000 families with interest-free loans for construction and purchase of housing in 1994 (*Informatsionno-analiticheskii Biulleten'* 1995: 17). Indeed, there is evidence that the process of granting loans is being speeded up and in one district of Ul'ianovsk city a migration service worker noted that in the first six months of 1995 loans had been given to eighty-five people for a mixture of construction, purchase of housing and contributions to cooperative housing ventures.

Despite its open recognition that it cannot resolve the problem of housing forced migrants and refugees permanently within the next ten to fifteen years, the FMS continues to prioritize housing in its budget allocation, correctly recognizing that it is the biggest single problem faced by returnees. A total of 4,153 flats and an additional 144 rooms were built or purchased for forced migrants and refugees in 1995. Given the budget short-fall which the FMS suffered this figure is impressive since it falls short of the target by only 655 (Komitet po delam SNG i sviaziam s sootechestvennikami 1996) and is significantly greater than the total of 2,398 new flats built in 1994[34] (*Informatsionno-analiticheskii Biulleten'* 1995: 4). The prioritization of housing is set to continue; it has already been suggested that 82 per cent of the budget for 1996 will be spent on housing-related items (loans, temporary centres and housing construction) (Dmitriev 1996a).

Compact settlements

Compact settlements are a controversial attempt simultaneously to resolve the housing, employment and socio-cultural adaptation problems of refugees and forced migrants. Traditionally such settlements have been promoted by NGOs and migrant associations while being treated sceptically by the FMS. The latter considered them to demand too much investment in infrastructure for a relatively small number of beneficiaries (Koshchueva 1994). The FMS also viewed them as potentially provoking rather than resolving problems of socio-cultural integration. Larisa Kablukova, a deputy director of the FMS, has warned that 'concentrated settlements could give rise to "Nagorno-Karabakhs" within Russia' (Rotar' 1993) while others suggested they would prevent proper integration by creating pockets of migrants from the same area trapped by their Tajik, Kazak or Latvian mentalities (Koshchueva 1994). Political objections have focused on the possibility of such settlements producing pro-Zhirinovskii supporters (Zhdakaev 1994) and on the implication of 'superiority' of the migrants over local Russians inherent in them (Koshchueva 1994).

There is, however, clear evidence that the FMS is changing its attitude to compact settlements. A clause in the amended Law on Forced Migrants notes the need to cooperate positively with migrant associations seeking to construct compact settlements and the FMS now claims to have helped financially in the construction of housing and social and engineering infrastructure in 107 compact settlements (Totskii 1996: 38).

Employment

Although part of the brief of the FMS is to help forced migrants and refugees find employment, no additional help is provided over and above that available to all Russian citizens; forced migrants (but not refugees) are entitled to grants during training and retraining and to normal unemployment benefits and services. The only benefit accruing to forced-migrant status thus appears to be that forced migrants may register with employment centres immediately whereas newcomers to an area usually have to wait six months after their official registration of residence before the centre will accept them.[35] Accordingly, employment-centre workers do not consider forced migrants to have any 'special needs'.

The 1995 amended Law on Forced Migrants omits the obligation of the state to offer tax concessions to enterprises and organizations employing forced migrants. As in housing, the emphasis has moved to supporting the entrepreneurial initiatives of forced migrants themselves; the FMS claims that by mid-1994 a system for this had been implemented by which money was awarded on a competitive basis (*Informatsionno-analiticheskii Biulleten'* 1995: 4). However, it also suggested that a job-creation scheme for forced migrants had been incorporated into the federal migration programme which would create 14,846 jobs at 327 enterprises in 38 regions of Russia and that 50 billion roubles had been allocated from the Federal Employment Service budget to provide employment for un-employed forced migrants (ibid.). The FMS claims to have helped create 3,698 jobs in 1994 and a further 1,968 in 1995 (Regent 1996: 35).

Counselling and psychological help

The first centre in Russia for the medical and psychological rehabilitation of refugees and forced migrants was reported to have opened in 1993 at a leisure complex outside Moscow (Baiduzhii 1993). In 1996 Tat'iana Regent referred to a second one working in Krasnodar territory (Airapetova 1996). Without doubt, however, often quite serious trauma among refugees and forced migrants goes completely unacknowledged and untreated.

Controlling migrational processes: from migration to policing service?

The FMS is evolving from an organization defending the rights of forced migrants and refugees into one which controls and polices migrational flows. This can be seen in the indications of the organization's priorities for 1995: the restriction of real aid to the most vulnerable; the devolution of much responsibility (such as for housing) to the regions; and an increased role for the FMS in controlling immigration and policing labour migration. Of the five priorities for 1995 stated by the FMS, two focus on aid to forced migrants and refugees but warn that the target is to aid those who are most vulnerable and that the housing problem, although a priority, cannot possibly be resolved within the next fifteen years. The other three priorities are concerned with the new control function of the organization ('Migratsiia v Rossiiu: Problemy ostaiutsia' 1995).

Controlling immigration: a new threat to Russia

During the Soviet period immigration was negligible and primarily utilized for propaganda purposes. In post-Soviet Russia, however, in-migration is being 'securitized' (Huysmans 1995) as elsewhere in Europe. In announcing new regulations regarding immigration control in 1994, the FMS declared that 'uncontrollable migration is acquiring a threatening character, aggravating the epidemiological, criminal and social situation in major cities and causing harm to the security of the country' (*Informatsionno-analiticheskii Biulleten'* 1995: 78). The concern is primarily over illegal migrants – an estimated 400,000 of them – from South East Asia, Africa, the Near and Middle East who, it is claimed, are abusing Russia's laxness in order to enter Scandinavian countries, Europe, Canada and the USA illegally (*Informatsionno-analiticheskii Biulleten'* 1995: 7–8). Interestingly, it is suggested that it is Russia's naivety regarding migrants which has been exploited – both by illegal migrants and by the west. In particular the naive accession of Russia to the 1951 UN Convention on Refugees is blamed for giving the signal to 'certain circles of African and Asian regions' that they could move to Russia and demand to legalize their stay in the Russian Federation (ibid.: 9). Moreover, the 'closed-door policy' of the west is blamed for allowing the passage of such 'transit migrants' to become blocked in Russia.

Measures to deal with the perceived threat are twofold. First, the problem of 'transparency of borders'[36] is to be resolved by the creation of posts of immigration control (PIK) on the borders. Reportedly forty-three of the planned fifty-three are already in operation.[37] In addition, three centres of temporary accommodation for immigrants (TsVRI) have been created and regional branches of the FMS have begun work looking at the applications for recognition as refugees. There is a clear indication that Russia is now learning from the west rapidly; it is reported that of 1,500 applications already considered, only twenty cases had been granted refugee status. Moreover, the FMS states clearly that it expects to be as tough as the west in closing doors; according to international practice refugee status realistically will be received by less than 2 per cent (ibid.: 8).

Second, immigration legislation is being drafted for consideration by the Russian parliament. The current Law on Refugees has been declared by the FMS to be 'more liberal' than the UN Convention of 1951 and to have left Russia unprotected from open borders with other CIS states, particularly along her southern frontier (ibid.: 82–3). The content of the new law on immigration is likely to follow precedents contained in existing executive statutes and regulations. In this case the presidential decree 'On measures for the introduction of immigration control' (of 16 December 1993) and the FMS statute of 1994 are indicative. Together they envisage:

- the establishment of immigration quotas for areas particularly attractive to refugees and migrants;
- the establishment of migration control points at entry points to the Russian Federation;
- the prevention of mass immigration through diplomatic efforts with other states whence flows are likely to come and through the establishment of an early warning system of potential large migration movements ('O merakh po vvedeniiu immigratsionnogo kontrolia' 1993; 'Polozhenie o federal'noi migratsionnoi sluzhbe Rossii' 1994).

Protecting Russian jobs

The second new priority for the FMS concerns the regulation of inward labour migration. There appear to be two concerns over the growth of foreign labour in Russia. First, that the financial benefits for the state of *regulated* employment of foreign workers should be fully exploited. And, second, that the process of 'the filling of individual regions of Russia with an unqualified, lumpenized and criminal workforce' which is overstraining the Russian labour market in several regions be ended (*Informatsionno-analiticheskii Biulleten'* 1995: 81). In the eyes of the FMS the current situation justifies the 'intolerance' and 'negative reaction' towards migrants in receiver communities (ibid.).

The growing impact of migrant labour on local labour markets and fears that it will encourage illegal residence has led to tighter controls being introduced on labour migration into Russia and it is the FMS which has been made responsible for monitoring and controlling this. Although precise figures are unavailable it is estimated that there are currently 350,000–400,000 'guest workers' in the Russian Federation – although the head of the administration for migrant workers of the FMS, G. Barabanov, suggests that this figure may be a great underestimate (Shmyganovskii 1994). Many such workers come from other member states of the CIS (Ukrainian workers for example attracted by the relative strength of the rouble). However, there are also guest workers from the 'far abroad'; between 1987 and 1989 Russia experimented with the 'import' of thousands of Vietnamese workers who were employed in low-skilled work (ibid.). Recently state concern both to control and maximize the benefit of the employment of guest workers has been rising, particularly in relation to the Russian Far East where there are periodic panics about the 'swamping' of the Russian population with Chinese guest workers. One outcome of this was a presidential decree 'On the attraction and use of foreign workers in the Russian Federation' (16 December 1993) which established in law that priority must be given to Russian citizens when hiring staff for job vacancies. The decree also stated that foreign citizens would be allowed to work only for the employer, and in the specific job, for which they were originally authorized and that their work permit of one year could be renewed only for one additional year. The FMS must ensure that the firm or organization is officially registered in Russia and that the contracts drawn up with guest workers guarantee their rights (ibid.). More 'direct action' was taken in 1995, however, when the Russian government returned home more than 10,000 Chinese from Russia's Maritime region as part of their 'Operation Foreigner' programme which ended in October 1995 (Helton 1996: 53).

While the issue of foreign workers lies beyond the scope of the current study, the introduction of stricter regulations and policing of such workers by the FMS has had spin-offs for refugees and forced migrants in Russia. The requirement that enterprises prioritize the local workforce in hiring labour (and, indeed, must pay for hiring foreign workers) means that enterprises are no longer prepared to take on forced migrants and refugees unless they are officially registered as such, and thus not likely to be classified as foreign workers. One migration service worker in Ul'ianovsk noted that much of her job was devoted to touring local employers and checking their books for foreign workers. Efforts are also being made to prevent the arrival of guest workers from hot spots and regions with high crime rates: shorthand for the Transcaucasus region. The deputy director of one Moscow bus depot admitted that Transcaucasians were not taken on at all (Shmyganovskii 1994).

The implications of this new prioritization of control outside the 'target areas' – for the work of the average TMS – is as yet unclear. An indication of the future, however, may well be found in the words of one migration service worker in Ul'ianovsk who noted having been informed that a 'migration police' was to be introduced. The growth of this control function must be seen in the context of deeper shifts in Russia's attitude to the countries of the 'near abroad' and to the changing priority ascribed to relations with the west. While, as yet, there appears to be no fundamental danger that Russia will withdraw from the obligations undertaken when she signed up to the 1951 United Nations Convention on the Status of Refugees, it is clear, nevertheless, that the domestic political scene is increasingly influential in determining migration policy and that this has had significant institutional impact already.

NON-GOVERNMENTAL ORGANIZATIONS

The shift in the role of the FMS indicates not only the rise of a more 'nationalist' macro politics in Russia but the emergence of a ground-level politics of self-help. To put it crudely, the retreat of the FMS from its original priorities of the defence of the rights of, and the provision of aid to, refugees and forced migrants has been facilitated by the emergence of third-sector provision for these social groups. By its nature such provision is often extremely localized and informal, consisting of a host of small, locally or regionally based self-help groups. However, in addition to international organizations (discussed separately below) two key, federal level, non-governmental organizations inputting into migration policy and implementation in Russia can be identified and these organizations are now considered in detail (see Figure 4.1).

The Coordinating Council for Aid to Refugees and Forced Migrants

The Coordinating Council for Aid to Refugees and Forced Migrants (CCARFM) was officially founded by a collective of forty-seven indi-viduals and twenty-nine organizations (twelve of them being migrant organizations) in April 1993 as an outcome of an international conference on 'The protection of refugees in Russia'. However, the Council's roots go back six years, growing out of the early work of the organization Civil Assistance (*Grazhdanskoe sodeistvie*) which had been formed originally by a group of ten individuals in reaction to events in Baku when the first 'Soviet refugees' emerged (Grafova 1995a).[38]

CCARFM states its chief aim in classic perestroika 'informal-group' style: 'to unite public efforts in order to resolve the problems of refugees and defend [their] interests in state and international organizations' (Sokolov 1994: 5). However, in fact the Council is active in two distinct ways: first, as a pressure group – providing feedback and critique of government policies; but second, as an umbrella organization for refugee self-help groups and a direct facilitator of aid provision.

In its first guise, CCARFM (or rather its committee and full-time staff) has conducted extensive work to influence FMS and government policy. This has been achieved via increasing participation in committees and commissions and through persistent inputting of their critiques to relevant government departments. The committee works out of offices of the literary newspaper *Literaturnaia Gazeta* and is chaired by the well-known journalist Lidiia Grafova. Undoubtably this has helped the organization to employ the media effectively to transmit an alternative approach to viewing the situation of the Russian diaspora (see Chapter 2). A recent communication by the Coordinating Committee to the head of the FMS, Tat'iana Regent, sets out the organization's current lobbying agenda succinctly:

- promotion of the right of refugees and forced migrants (in practice, not just in principle) to choose freely whether to remain in a former place of residence or to move to another republic;
- the acceptance by Russia of her responsibility for all former Soviet citizens wishing to become citizens of Russia and the organization of a long-term campaign in the media to create a favourable climate for their reception;[39]
- the acceptance by Russia that current migratory processes are essentially those of *repatriation* and the adoption of a law 'On repatriation' to recognize this;
- the recognition of the need for greater input from international organizations in developing a strategy and tactical approach to migration in the post-Soviet space and, in particular, the establishment of a permanent working body under the auspices of UNHCR, the International Organization for Migration (IOM) and the Organization for Security and Cooperation in Europe (OSCE);
- the recognition of the positive input of refugees and forced migrants into Russian society;
- the placing of displaced persons from Chechnia under the protection of UNHCR;
- the creation of regional representatives of OSCE to defend the rights of national minorities and help prevent migrational flows;
- the recognition and support of the work of NGOs (Pravlenie Koordinatsionnogo Soveta 1995).

In its second guise – as umbrella organization and direct facilitator – the Council's work has been concerned primarily with the development of compact settlements. The idea of compact settlements was first raised in *Literaturnaia Gazeta* in July 1990 and was subsequently taken up by potential migrants in various republics. The construction of compact settlements began in 1991–2 and about sixty[40] are now under way in various regions of Russia, although they vary in size, productive activity, the extent and type of housing they construct and their place in the local community (Koordinatsionnii Sovet pomoshchi bezhentsam i vynuzhdenim pereselentsam 1995).

In contrast to the FMS (whose initial opposition to compact settlements was noted above), CCARFM has always promoted the movement as an important means of resolving the integrated problems faced by migrants in the current economic and political climate in Russia. In particular the organization notes that the absence of compensation for housing left in the republics and the lack of state support for buying or constructing new housing in Russia means that compact settlements provide a way of pooling resources among migrants to construct housing collectively. Tax concessions given to such organizations enable them to buy cheap building materials. The compact settlement is also seen as providing an environment of mutual support for people united by a common fate and common tragedy and as helping them survive in an indifferent and hostile environment. Finally, the compact settlement allows migrants to retain a sense of their own identity – the unique ethno-cultural community developed in the republics over several generations of 'Tajik', 'Uzbek' or 'Kazak' Russians – and a space to prove that they are not 'parasites' but talented and able workers prepared to make a contribution to Russia.

The most positive example of such settlements is that of KhOKO – comprising more than 4,000 forced migrants and refugees mostly from Tajikistan – formed in 1990 just outside the medium-size farming town of Borisoglebsk in Voronezh region. The settlement boasts seventeen companies (working in numerous fields including architectural design, woodworking and printing) and employees are reported to earn monthly salaries of up to 200 US dollars. Housing construction is funded via contributions from wages from employees which is offset against the cost of buying a flat or having a cottage built by the collective (Owen 1995b). However, CCARFM is fully aware of the many problems still faced by even the most successful of such settlements and continues to call for their real support at state level (Grafova 1993, 1996).

In addition to the promotion of compact settlements, CCARFM hosts weekly receptions of refugees and forced migrants in the basement of *Literaturnaia Gazeta*'s offices. In the first half of 1995 more than 2,000 people were received and 806 families received financial aid. More than 100 people were given psychological and psychiatric assistance. Although many of these were treated with anti-depressants and sleeping tablets the Council has also developed a programme of therapy aimed at improving the psychological climate in migrant groups. The Council has been particularly concerned to provide legal assistance to refugees and forced migrants and has helped 318 Chechen refugees sue the Russian government for compensation for moral and material damage. The handbook for forced migrants *Kompas*, published by CCARFM, also outlines in detail the rights of forced migrants and refugees and includes reprints of all significant legislation concerning them. The first print run consisted of 1,000 copies distributed free of charge, and a second edition was published at the beginning of 1995 with a print run of 10,000.

The highly critical stance adopted by CCARFM in its lobbying role has brought it into conflict rather than cooperation with the FMS, particularly with its leadership. Grafova describes the FMS and CCARFM as 'antagonistically opposed' since the latter seeks to 'defend the rights of refugees' while the FMS has an interest in 'keeping them as hostages' (Grafova 1995a). To some extent this is a personal feud between Grafova and Regent[41] and, according to CCARFM at least, relations with many departments of the FMS at a more practical level remain very good. In particular the reception department of the FMS in Moscow frequently directs refugees to CCARFM since, as a result of increasing cooperation with international organizations, the Council has been in a better position to provide concrete help (financial, material, legal and psychological support) than the FMS in Moscow. CCARFM also has very good relations with a number of territorial migration services (such as Orenburg region) where they are particularly active, as well as a number of other state bodies, especially the Presidential Commission on Human Rights, the Presidential Commission on Citizenship and with (parts of) the Ministry of Foreign Affairs.

Having relied on voluntary help for most of its existence, CCARFM is now beginning to strengthen its position through the establishment of outside contacts. Links with international organizations are a priority for the Council and help its work in three fundamental ways. First, in its lobbying activity, reference to the need to uphold policies and recommendations of the international community can be mobilized to support the Council's criticism of state policy. Second, recognition as a key NGO in Russia can bring material and status gains; recent recognition by the UNHCR, for example, has led to the receipt of a small budget from them for hardware, staff and administrative costs, rent payments, fees for lawyers and direct material support to refugees. Three branches of CCARFM opened in summer 1995 in Voronezh, Lipetsk and Sverdlovsk regions. Third, international organizations may help fund key projects. Recent examples of success are the decision in March 1995 by the Swiss Red Cross to invest 500,000 Swiss francs in the construction of a social centre in the compact settlement 'Novosel' in Kaluga region – the first compact settlement in Russia – formed by migrants (mainly Russian) from Tajikistan, and the increasing involvement of the IOM in the compact-settlement programme. Indeed, such international involvement may have unanticipated benefits. As Richard Morris of the IOM points out, quite often the simple presence of a western representative may serve as a catalyst in bringing together migrant associations with reluctant local leaders and thus reduce friction between them (Morris 1995: 8).

The Compatriots' Fund (Russian Fund for Aid to Refugees)

The Compatriots' Fund has a rather more ambiguous position and role than CCARFM. The Fund was registered officially in 1991 as a non-commercial organization designed to ensure the legal protection of refugees and forced migrants and assist their settlement and employment. However, in reality it was always a semi-state organization and a government decree of 1992 ordered local administrations, ministries and departments to set up territorial branches of the Fund and help it meet its aims. Consequently many representatives of the Fund worked hand in glove with the TMS, literally in the same office (as in Orel region), or, in the case of Ul'ianovsk the head of the TMS and the Fund representative were one and the same person. However, increasingly the Fund has taken up a more critical position *vis-à-vis* the FMS and, for its efforts, has had its state funding withdrawn (Grafova 1995a; Mukomel' 1995a), making it a real non-governmental organization.

Under its new head, Boris Sergeev, the Fund is asserting its independence. It currently consists of thirty-four regional affiliates and about 700 migrant production enterprises and it is seeking to bring together all migrant production facilities in a general movement for the economic revival of Russia. The Fund organized the first Congress of Refugees and Forced Migrants from the 'Near Abroad', which took place in Moscow on 2–3 June 1994, and was attended by 500 delegates of its regional branches. Under the slogan of the Congress 'Migrants, help yourselves!' (Nekrasova 1994a), the Fund used the Congress to pass a resolution calling for its own recognition as the official mediator between migration organizations, the Russian government and local organs of power. Subsidies from Moscow for the construction of housing and production organizations for refugees, it suggested, should be directed to the Fund. This would have effectively cut out the FMS altogether and passed its resettlement functions to the Fund (Rotar' 1994b).

However, not everyone is impressed by the efforts of the 'Compatriots' to revitalize and redirect themselves. A minor criticism of the Fund is that it is elitist; it will only deal with those who have official status and money (Koshchueva 1994). More serious allegations concern the way in which the Fund's management has used budget allocations. Here it must be remembered that the Fund was originally established to handle the construction of housing and production units for groups of migrants and thus much of the budget allocated by the state passed through its hands. In 1993 alone the Fund received 8 billion roubles from the FMS to help migrants and, according to its deputy executive director, the Fund had helped 50,000 migrants and organized around 500 production complexes (Koshchueva

1994). Due to the tax concessions accorded them, NGOs in Russia are frequently criticized for corruption, and the specific brief of the Compatriots' Fund to handle the funding side of migration projects has, not surprisingly, led to many accusations of misuse of funds. In particular concern has been expressed over the heavy investment of the fund in a number of commercial organizations. Although this in itself is not illegal, commercial organizations may only be set up under the Fund's auspices if the money invested comes from the income of the Fund; the Fund is not allowed to use budget money for commercial purposes. The former president of the Compatriots' Fund, however, claims that budget money was often paid into such firms (ibid.). Similar accusations of non-legitimate use of government funds have been directed at individual production and housing complexes set up by migrants and funded by the Compatriots' Fund (such as 'Novosel' in Kaluga region) and local branches of the Fund, such as that of the generally praised Pskov branch (ibid.).

Although it would be naive to expect any complete eradication of corruption from the NGO sphere, nevertheless the distancing of the Compatriots' Fund from the FMS, in itself, will break the monopoly control of the funding of migrant production units and thereby much of the opportunity for misuse of funds. There is also evidence from the regions that a reborn Fund has emerged separate from the FMS structure. In Ul'ianovsk, at least, a new Compatriots' Fund organization has emerged and is seeking to mobilize refugees themselves in concrete activities (buying land and setting up production facilities). The Fund has also been busy defining new relationships with other institutions, now that its status is no longer guaranteed by the FMS. Sergeev claims that agreements on cooperation in helping forced migrants and refugees were being drawn up with the heads of administration of twenty-seven regions of Russia and that an agreement had been signed already with the Department of Employment (Sootechestvenniki 1996: 3).

Regional and local organizations and 'compact settlements'

The handbook for forced migrants and refugees published by CCARFM lists seventeen Russian organizations providing aid to displaced persons (Sokolov 1995). In addition there is a variety of social and charitable organizations dealing with the problem of refugees on a local level – supplying information to potential migrants, providing emergency relief and supporting local resettlement projects. Some of these organizations have launched commercial ventures as a way of funding their activities since they cannot rely on charitable donations. Some of the most prominent are the Tajikistan Migration Society, the Kasparov Fund (for Armenian refugees), the Sakharov Charity, the Native Expanses Association, and the Society of Russian Refugees in St Petersburg[42] (Marnie and Slater 1993). Many smaller groups form in the country of origin and are based around compact-settlement projects such as the 'Migration Society' formed in Tajikistan which set up the TOO Novosel in Kaluga region, headed by Galina Belgorodskaia, or the 'Zov' organization of migrants from Kazakstan, headed by Olimpiada Ignatenko, which set up a compact settlement in Lipetsk region. Others emerge in the place of resettlement such as the 'Tulitsa' fund and organization designed to help integration of migrants and refugees in Tula region (Zhdakaev 1994). In all, according to Boris Sergeev, by the end of the third wave of migration in 1993 there were 700 migrant communities in Russia with an average size of fifty families (Sokolov 1994: 71). Estimates in 1996 suggested there were more than 1,000 migrant communities in Russia involved in housing construction, production, commerce and social and welfare work.

KhOKO is still considered to be the most successful of the compact settlements of migrants; rather than being a drain on the state, it actually contributed 1.5 billion roubles in taxes to the Voronezh regional budget in 1994. New success stories are 'Servistsentr' of Sergiev Posad and 'Grinvud' of Vladimir region. Pskov continues to be praised as one of the most active regions; sixty-two migrant enterprises have been established there employing 724 families (primarily returnees from the Baltic states) (Sootechestvenniki 1996: 5). Pskov's success may be connected to the fact that the head of the Pskov branch of the Fund of Compatriots, V. S. Nikitin, is active within the policy-making arena, being a deputy of the Duma and chair of CIS Affairs' subcommittee on cooperation with refugees and forced migrants.

A recent trend towards networking has encouraged the emergence of regional associations bringing together local migrant organizations. The model developed by the Urals Association of Refugees and the Association 'Saratovskii istochnik' were praised at the forum of migrant associations in April 1996 and adopted for recommendation to other groups. The effectiveness of the Saratov association – which includes fifty-five enterprises – might be judged by the fact that Saratov region was the only region in 1995 to receive the money apparently allocated by the employment service to the FMS for funding additional jobs for forced migrants. According to the leader of the Saratov association, this success was due to constant lobbying conducted by the local administration.

At the federal level the networking which produced the forum of migrant associations held in April 1996 may also have a permanent outcome. The forum concluded with the creation of what was described as a 'mass social movement' called the Forum of Migrant Organizations. This, it was agreed, should have a permanently active executive committee which would lobby the interests of forced migrants in government and legislative institutions and participate in developing and implementing migration policy and programmes as well as providing social support for migrants, protecting their rights against bureaucrats and acting as a source of public control over funds granted from the state and private business. It also pledged to foster a positive public opinion towards migrants and furnish state, international and migrant organizations with information and to establish a training centre for migrant leaders and a teaching centre on enterprise and a socio-psychological rehabilitation service (Ispolkom foruma pereselencheskikh organizatsii 1996).

It would appear that the forum provides a significant opportunity for the myriad local migrant associations to exchange experience, information and mutual support which may help individual organizations to overcome what have hitherto appeared insurmountable, localized problems. It may also succeed in ending the competition for national representation of migrants previously conducted between CCARFM and the Compatriots' Fund since the executive committee includes both organizations and leaders of the most successful migrant associations. Perhaps just as importantly, however, the executive committee provides a visible and permanent body which can be drawn into policy-making circles. The fact that the forum was concluded by a parliamentary debate which managed to produce a joint final document reflecting many of the suggestions made during the forum is a positive sign. The priority areas in legislation were declared to be the formulation of a law 'On migration policy of the Russian Federation', a law 'On migrant associations' and the introduction of amendments to existing tax laws to provide concessions for forced migrants involved in the construction of housing. The document also called for state support for migrant associations and enterprises and for the inclusion of the Compatriots' Fund, CCARFM and other non-commercial migrant organizations and their regional associations in the implementation of federal migration policy. Finally, the document pledged to hold a special parliamentary debate on the plight of refugees in Chechnia, hitherto a question which the state has largely chosen to ignore.

INTERNATIONAL ORGANIZATIONS

Although the primary object of this chapter has been to map the peculiar institutional framework of migration-policy formulation and implementation in post-Soviet Russia, it is essential that the global context of the Russian approach and provision is not ignored.

As was noted in Chapter 2, the current hysteria about the potential inflow of migrants from the former Soviet Union and Eastern Europe into Western Europe forms part of the discursive framework of the refugees and forced-migrant debate in post-Soviet Russia. The current concern in Europe with drawing up a harmonized and effective procedure to prevent 'the abuse of asylum systems' and the widespread establishment of the 'safe-country' principle (Widgren 1994: 41) to protect themselves from emigrating former Soviet citizens is not only hurtful to great Russian pride, it is also being copied by Russia itself in order to limit immigration into Russia. The FMS is fully aware of the turn-about in policy towards refugees in the west during the 1990s (*Informatsionno-analiticheskii Biulleten'* 1995: 85) and the intention to follow suit has already been put into practice. A presidential decree on political asylum signed on 27 July 1995 effectively establishes the 'safe-country' principle for Russia and requires that each application for political asylum is granted only by the president himself (see Chapter 3).

At the institutional level, the global community is significant in both its presence and its absence. Although excluded from Figure 4.1, international bodies concerned with displaced persons do play a role in Russia and the precise nature of that role is discussed below. Nevertheless, international organizations have appeared reluctant to involve themselves in regulating migration issues in the post-Soviet space and this is suggestive both of a growing overload on international organizations set up originally in quite different circumstances and a counter-tendency among the most powerful members of such organizations to prioritize peculiar national interests over global humanitarian goals. The minimalist role adopted by the global community has led the Russian non-governmental organization CCARFM to call upon international organizations to take up a more vigorous role in scrutinizing Russian government policy from a human rights angle, to establish an arbitration court to settle disputes over violation of migrants' rights, to insist that money from loans issued to Russia be set aside to deal with migration problems and to establish a body under the auspices of the UNHCR, IOM and OSCE to implement decisions adopted at international forums concerning migration and refugee issues in the former Soviet space (Grafova 1995d). Schwarz goes even further in suggesting that international organizations and agencies (UNHCR, IOM and CSCE High Commissioner on National Minorities) are making the CIS a testing-ground for their previously virtually unimplemented 'early warning strategies'. On the ground level, he argues, international aid directed at non-governmental self-help groups is inefficiently handled and patronizing in attitude (Schwarz 1995: 13–19). Whether or not these criticisms are justified, Kolstoe is right to suggest that the very fact that Russia as the 'historical homeland' is playing such a key role in regulating migration issues in the post-Soviet space suggests a failure on the part of the international community (Kolstoe 1995: 289). The latter does not officially envisage any special role for the 'external homelands' of diaspora groups in the monitoring of minority rights which should, ideally, be guaranteed via global and regional supra-state organs such as the UN, the Council of Europe, the CSCE (Conference on Security and Cooperation in Europe) and non-governmental organizations (ibid.).

Mapping the role of international organizations

In relation to the former Soviet Union, the chief international actors are: the United Nations High Commissioner for Refugees (UNHCR), the International Organization for Migration (IOM), the International Labour Organization (ILO) and the Red Cross and Red Crescent. The mandate for their involvement arises from the fact that four of the countries in the region have become parties to the 1951 UN Convention relating to the Status of Refugees and its 1967 Protocol, thus undertaking a series of commitments towards those defined as refugees who fear persecution (Open Society Institute 1995a).[43]

The IOM has an office in Moscow which consults with state bodies and NGOs in Russia on migration and aid to migrants including refugees and forced migrants. It employs its international links to draw on experts from across the world to consult on: institution building (including drafting legislation, citizenship issues and policies on NGOs); developing reliable information systems; and observing, advising on and seeking support for resettlement programmes (Morris 1995: 7). It currently has a fieldworker actively involved in developing and monitoring compact settlements under a programme called 'Direct Help', designed to assist migrants in overcoming various current problems and in obtaining equipment and premises for setting up production (Sokolov 1994: 68). Under a broader programme of 'Migration as development' the IOM has supported two pilot projects in cooperation with Tambov and Novgorod regional authorities (Sokolov 1994: 73). The IOM also has offices in Armenia, Tajikistan and Georgia and has played an important facilitating role between former Soviet republics. In April 1993 an IOM conference on 'Mass migration and the health of the population' held in Moscow brought together for the first time delegations from all the republics of the former Union and representatives from the majority of Russian departments handling problems of refugees and migration (Anatol'ev 1993).

International efforts at the diplomatic and policy-making level have been concentrated in the recent period on the 'International conference on refugees, returnees, displaced persons and related migratory movements in the CIS and relevant neighbouring states' held in Geneva at the end of May 1996 and organized under the auspices of the UNHCR, the IOM and the Organization for Security and Cooperation in Europe (OSCE). The initiative for this conference was taken by the Russian Federation itself; in spring 1994, Andrei Kozyrev wrote to the UN High Commissioner for Refugees, Sadako Ogata, requesting that UNHCR organize a conference on migration and displacement issues in the CIS and neighbouring states (Open Society Institute 1995a). There were high hopes for this conference whose aim was to provide a framework for the international community to address questions concerning the dynamics of population displacements, the immediate needs of displaced persons for legal protection and practical assistance, as well as prevention, early warning, and possible long-term solutions to such problems. As preparation for the conference, a series of governmental sub-regional meetings to consult governments on displace-ment and migration-related issues were conducted as well as parallel sub-regional meetings of local non-governmental actors and independent experts whose concerns were to be forwarded to governments and the conference secretariat for further consideration (Open Society Institute 1995b).

These hopes appear to have been frustrated, however. Although the conference was well attended – boasting representatives of seventy-seven governments, twenty-seven international organizations and seventy-one NGOs – lack of either clarity in objectives or commitment by governments meant the conference ended without meeting its declared aims (Helton 1996: 52). Helton also criticizes Western European states for blocking the inclusion in the final document of a broadened definition of refugees – in line with that adopted by African states – fearing that this might be used against them in challenging their own restrictive asylum policies in the future (ibid.: 53). Following the conference the UNHCR and IOM took a joint programme for the assistance of refugees in CIS countries to the mem-ber states of the UN with a request for $7.6 million for its implementation (International Refugee Documentation Network Newsletter 1996).

This should not diminish the value of international efforts *per se*, however. A government data-collection effort initiated in February 1995 by UNHCR has been completed providing important data on refugee-producing states in the region. The UNHCR has a representation in Moscow (serving Russia, Belarus, Moldova and Ukraine) which gives consultations to state bodies and NGOs in Russia on questions of the legal protection of, and aid to, refugees and people seeking refuge. It helps refugees and asylum-seekers arriving from the 'far abroad' drawing on aid from foreign and, to some extent, Russian charitable organizations. As part of this effort UNHCR has established four transit camps for refugees around Moscow (Slater 1994: 40). The UNHCR also promotes the norms of international law on refugees and the experience of international organizations in helping refugees, and helps Russian governmental bodies and NGOs in training workers for work with refugees.

Delegations of the International Committee of the Red Cross exist across the former Soviet Union – Moscow, Nal'chik, Baku, Yerevan, Dushanbe and Tashkent – and, in accordance with its mandate, the organization tries to ensure the maintenance of internationally agreed rules of the conduct of war and humanitarian norms during armed conflicts. The organization conducts searches for missing people on the individual request of relatives. The International Federation of Societies of the Red Cross and Red Crescent also has a delegation in Moscow and controls programmes of humanitarian and medical aid to Russia via the Red Cross Movement, although it does not give individual help. It has published a handbook for staff and volunteers of the Red Cross and Red Crescent in Russian (translated from the English), providing guidelines for working with refugees and displaced persons including chapters on the problems of stress, cultural adaptation of refugees, and on the particular problems of female, elderly, young and disabled refugees. The handbook also sets out its own policy, forms of help offered and legal positions (League of Red Cross and Red Crescent Societies 1992).

Caritas (International Confederation of Catholic Organizations of Church Charity and Social Help) also helps refugees on the recommendation of the International Catholic Commission on Migration. Independent national organizations of Caritas have already been created in a number of former republics of the USSR.

In terms of concrete input into migration-policy formulation and implementation in Russia, international organizations have played a minimal role, preferring to allow Russia to take up the position of 'internal regulator' which it feels accrues to it as a result of its great-nation status in the region.[44] Given the massive problems of refugees across the globe and current burdens on international organizations, this is hardly surprising. Nevertheless, this minimalist role may only be tenable as long as western-oriented ministers remain in power and democratically committed NGOs can provide a channel for concrete aid programmes. Thus far, for example, Kozyrev's concern to appeal to the global community in support of the protection of Russian minorities abroad has meant that Russia itself has been obliged to abide by the norms it is advocating be adhered to elsewhere. As suggested above, however, the growing disillusionment with the west's failure to help in a material way has led to veiled threats that Russia might suspend its accession to the 1951 Convention and 1967 Protocol, or at least individual articles of it, and there are suggestions that such a move has been approved by the head of the Federal Migration Service (Korkeakivi 1996: 21).

CONCLUSION

Post-Soviet Russia is not unusual in its dilemmas concerning migration policy and provision. It is torn like a number of other countries between meeting obligations borne of an imperial heritage and its own severely limited resources and domestic political considerations. Not surprisingly, therefore, after a first flush of extremely liberal policy and practice, it has chosen to tread the familiar path of tightening borders, referring to the threat of rising crime and the economic and political instability which could arise from mass immigration.[45] There are a number of factors which make the Russian situation unusual, however.

First, there is a uniquely delicate political configuration around the issue of refugees and forced migrants emanating from the 'near abroad'. There is little international 'best practice' to follow in the sphere of displaced persons of this kind, while the economic burden of accepting the full obligations of its own imperial past is inhibiting Russia in seeking its own 'democratic' policy. The FMS openly states that economic constraints mean that the requisite financial and material aid to returnees and refugees is simply not possible (*Informatsionno-analiticheskii Biulleten'* 1995: 18). This has called for the promotion of other means of resolving the migrant crisis, including: the improvement of the position of the Russian-speaking population in the 'near abroad' to prevent mass migration in the first place; the greater control of immigration into Russia; the better classification of categories of forced migrants to facilitate the differentiation of state support; the development of regional policies to curtail the outflow of the local population from the far north and east; and the 'harmonization' of national, regional and individual interests in the regulation of migrational flows (ibid.).

In practice this means a rapid uncoupling of notions of 'economic migrants' (Russians wishing to return to Russia because of the economic weakness of the newly independent states in the wake of the collapse of the Soviet Union) and 'real' refugees and forced migrants fleeing ethnic and political conflict in the former republics. This is accompanied by the withdrawal of aid to those considered to be 'economic' migrants and a battening down of the hatches against refugees from the 'far abroad'. Those who are admitted have their interests 'harmonized' with those of society by resettlement in those parts of the country with population outflow and poor infrastructure development.

Second, there is the problem of the role of the Federal Migration Service in the formulation and implementation of migration policy overall. The FMS has been criticized for 'departmentalism'; an age-old Russian and Soviet tradition whereby an institution seeks its own aggrandizement often via the centralization of the allocation of resources. It is identified in the FMS both by other government bodies and by NGOs who criticize the service for attempting to include within its remit the whole sphere of migration, including labour migration and the prevention of illegal migration, as well as immigration control and customs (Mukomel' 1995a; Marnie and Slater 1993: 50–3). The attempt by the FMS to monopolize the sphere of migration-policy implementation has encroached above all on the territory of the NGOs. Independent migrant associations and their NGO representatives have been highly critical of the FMS and accused it of seeking primarily to raise its own status as an institution rather than to ensure effective aid to migrants.

Such criticisms generally fail to recognize the real problem faced by the FMS in its double identity as a government agency (requiring it to act in the interests of the state) *and* an organization designed to protect and assist refugees and forced migrants (individuals who often have real grievances against that state). Perhaps Grafova is right to accuse the Moscow bureaucrats of callously abandoning the people it set out to help, but at the regional level at least many migration service workers experience deep distress at not being able to provide the service they would like to and recognize their fundamentally ambiguous position. Indeed, despite the frequent exchange of fire between NGOs and the FMS the former do sympathize with the appalling lack of resources which the FMS confronts daily. In turn the FMS has begun to show signs of making space for a more meaningful contribution to the legislative and executive processes of migration policy by non-governmental organizations.

Although, in theory, therefore, the fact that the FMS has increasingly been divested of the role of providing for the political, social and economic integration of returning Russians and other former Soviet citizens should be evaluated positively, such approval needs qualification. This arises from the fact that the 'third sector', which is increasingly taking on the welfare-provision role, is extremely weak and poorly supported by the international community. Moreover, the FMS has replaced this 'double burden' with another by taking on the function of immigration control instead. This additional role, it has been suggested in this chapter, is an even more worrying tendency, not only from a humanitarian perspective, but also since it is likely to fuel still further the sense of abandonment among both Russian communities abroad and returnees, and thus to increase rather than lessen social tension at home. Evidence from expert interviews with migration workers and from interviews with refugees and forced migrants themselves showed a belief that the government had no coherent migration policy. Territorial Migration Service (TMS) staff in Ul'ianovsk clearly felt that out-migration was being encouraged by a failure on the part of the Russian government to ensure protection for its diaspora in the 'near abroad' and to prevent discrimination against Russians in the former republics. At home, they said, the government had failed to develop a clearly thought-through policy towards refugees and forced migrants, had insufficient resources to ensure implementation of those laws it had passed to protect refugees and forced migrants in the Russian Federation and had no mechanism for keeping the centre informed about the situation at the local level. Evidence from those dealing with communities in the 'near abroad' (such as diplomatic representatives of Russia in the former republics) also suggests that the Russian government has not succeeded in its aim to make inter-state agreements and provision for Russian communities in the near abroad effective enough to halt the out-migration of the Russian population. Indeed, where the outflow of Russian-speaking populations has fallen sharply it is less to do with the stabilization of inter-ethnic relations there than the exhaustion of the mobile sections of the Russian-speaking communities.[46] The support for Russian communities in the former republics espoused in Russia's 'dual policy' on the Russian diaspora is also failing to impress those it targets. Forced migrants perceive Russian aid as being given to the former republics rather than their Russian communities while the inter-state agreements drawn up supposedly to protect ethnic minorities in the former republics appear meaningless.[47]

Upon return to Russia, forced migrants are bitter about what they perceive to be their abandonment or, still worse, 'exploitation' by the Russian government. They are particularly resentful of the policy of re-settling them in Russia's rural backwaters; for the Russian diaspora the first journey to the former republics is seen as their personal sacrifice in order to 'raise' the economic and cultural level of the Soviet Union and to be asked to repeat that sacrifice to revive Russia's abandoned countryside fits unhappily in the group narrative.[48] The irrationality of trying to use returnees from the 'near abroad' to repopulate abandoned rural areas, given the gross mismatch of people and skills to jobs and lifestyle which this involves, is a recurrent criticism of the government advanced by the Russian academic community. One critic argues that the places to which migrants are directed are precisely those where it is impossible to expand production and agriculture. It would be much more effective to fund economic stabilization measures in their countries of exit while seeking to employ those who do choose to return where their skills are most useful: in the service sector, in new, modernized industries and tourist resorts. Instead, it is argued, forced migrants and refugees are stubbornly offered only rural backwaters while foreign labour is invited into the large cities where they are somehow found housing which reportedly does not exist for refugees and forced migrants (Kozlov 1994).

Given the fact that post-Soviet Russia inherited no existing migration regime at all, these criticisms may be misplaced. The government has succeeded in rapidly generating a migration regime and its centrepiece – the Federal Migration Service – is up and running. Moreover, in day-to-day policy-making and policy implementation, there appears to be relatively good cooperation between this government agency and other key institutions (parliamentary committees and commissions, other ministries, NGOs, etc.). There are forums for the exchange of opinion, data and expertise between legislative, presidential apparatus and government bodies and even where conflicts do exist, they do not become institutionalized (Mukomel' 1995a; Grafova 1995a). However, this state of affairs has been made possible, it has been argued here, primarily by the false distinction drawn by the government between social and political issues relating to migration. The social management of arrivees was portrayed as a question of 'rational distribution' – the resettlement of refugees and forced migrants for maximum benefit to the country's economic interests – while the political issue was perceived to be one of ensuring the 'right to stay' of Russians in the 'near abroad'. Partially as a result of political winds whipping up debates around forced migrants and refugees during parliamentary and presidential elections and partially as a consequence of economic constraints on the FMS alongside the growing organizational capacity of the non-governmental sector, these two issues have become increasingly fused. The result is the gradual, but real, reconfiguration of the migration regime outlined above founded on a 'securitizing' of the migration issue not so much around the image of the cultural 'otherness' of the immigrant but around a rather more physical securing of Russia's post-Soviet borders.

5 Putting policy into practice

A regional comparison

All the regions of Russia except Kamchatka, Magadan and Sakhalin regions have experienced a population increase as a result of the inflow of refugees and forced migrants (*Informatsionno-analiticheskii Biulleten'* 1995: 21). However, regional variations in reception have been significant. The early burden of refugees from troubled areas of the Transcaucasian republics fell on the southern areas of Russia and the Northern Caucasus. Up to 1992, three-quarters of forced migrants and refugees fled to the Northern Caucasus (especially North Osetiia, Krasnodar territory and Stavropol' territory) (Vitkovskaia 1993: 47). Parts of central Russia, especially Belgorod region, became increasingly popular as housing became more difficult to obtain in the south of the country. As the refugee-producing regions have changed, however, so too have the regions of Russia receiving the greatest number of displaced people and by 1994 the centre of gravity for attraction of forced migrants had moved east, to those areas adjacent to Kazakstan and Central Asia. This has meant an increased burden on the Southern Siberian, Ural and Volga regions of the country which have now joined the list of regions with the highest concentrations of refugees and forced migrants alongside the traditionally popular regions of Moscow, the Central Black Earth region and the Northern Caucasus.[1]

Regional variation in the implementation of migration policy, however, is more than a direct reflection of the size or nature of the phenomenon in a particular region. The unitary system of migration services headed by the Federal Migration Service in Moscow described in Chapter 4 leaves considerable scope for the formulation in practice of very different regional approaches to the resettlement of forced migrants and refugees. This chapter begins with a brief discussion of two regions where migration has become an important local political issue leading to the declaration of 'emergency' measures to resolve perceived acute problems. It then compares and contrasts two regions of Russia with non-exceptional situations to illustrate the ways in which regional administrations work migration policy into their own distinct political agendas, and the implications this has for returnees.

EXCEPTIONAL CIRCUMSTANCES? THE CASES OF MOSCOW AND KRASNODAR

The peculiar way in which migration policy in Moscow has developed is a result of the city's exceptional status rather than any acuteness of its refugee situation. Moscow does not have a particularly large refugee and forced-migrant community in relation to its population size. According to Sergei Kovalev the proportion of forced migrants and refugees among the population of Moscow is 2.4 times less than for the country as a whole (Kovalev 1994: 3). This is confirmed by Federal Migration Service figures which calculated the average number of forced migrants and refugees per 10,000 population for Russia as a whole at 47.4, whereas for the city of Moscow it is just 16.9 (*Vynuzhdennie Pereselentsy v Rossii* 1995: 15). However, since the advent of the 'refugee problem' and the construction of tent cities in the capital by displaced people in order to draw attention to their plight, the fear that displaced persons will concentrate in Moscow has been widespread and this popular perception has been aggravated by the nature of the refugee population there.

The capital's forced-migrant and refugee community is a highly visible one. Most arrived in the early years of migrational flow before Moscow had managed to shut its doors and thus the majority are from the Transcaucasian republics; in 1992, 80 per cent of forced migrants in Moscow were Armenians from Azerbaijan (Kolesnikova 1994). The visibility of such refugees and forced migrants is reinforced by their employment and housing situation. They tend to find work in trade (in commercial stores, at markets or as street vendors) which effectively reinforces dominant stereotypes of Transcaucasian 'swindlers'. Moreover, the failure to provide refugees with permanent housing means that many (around 2,500 in 1994) remained in the hotels and hostels in which they were originally, temporarily, placed (ibid.). Not only is this unsatisfactory accommodation for any length of time but it is bad for public relations: the cost to the city of maintaining families in this type of accommodation in 1993 was 4 billion roubles.

Moscow also plays host to the majority of refugees from the 'far abroad'. The UNHCR in Moscow estimates that there are currently more than 28,000 refugees[2] living illegally in the capital (although the Russian press has put the figure for illegal immigrants at 100,000).[3] This external refugee problem is becoming increasingly visible; in August 1993 300 Somalis camped outside the office of the UNHCR in Moscow to protest against the poor conditions in which they were being kept, clashing with the Moscow police in the process (Slater 1994: 40). This, coupled with the attraction of Moscow to potential migrants, has led the city authorities to impose special restrictions on settling in Moscow. The chief tool of limiting access to the city has been the residence permit;[4] during the first half of 1995 only 350 of the 5,000 people issued migrant status in Moscow were granted residence permits (Open Society Institute 1995c). Moscow has pursued this policy with apparent disdain for Federal Migration Service regulations, not to mention federal legislation on refugees and forced migrants. The head of the Moscow migration service, Sergei Smidovich, has justified the policy on the grounds that legislation not supported with adequate resources does little more than rub salt into the wounds of refugees and forced migrants (Kolesnikova 1994).[5] Given the dual subordination of territorial migration services discussed in Chapter 4, however, it is difficult to see this as a principled stand on behalf of refugees; the interests of refugees and forced migrants are rather being subordinated to the protectionist concerns of the city authorities.[6] The latter were made apparent in March 1996 when – perhaps as a populist move in the run up to his re-election as Mayor – Iurii Luzhkov issued a direct instruction providing for the granting of forced-migrant status in Moscow only to those who had close relatives officially registered (*propisany*) in the capital willing to allow them to be registered in their housing for at least a year. Refugee status, the order stated, was to be available only to those with registered residence in Moscow ('Status bezhentsev v stolitse budut davat' lish' rodstvennikam moskvichei' 1996; Rutland 1996). In June of the same year the Moscow city government announced that it would impose a strict limit to the number of foreign workers in the city to avoid an increase in unemployment among Muscovites; the number of registered foreigners would be restricted to 5 per cent of the labour force (Gurushina 1996).[7]

While populist in form, the city authorities' policy *vis-à-vis* incomers has been hostile, if not racist, in content. In October 1993 the Moscow authorities used the 'emergency situation' declared by Yeltsin during the national political crisis to initiate a Russian government decree which provided for the resettlement of Baku refugees from the Moscow hotels and hostels in which many had been living since their flight in 1990 into vacated military camps (in Siberia). The decree also included a clause suggesting that the Ministry of Foreign Affairs and the Federal Migration Service conduct talks with states from which refugees had fled about their voluntary return; a clear violation of both the international convention on the status of refugees and the Russian Federation law on refugees (ibid.; Lebedeva 1994). This decree remains unrepealed (despite the end of the state of emergency in Moscow), although active intervention by a number of human rights organizations forced the government in Moscow to re-register refugees.[8] Refugees living in hostels in the suburbs of Moscow were evicted, however, many being left homeless (Gannushkina 1996b).

The Moscow authorities justified their actions by reference to the link between forced migrants and political extremists (reportedly pro-Russian fighters from Moldova were among those outside the White House) as well as playing on a general stereotyping of Transcaucasians (see Chapter 2), linking them to crime in the city. In fact, according to the Moscow prosecutor's office, the crime rate among refugees in Moscow is 2.5 times lower than among Muscovites as a whole (ibid.). Thus, it seems that the emergency situation simply allowed Luzhkov to push through a restrictive residence policy which had been rejected earlier that year (February) by the Moscow city council. Following the dissolution of the council as a result of the constitutional crisis, Luzhkov was able also to introduce arbitrarily the special regulations for visits to the capital by non-Russian citizens he had been seeking (Kamyshev and Zhukov 1995).[9] Although Luzhkov's order officially affected *all* those living without residence permits in the city, reports of human rights abuses by the police during the state of emergency spoke particularly of the maltreatment of Transcaucasian and Central Asian immigrants, of whom some 14,000 were detained and between 5,000 and 10,000 deported (Slater 1994: 41). This kind of officially sanctioned racism gives a clear message to those implementing the law and in July 1996 it was reported that forty Azerbaijani traders were beaten up at a market in the south of Moscow by police ostensibly checking their residence papers. Prospects for the future look no brighter. Gannushkina reports that in 1995 the city government again tried to use re-registration to empty hotels of refugees (Gannushkina 1996b). Meanwhile, the ongoing Chechen crisis provides the perfect justification for arbitrary detentions of those of Transcaucasian nationality. Six thousand people were detained in the aftermath of the bombing in Moscow on 12 July 1996 when Luzhkov pledged to evict the entire Chechen diaspora from Moscow (Morvant 1996e).

A truly exceptional case is that of Krasnodar territory which has received a disproportionate number of refugees and forced migrants, partly because of its position as a border territory with refugee-producing areas, and partly because of its attractiveness to refugees seeking to settle in a region with relatively similar climatic conditions to their former place of residence. The inflow of migrants into Krasnodar territory began in the 1970s and 1980s when Crimean Tatars, Turkish Mskhetians, and Kurds moved to the region. However, there were significant new flows of Mskhetians after the Fergana pogroms in 1989, of Armenians following the earthquake in Armenia in 1988, the genocides in Sumgait and Baku and the war in Karabakh, and of Russians, Armenians and others as a result of the Abkhazian–Georgian War. By 1991 the region was one of only three with what was considered to be a problematic refugee population,[10] having received 41,000 refugees and forced migrants. The high proportion of refugees in the population is aggravated by the complex ethnic composition of the region which comprises 4 million Russians as well as another twenty-two ethnic groups living usually in relatively compact and ethnically homogeneous communities. Reportedly, the arrival of new flows of refugees and forced migrants – many of whom are not officially registered and not working – has aggravated inter-ethnic relations, especially between the Russians and Armenians, the Russians and the Adygs and between Cossacks and the rest of the population, resulting in calls for the deportation of Armenians and Turkish Mskhetians (Toshchenko 1994).

In order to manage the potential conflict, a special decree was issued by the Russian government in September 1994 ('On additional measures for the state regulation of migrational processes in Krasnodar territory', 8 September 1994, no. 1019) which demanded that, in consultation with the FMS, the regional authorities should determine the maximum possible number of migrants to be received in the region.[11] In fact the regional government had been taking the matter into its own hands for some time before this; as early as 1991 there were complaints by refugees that their belongings were being returned to their point of origin, that they could not get jobs and that if they complained their water and electricity were cut off (Livshin 1991).

Moscow and Krasnodar have practised exclusionary policies with regard to refugees and forced migrants regardless of the 1993 federal legislation on forced migrants and refugees. They have justified their actions by reference to the exceptional situations of their regions and increasingly they have supported this practice with local legislation which has overridden federal law (see Chapter 3). The re-election of Iurii Luzhkov – the iron hand of Moscow – in June 1996,[12] as well as the reappointment of Nikolai Yegorov as governor of Krasnodar region,[13] following his spell in federal government, bodes ill for the future; in the name of the protection of law and order, both are likely to 'cleanse' their regions of unwanted newcomers.

REGIONAL APPROACHES TO MIGRATION: OREL AND UL'IANOVSK

Such blatant policies of exclusion and control, which have been the hallmark of regions considering themselves 'under threat' from refugees, are far from the norm across Russia. In other regions it has not been the ethnic factor which has been determining; rather the forced-migrant and refugee issue has been woven into wider regional policies of economic recovery. The forms this has taken are illustrated below by comparing two very different regional approaches to migration policy in Orel region and Ul'ianovsk region (see Table 5.1).

Table 5.1 A socio-demographic profile of Orel and Ul'ianovsk regions

Feature	Orel	Ul'ianovsk
Location	Central region	Volga region
Size	24,700 sq km	37,300 sq km
Population	903,000 (of whom 347,000 live in Orel city)	1,444,000 (of whom 656,000 live in Ul'ianovsk city)
Main industrial and agricultural production	*Industry*: machine building, metallurgic, chemical, light, food. *Agriculture*: grain, hemp, sugar beet, livestock, poultry.	*Industry*: machine building, light, building materials, timber, manufacturing. *Agriculture*: grain, livestock, sugar beet, sunflowers.
Distinguishing features	Like other regions in Central Russia, Orel has suffered large population loss (especially youth) in the post-war period	Protectionist economic policy led to reputation for extremely low cost of living after 1992.
Population trends	Negative natural growth of –2.4 (1991)	Positive natural growth of +1.3 (1991)
Number of refugees and forced migrants registered in region per 10,000 of permanent population on 01/01/95	78.1 (total) 41.2 (urban areas) 140.0 (rural areas) (Average for Russia as a whole is 47.4 (total), 39.2 (urban areas) and 69.7 (rural areas))	83.4 (total) 82.3 (urban areas) 86.4 (rural areas)
Type of regional government	Strong. Head of administration is former First Secretary of the Communist Party of Orel region, E.S. Stroev	Strong. Head of administration is former First Party Secretary V. Goriiachev

Sources: Vachnadze 1995: 55–7; *Vynuzhdennie Pereselntsy v Rosii*, 5: 15–16

Setting regional migration policies in context

When these two regions were selected for comparison in early 1993, the main criterion was their unspectacular nature. Neither region had experienced unusual migrational flows into the region nor was either included on lists of regions designated (ordered from Moscow) to receive significant flows. Geographically neither region bordered an area of significant outflow (making it susceptible to the 'push factors' apparent in Krasnodar territory) and neither was particularly sought after for residence (the 'pull factors' affecting Moscow). Since 1993, however, both regions have had territorial migration services in operation which have been actively working with refugees and forced migrants coming into the regions.

Although superficially unremarkable as regions and apparently similar in profile, the aims and objectives of the two regions' migrational policy have been very different. This is essentially explained by the political implications of each region's demographic situation. Orel region perceives its demographic decline to be seriously inhibiting its social and economic development and thus to be a destabilizing factor while Ul'ianovsk region considers population growth a likely cause of increased competition for limited resources and thus a potential threat to social stability.[14]

Orel region is predominantly agricultural. However, in the last thirty-five years 700 villages have disappeared and the number of children under the age of 16 has fallen from 225,000 to 70,000. This conforms to a well-established pattern of out-migration from the rural areas of Central Russia; the rural population of the seventeen regions of Central Russia fell from 16.5 million in 1959 to 9.6 million by the beginning of 1994 (Vachnadze 1995). In these circumstances the influx of a well-qualified and 'highly cultured' new workforce – in the form of refugees and forced migrants – may be viewed as an opportunity to revive the Russian village. This has been the open policy of Egor Stroev (the former first secretary of the Orel Region Communist Party Committee and popularly elected head of administration since April 1993), who has declared his aim to revive flagging agriculture by, among other things, accepting into the region half a million new residents. In a keenly pragmatic approach to the collapse of the Union, he has suggested that Russia may actually have been strengthened rather than weakened by the Union's disintegration since the process has brought 'persecuted people . . . from the periphery into its heart'. These people, according to Stroev, 'constitute the intellectual part of the population which . . . lends power to the state' (Ziat'kov 1994). The open-door policy to migrants has been used also as a bargaining chip with Moscow for the extraction of funds for agricultural development. Stroev's regional-development policy has concentrated on creating direct links with the centre and his links with Prime Minister Chernomyrdin have long been a central theme of political discussion in the region (Iakovleva 1994). Not surprisingly Stroev signed up to the 'Our Home is Russia' bloc for the parliamentary elections in December 1995 and in January 1996 was elected chair of the upper house (the Federation Council) (Orttung 1996), from where he is likely to continue to seek direct help for the region.

The genesis of migration policy in Ul'ianovsk region must be seen in the light of the 'Ul'ianovsk phenomenon' as a whole. Behind the famous low cost of living[15] is a regional administration committed to 'social partnership in the interests of the individual' (Burkin 1993) by which is meant the prioritization of social stability and social guarantees in order to prevent social and economic disruption. This prioritization of social order and stability extends to migration policy and the contrast with Orel is immediately apparent. In Orel the head of the Territorial Migration Service is a forced migrant herself and policy is directed to extracting money from all possible sources and encouraging attempts at all levels to get things done (seeing in migrants a possible force for accelerating economic development). In Ul'ianovsk, in contrast, the Territorial Migration Service is staffed by loyal regional administration workers whose chief concern is that forced migrants do not rock the Ul'ianovsk boat and throw off course what they see to be the administration's currently successful economic programme.

In contrast to Orel, Ul'ianovsk regional policy is clearly oriented towards the control – or policing – of migration. This kind of protectionism reflects the wider policy of a region which has more or less shut its doors in an effort to pursue an already semi-autarkic economic policy in place since the 1970s. This has been achieved by employing subsidies to restrain prices and continued rationing, by developing its own resources for investment into the region's economy and imposing heavy fines and taxes on advertising, market trade and excess profit of monopolies (Ivanov 1993: 43–5). Statements by the TMS head Vladimir Il'ich Svaev indicate the priorities of migration policy in Ul'ianovsk to be: controlling the influx; weeding out unworthy applicants; and destroying the myth of Ul'ianovsk's wealth (and thus deterring new applicants). His concern about 'pull factors' stems from the reputation of Ul'ianovsk as a cheap place to live promoted in the media and Svaev openly seeks to counteract this by emphasizing the shortage of housing and poor employment prospects in the region and discouraging those who write to the service enquiring about prospects for moving there (Belozertsev 1994). It is also a reaction to the perceived threat to the region of becoming swamped with returning military personnel. This is partly due to the general process of the resettlement of military units being withdrawn from the CIS in the Volga region but also to the spontaneous resettlement of military personnel; there are numerous military colleges in the region and graduates of them are attracted back there by the presence of family and friends.[16]

Implementation of policy: incentives and obstacles to immigration

The fact that regions have distinct aims and objectives *vis-à-vis* migration does not imply that they have pursued migration programmes openly at odds with that of the FMS. Rather they have interpreted and implemented the policy handed down from Moscow in a way which suits their own needs. How this has been achieved in practice is illustrated below by examining the presentation of migration issues in the media, the process of registration and treatment of refugees and forced migrants in the implementation of migration policy and the relation of migration policy to other socio-economic policy priorities.

Constructing the 'happy home': the local media and forced migration

In both regions of the case-study the media have been tightly controlled in an attempt to show how the aims of regional migration policy are being met. This takes the form neither of a crude manipulation of facts nor outright censorship of the pre-perestroika type but of a controlled flow of information which highlights the region's policy aims and its success in achieving those aims while silencing those aspects of the phenomenon which might suggest otherwise.

The use of the local media to stress the aims and achievements of regional migration policy is clearer in the case of Orel region where the portrait painted of the process of migration to the region is extremely positive, suggesting a highly effective regional programme of support. Excessive praise for the Stroev administration in the local media is not unusual according to the governor's critics (Iudin 1995);[17] nevertheless, a number of specific reasons are elaborated to explain why the reception of migrants in Orel was proving so successful:

- a good starting base – this relates specifically to the '100 programme' begun by Stroev in the early 1980s and aimed at building 100 new houses on each farm in order to attract new workers and encourage youth to stay in the villages (Poliakova 1994);
- an effective monitoring system – the TMS and local district branches of employment and migration services were reported to visit places where migrants settle and elicit their experiences and emergent problems (Izvekov 1994);

- the existence of integrated social programmes on a district basis to aid incoming families. One article was dedicated to the success of Livny district's programme where the district head of administration, Vladimir Tarnavskii, claimed that rather than constituting a financial burden, the migration programme was effectively helping solve the shortages of labour in agriculture as well as successfully rejuvenating the district's depopulated villages (Poliakova 1994);
- the initiative of individual farm managers who have shown an 'ability to take risks fearlessly' and to use the construction of new housing to attract newcomers (Kim 1994).

It is emphasized, therefore, that the migration programme is effective in Orel because of the pooling of efforts and resources from the federal, regional and individual farm level. Money allocated from federal funds is used for basic housing construction but is matched by investment from individual farms and the efforts of the new residents themselves who are given the key to 'four walls and a roof' and are asked to complete the building. In order to substantiate these claims individual district heads, farm directors and even forced migrants themselves are credited with positive statements about regional policy aims and achievements (Kim 1994; Izvekov 1994). Some articles appear to be eulogies to the spirit of 'revival'. Kim's article, for example, brims with references to 'young talent', 'new technology', 'new blood' and 'new beautiful houses' which are designed to give an impression of an oasis of new life providing a model for the revival of the region as a whole and generating a 'confidence about the future' (Kim 1994).

In Ul'ianovsk, in contrast, while the generally positive picture of conditions for migrants is preserved – after all Ul'ianovsk region prides itself on its social order, social welfare and lack of social tension – there is concern not to 'advertise' the situation for fear it will attract increasing numbers of migrants. Potential migrants are warned that 'the prices are the same as in other regions, there is no housing, [and] the number of employment places is also limited' (Belozertsev 1994). The content analysis of the Ul'ianovsk press (see Chapter 2) found that none of the articles discussing forced migration raised the issue of 'legal adaptation'. In effect this means that there is no reference to the rights and benefits available to refugees and forced migrants and serves the purpose of not publicizing their availability. In this way claimants are discouraged and potential resentment of any perceived special treatment of forced migrants among other sections of the community is avoided.

Despite the deterrent aim of migration policy in Ul'ianovsk, over 80 per cent of reports on forced migration in the local papers studied noted a positive attitude to forced migrants and refugees and only 9 per cent reflected negative attitudes. Thus, the claim made by NGO leaders that a consistently negative picture is painted of migrant experience in order to deter future returnees is refuted at the local as well as the central level, even in a region consciously seeking to discourage migrants. The absence of crude bias, however, does not mean the local media have refrained from constructing the issue of forced migration in particular ways. In Ul'ianovsk the local media have effectively ignored forced migration as an issue for the region. Two chief editors (of the weekly paper *Skify* and the extremely popular daily paper *Narodnaia Gazeta*) stated that they had not had to deal with solving problems of forced migrants and refugees in the course of their work,[18] and neither had given the issue any serious thought on either the political or social level. One explanation for this 'absence' might lie in what one editor called the great 'caution' of the regional administration in releasing any information which touched on ethnic or nationality issues.[19]

In Orel region – where a policy of encouraging migrants was being promoted – there was much more interest in the issue of migration and articles appeared more frequently than in Ul'ianovsk. Indeed, one weekly paper which was preparing for its first edition in spring 1993 – *Prostory Rossii* – declared an open intention to devote a regular column to the issue. However, even in Orel media workers were being asked to exhibit extreme caution in reporting issues concerning the influx of migrants, and the release of information by the authorities was tightly controlled. The head of the TMS in Orel stated this openly, saying that it was a conscious policy to release only small amounts of selected information, under her direct control. This was necessitated, she said, because the issue was one which could potentially cause social tension and impact negatively on the situation of the migrants themselves, not to mention the regional migration programme.

Finally, it is worth noting that media manipulation and control would appear to be confirmed by spontaneous respondent comments reflecting deep mistrust of the media, often based on personal experience. One couple interviewed in Orel region described the article by Kim cited above as a 'deceit' since it had completely misrepresented the help they had been given by the farm, the condition in which they had received the housing they were still building and what they could expect in the future. There was a general feeling among respondents on this farm that journalists were brought in by the farm director to promote himself, wrote what they were told to, and not only did not seek the truth but consciously manipulated facts to suit their story.

Implementing policy: the power of pen and purse

In implementing migration policy, Orel and Ul'ianovsk interpret the rules on registration and welfare provision for refugees and forced migrants differently in order to suit their overall policy aims. In Orel registration policy was applied liberally. In the case of migrants from Kazakstan, for example, it appears to have been an exception to be refused status rather than granted it – a very different policy from other regions.[20]

In Ul'ianovsk the implementation of regional migration policy has reflected rather the closed doors aims of the policy set out above. The most vivid illustration of Ul'ianovsk policy in practice occurred in 1993 when the Russian 104th Parachute Division returning from station in Azerbaijan was refused permission to land in Ul'ianovsk; they had been intending to settle their returnees in a newly vacated military camp in the region (Vachnadze 1995). This is just one incident, however, reflecting a wider migration policy which carries out the duty of the TMS to 'receive' migrants only in so far as the regional administration's policy aims of 'preserving socio-economic stability in the region' and 'regulating crime' permit.[21]

From interviews with TMS staff in the city, it is clear that the control of entry to Ul'ianovsk has been systematized in their procedures for registering all forced migrants and refugees. First, the region tries to screen out potential migrants wanting to settle in Ul'ianovsk using its links with Russian consulates in the former republics. The head of the TMS, Svaev, stated during an interview that not a single advance application for forced-migrant status had been authorized by the region because such advance agreement obliged the region subsequently 'to register [*propisat'*] them and provide work'. In the process of considering applications information is received from a wide range of sources, including the state security service, police organs, television, newspapers and personal documents, to verify whether the claims of the applicant are genuine. Also, in contradiction to federal regulations for the registration of refugees and forced migrants, it is insisted that applicants are de-registered (*vypisat'sia*) from their former place of residence before they are granted a residence permit in Ul'ianovsk. Second, as in a number of other regions, the residence permit continues to be used to ensure that only those refugees and forced migrants with relatives in the region (and whose relatives agree to register them in their flat) are registered. Anybody else arriving in the region is directed to a temporary accommodation centre (usually in Saratov, Perm' or Tver').[22] Third, applications for status are refused for a wide range of reasons not specified in the legislation. Grounds for the rejection of applications included: lateness of application; region of origin;[23] family reunion where a spouse had been working in the region for more than eighteen months; arrival without one's whole family; and arrival from another region where the applicants had already registered. Some of these reasons for rejection of applications became legal when the amendments to the Law on Forced Migrants were passed in December 1995, but were not legislated for in summer 1994 when these interviews were conducted.

There is also a clear policy of differentiation towards refugees and forced migrants. In order to limit inward migration and to hold down the crime rate in the region an attempt is made to distinguish potential 'trouble-makers' from among potential migrants. For Svaev the favourite whipping boy is 'people of Caucasian nationality' whom, he states, the TMS tries to avoid registering (Belozertsev 1994). Another strategy is, where possible, to encourage refugees to return. Although the use of deportation is denied, some arrivees had been subjected to immediate 'redirection', that is, were sent straight from the station to another city considered better able to accommodate them. In such instances migrants are actually bought tickets by the TMS; a strategy known to have been used to facilitate the return of refugees to Chechnia.

People of Caucasian nationality are a particular target for potential expulsion; an order from the head of administration (according to one TMS worker) meant that in the districts of the city TMS workers were now involved in establishing how many people of Caucasian nationality there are in the district and how many are registered. Indeed, TMS workers noted that they were increasingly engaged in seeking out foreigners employed by firms and ensuring that firms were paying the levy on this. If they did not, then the region reserved the right to dismiss and even deport the employee.

It is clear from monitoring the work of territorial migration services in Orel and Ul'ianovsk regions that the interpretation of the main tasks of the service varies according to regional priorities. In Orel the registration and welfare-provision functions were emphasized and this was reflected in more inclusive registration criteria and more universal supply of minimal welfare provision. In contrast the new monitoring and control functions of the migration service prevailed in Ul'ianovsk.

Migration and regional development: fits and misfits

In some regions migration forms a central part of regional-development plans and migrational policy can be manipulated to the advantage of the region. This is the case in Orel region where the already-established '100 programme' was adapted to the needs of migrants who became the targets of a reformulated rural-revival programme. Even at regional district level there are 'integrated programmes' in which migration policy is central to job-creation and retraining schemes, the revival of village schools and the upgrading of medical points and housing (Poliakova 1994). The region thus measures its own success *vis-à-vis* migration by the numbers it has managed to attract. Head of the regional administration, Egor Stroev, has boasted of the 500,000 for whom there is room in the region and claims that since 1993, Orel region had received more than 10,000 (Vachnadze 1995).[24] In so doing a net migration deficit of −13 (per 10,000 population) between 1979 and 1988 has been transformed into a positive rate of +81 between 1989 and 1994 (Goskomstat 1995: 428).

Orel is additionally fortunate in that its policy orientation is in harmony with federal policy aims to direct migrants towards rural areas but away from the Black Earth zone. By April 1995, 7,797 refugees and forced migrants had been registered by the Orel TMS, of whom two-thirds had settled in rural areas (*Informatsionno-analiticheskii Biulleten'* 1995: 97, 104). This coincidence of interests, as well as the careful development of governmental links by Stroev, probably explains the personal visits made by figures prominently placed in the FMS to the region to assess its needs (Poliakova 1994) and why individual districts of the region have had success in negotiating directly with the FMS to help cater for migrants, especially their housing needs.[25]

In contrast Ul'ianovsk region's prioritization of social stability and social welfare has made it extremely cautious with regard to the reception of migrants even into its rural areas. Migration workers have no sense of a clear, positive directive on migration other than the obligations set down by Moscow. However, concerns of the regional administration have led them to devote considerable energy to seeking out unregistered 'foreign workers' and the head of the Ul'ianovsk TMS emphasizes the role of the service in maintaining social order and helping reduce the level of crime; a practice increasingly in line with new Moscow directives. The TMS thus measures its own success in terms of its ability to *reduce* in-migration. Belozertsev notes that the service had succeeded in lowering migration into the region between 1992 and October 1994; the sharp increase in in-migration of forced migrants between 1992 and 1993 had been turned around in 1994 (Belozertsev 1994).[26]

Despite the more receptive nature of Orel region and its support from the FMS, however, the migrational flow into Ul'ianovsk region remains higher than into Orel. By 1 April 1995, 14,138 refugees and forced migrants had been registered in the Ul'ianovsk region, 70 per cent of whom had settled in urban areas (*Informatsionno-analiticheskii Biulleten'* 1995: 97, 104). Moreover, the level of satisfaction of refugees and forced migrants with their new lives is higher in Ul'ianovsk. Despite concerns by Orel to emphasize the positive aspects of in-migration there is resentment from the local community; Tat'iana Regent singled out the problem in Orel, noting that she had observed 'envy, slander and malice' directed towards refugees from Dushanbe who had built themselves housing of a better quality than that of local residents (Karkavtsev 1993). Of course, the situation in Ul'ianovsk is far from perfect either but resentment is generally directed at official circles not the receiver community in general.

CONCLUSION

Examination of the implementation of migration policy at the regional level shows that federal policy is implemented quite differently and the vertical chain of command of the FMS is far from secure. Indeed, the Federal Migration Service itself admits that relations between the FMS central apparatus and regional administrations have been complicated by the failure of regional leaders to 'correspond to the principles of state policy on migration' (*Informatsionno-analiticheskii Biulleten'* 1995: 13). Although such regions as Moscow and Krasnodar are exceptional, nevertheless, the trend towards migration restriction is widespread. Gannushkina suggests that more than twenty regions limit admission to refugees and confirms that in those regions where there is no extra financing for reception centres, regional migration policies are formulated and implemented at least with as much attention to the regional authorities as to Moscow (Gannushkina 1996c).

The Federal Migration Service is aware of the situation and although apparently not prepared to challenge the legality of regional activities, it is planning an incentive policy for regions positively assisting forced migrants and refugees in their settlement. From 1996 a 'differentiated mechanism for assistance to forced migrants' will be introduced by the FMS which will ensure that those regions accepting migrants will be given financial assistance while those who close their doors will not (Regent 1996: 36).

The interaction of factors influencing the way in which refugees and forced migrants are treated on return to Russia is explored in much greater detail in the second part of this book. Here it is worth noting only that the roots of regional policy are complex and must not be reduced to simple political dichotomies. Despite its communist heritage and reputation, for example, Ul'ianovsk region proved less 'red' than Orel region in the 1995 parliamentary elections (the communist vote in Ul'ianovsk region was 37.2 per cent while in Orel region it was 44.9 per cent). Thus the 'open door' to Orel is not explained by its democratic orientation towards the reception of returnees as victims of empire. Moreover, there is no straight line between policy *vis-à-vis* forced migrants and their satisfaction with their new lives. The general social profile of migrants (who are predominantly from urban areas and highly educated) means that they are likely to experience significantly less difficulty adjusting to life in urban Ul'ianovsk than rural areas of Orel region and thus, despite their less than enthusiastic welcome, those settling in Ul'ianovsk city are likely to be more positive than those welcomed, with open arms, to the villages of Orel region.

Part II

Going home? Social and cultural adaptation of refugees and forced migrants

Introduction
Into the field . . .

The empirical project which forms the basis of Part II of the book was conducted between July and December 1994. It applied a combination of qualitative research methods to gather data among migrant communities in two regions of Russia. Data were gathered from a total of 195 respondents, 144 of whom were settled in four rural settlements in the Orel region, Central Russia, the remaining 51 of whom were resident in the city of Ul'ianovsk in the Middle Volga region of Russia.

A SOCIO-DEMOGRAPHIC PROFILE OF RESPONDENTS

Respondents were not selected by sampling. The two regions in which fieldwork was conducted were selected according to the criteria described in Chapter 5; neither had special status as an area for the reception of refugees and forced migrants and both had 'average' levels of reception on commencement of the project. However, the heavy depopulation of Central Russia as compared to the attractive nature of Ul'ianovsk city, given its reputation for social stability and low cost of living, provided contrasting migration regimes at the regional level.

In Orel region one main fieldwork base, near to the town of Livny, was selected where the researcher lived with one of the migrant families. Here a preliminary 'map' of the location of migrant families was drawn up and those identified were systematically approached and interviewed. Migrants in three other villages, all near to the district centre of Zmievka, were also interviewed. These bases were chosen since they involved different forms of settlement; in one the collective farm had been dissolved, in another a migrant-run agricultural firm employed some of the respondents. These bases were travelled to daily from the regional centre, Orel. In all of the rural bases migrant families had settled independently (not as a compact settlement) although networking processes had brought relatives, friends, colleagues and acquaintances from the former place of residence to the same place in Russia. In Ul'ianovsk city, where accessing respondents was more difficult, snowballing techniques were employed. This led to a certain clustering of respondents by former place of residence, ethnicity and current place of employment and residence.[1]

Respondents were not sampled according to socio-demographic characteristics but these were monitored *post factum*.[2] There were few major deviations from the general profile of registered refugees and forced migrants provided by Federal Migration Service data. One exception to this was the higher educational level registered among my respondents in Ul'ianovsk than among registered forced migrants and refugees in general.[3]

Respondents had all settled in their new place of residence in Russia between 1988 and 1994. Almost three-quarters (73 per cent) of the 195 respondents stated their nationality to be Russian, which corresponds exactly to the proportion of Russians among registered refugees and forced migrants across the country at the end of 1994. However, there was considerable difference between the two regions: in Orel region 81 per cent of respondents were Russian (compared to 86 per cent of those registered by the Federal Migration Service) and in Ul'ianovsk 49 per cent were Russian (compared to 67 per cent of registered refugees and forced migrants). The relatively smaller number of Russians in Ul'ianovsk is accounted for by the large number of ethnic Tatars moving to this region, reflecting the Volga region's status as 'historical homeland' for the Tatar community. Both in Federal Migration Service data and among my respondents Tatars accounted for 22 per cent of refugees and forced migrants in Ul'ianovsk region, compared to only 8 per cent for the country as a whole. In my study in 1994, therefore, it is not the number of Tatars, but the high proportion of Armenian respondents (14 per cent compared to 3 per cent recorded by the Federal Migration Service) which deviates from the Federal Migration Service profile.

The region of origin of respondents was in line with the general trend (see Figure 1.3); the majority came from Central Asia and the Transcaucasus (24 per cent had come from Tajikistan, 24 per cent from Kazakstan, 16 per cent from Kyrgyzstan, 15 per cent from Azerbaijan and 13 per cent from Uzbekistan). Relatively few had come from republics within the Russian Federation (including Chechnia) (3 per cent) which is explained by the timing of the fieldwork which was completed just prior to the Russian military action in Chechnia of December 1994. Most significant is the complete absence in my study of forced migrants from the Baltic republics which is explained by the regions of resettlement selected for the study – which are geographically distant from these states – and the relative prosperity of forced migrants from these areas which would afford them greater choice in area of resettlement.

DATA COLLECTION AND ANALYSIS

Three methods of qualitative data gathering were used in conjunction: semi-structured interviews; questionnaires completed in interview form; and field observations. First interviews with migrants covered four areas: short 'life-histories'; motivations for leaving the former place of residence; material situation and help received; and experience of reception in Russia. A preliminary analysis of interviews was completed before repeat interviews were conducted. Repeat interviews focused on key areas of interest identified by the first interviews. Three themes were followed up in these interviews: national identification (using the categories outlined in Chapters 8 and 9); problems of cultural adaptation; and gender differences in the experience of resettlement.

Interviews were also carried out with non-migrant (local) residents in the main rural base of fieldwork. Semi-structured interviews covered questions of: the impact of the arrival of refugees and forced migrants on the local community; the level of empathy with forced migrants; and sources of conflict or potential conflict between the two communities (see Chapter 8).

A total of 139 interviews were transcribed in full and analysed in Russian. The analysis of interviews from the two regional bases was conducted separately since difference of experience between refugees and forced migrants having settled in rural and in urban locations was a key comparative dimension of the project. Particular attention was also paid to gender difference during analysis.

Although in this volume some data have been tabulated and illustrated with charts, it is important to note that the data were not analysed statistically; that is, conclusions are not drawn on the basis of the isolation and correlation of variables. The respondent set was neither large enough nor appropriately selected for such an analysis. Statistical calculations and charts are used for *illustrative* purposes only; they encapsulate and represent conclusions which have been drawn on the basis of textual analysis of interviews, field notes and questionnaire responses.[4] The triangulation of methods also means that the total respondent set varies; in some cases it draws on the eighty-three questionnaires completed in interview form in Orel region, since these provide the most easily quantifiable data. In other cases data from all 195 respondents are drawn upon. The total respondent set and the region of resettlement of respondents are indicated on each chart. The real 'data' from the empirical project are presented, however, in the form of citations from interview transcripts. In the interests of confidentiality respondents are not identified other than by the number assigned to them in the data-base collating demographic data on all respondents which is given in brackets after the citation.

For the reasons described in Chapter 8, views of the local (non-migrant) population in Ul'ianovsk were studied using a small-scale but representative survey conducted under the auspices of the project by sociologists working in the research centre 'Region' of Ul'ianovsk State University. A representative sample was constructed on the basis of sex, age and district of residence, employing a formula previously used for public-opinion surveys of the region's population by the researchers involved. A total of 370 respondents (45 per cent male, 55 per cent female) returned questionnaires, 291 (78 per cent) of whom were city and 79 (22 per cent) were rural residents (the latter were from two rural settlements in the region). Questions concerned: the rating of the issue of 'immigration' as a problem; attitudes to the reception of refugees; the perceived impact of the arrival of refugees and forced migrants on the local socio-economic situation; stereotypes and images of refugees and forced migrants; levels of empathy with refugees and forced migrants; and personal contact with actual or potential refugees and forced migrants.

TURNING PEOPLE INTO DATA?

Despite widespread beliefs about the reluctance of the former Soviet population to talk openly due to the legacy of the split between 'public' and 'private' modes of articulation in the Soviet period (Shlapentokh 1989), no significant problem of non-respondence was encountered; refusals to give interviews were isolated. Indeed, over-response was probably a greater problem than lack of response; interviews of two or three hours in length had to be transcribed and analysed. The interview clearly played a cathartic role for many respondents who were in a state of physical and mental dislocation. As one respondent noted, there was not really anyone to whom they could tell their stories: the other migrants had their own losses to deal with while the locals were not interested.

The decision to use qualitative research methods helped minimize non-respondence, since the researcher was not eliciting information but *listening to* the respondent. These same methods raised a number of other problems, however, which are discussed in a separate publication (Pilkington and Omel'chenko 1997). One or two are noted here as they must be taken into account by the reader in evaluating the findings which will be presented in the following chapters. The first concerns the impact of the researcher upon the research process and the second the lack of generalizability of the research findings.

Although there was no overall problem of non-respondence, there was a gender imbalance among respondents: 62 per cent were female and 38 per cent male. This was not by design but due to the fact that women –

especially in the rural fieldwork bases – were more often to be found at home and were more willing to find time to give interviews. Men, in contrast, were less willing to talk because, they claimed, their wives 'talked better' and proved more difficult to pin down because they were less frequently at home. Interviews with the local population in rural areas were also problematic, in this case because of the researcher's prior association with the migrant community which reduced the level of trust between researcher and interviewees. As is indicated in Chapter 8 the dialogue in these interviews was not of the quality necessary to give an adequate representation of the reception of migrants by the local communities.

Given the qualitative nature of the research, it is essential to bear in mind the researcher's impact on the respondents more generally, and this is discussed at length elsewhere (Pilkington and Omel'chenko 1997). Respondents were particularly concerned about where the information they gave would go and upon whose authority the researcher was acting; this reflects the often dependent relationship migrants have with their employers (see Chapter 7). For some the 'unhealthy' interest of a foreign researcher in their problems was also an issue of concern. They felt a pressure from outside not to 'run down' their country. In other ways, however, being a foreigner allowed a more neutrally academic positioning *vis-à-vis* respondents since the expectations to provide practical help or support, with which Russian researchers collaborating on the project were met, were reduced.

The range of methods employed in this study make it apparent that generalizability and comprehensiveness were subordinate to validity in the project design. The aim was to present an accurate, although partial, picture of the experience of selected refugees and forced migrants upon resettlement to Russia. However, since the author is aware that regardless of intention, readers will seek to generalize the picture presented here, it is worth reiterating the dangers of such a misreading of the findings.

First, the project was exploratory and had a specific agenda (see Chapter 1) which led to decisions to employ self-definitions of forced-migrant status and to isolate an undifferentiated group of migrants (in terms of ethnicity, legal status, region of origin and length of time in Russia) *after* their return to Russia. Taken out of context the research might appear to obscure the difference between Russian-speaking populations in the former republics as well as the different attitudes among receiver communities to refugees and forced migrants, or indeed to Russians and non-Russian ethnic groups. Since the respondent set was not large enough to justify comparing attitudes by place of origin, ethnic identity, rural/urban former residence and so on, the problem cannot be resolved using *post factum* analyses of the data. The findings must, therefore, be read for that which they do explore rather than that which they do not and the reader is directed to published work using survey methods where this may be illuminating.

Second, the resettlement experience of migrants varies significantly according to the region and mode of that settlement. In particular the experience of migrants who settle in compact settlements will vary significantly from that described in this study, where migrants had settled individually or in places where they had friends or relatives. Respondents in this study would have suffered less socio-economic dislocation, although potentially greater isolation. Migrants settling in compact settlements, on the contrary, often feel greater support psychologically but suffer many years of appalling living conditions as they build housing and employment opportunities from scratch. The fieldwork approach adopted for the purposes of this project could not possibly capture the range of experience of forced migrants and refugees which varies from those fleeing direct persecution or military conflict who are channelled through emergency reception centres, to those who move to identified jobs and housing. The regional and urban/rural comparisons built into the project design allow for some differentiation of experience but further case-studies would greatly enhance a fuller understanding.

Despite the relatively large respondent set – 195 forced migrants and refugees – it should not be forgotten that the empirical work described in the following chapters was fieldwork. Fieldwork is dirty work, and although, in the process of writing up, the 'data' have been sanitized into neat numbers and polished interpretations, it would be pointless to deny the far from ideal conditions of their collection. Daily confrontation of the same problems facing one's respondents hinders data gathering, from the two-mile walk to the village each day to the drunkenness of would-be interviewees, from hostel managers refusing permission to talk to residents to trying to conduct 'individual' interviews in the single room shared by three generations of a family, from dealing with the distress of respondents during interviews to handling the local gossip directed at you. To some extent the researcher can console herself with the knowledge that what might appear to be methodological weaknesses to some extent raise the quality of the data gathered since being in the same physical situation – even for a short time – helped secure trust among respondents, as well as actually introducing the researcher to the reality of urban–rural 'down-shifting'. In practice, however, the research process was less one of 'data gathering' than a process of learning from interviewees the strategies they had devised for coping with their displacement which, particularly in the rural fieldwork base, I had more than an academic interest in assimilating. It is the impact of displacement on the lives of specific individuals, therefore, which is described in the following chapters.

6 More push than pull?

Motivations for migration

The motivations for migration and future migrational intent have been studied more than any other aspect of migration from the former republics of the Soviet Union to Russia. The reasons for this are outlined in Chapter 1 and are rooted in the premises of the 'push' and 'pull' model of migration as well as the interest which institutions of the migration regime have in both predicting the size, geographical origin and socio-demographic characteristics of future migrational flows and distinguishing between economic and political motivations for leaving the republic of origin and resettling in Russia.

Using statistical records of migrational flows, published quantitative sociological research into migrational intent among Russians in the 'near abroad' and data from respondents in the author's own study, this chapter explores the reasons why Russians in the 'near abroad' are currently returning to Russia in such large numbers. The first section draws primarily on published academic material and argues that, although in general terms, the return of the Slavic population from the Transcaucasian and Central Asian republics of the former Soviet Union had certainly begun well before the ethnic conflicts of the mid-1980s, none the less, the size, direction and composition of current migrational flows suggest a significant break in established patterns of migration on the territory of the former Soviet Union. The second section refers to the findings of the author's own fieldwork (see the introduction to Part II of the book for details) which suggest that subjective indicators – the expectations with which migrants move, the lack of prospect of return, the chaotic nature of the move and the severe drop in living standard they experience upon arrival – support the hypothesis suggested in Chapter 1 that current migrations from the former republics to Russia are more than an acceleration of established patterns of decolonization.

MIGRATIONAL FLOWS: EXPLAINING THE STATISTICS

Since 1989 there have been a number of apparent deviations from traditional migration flows on the territory of the former Soviet Union. As was
suggested in Chapter 1, some of these anomalies – such as the temporary
decline in net migration in Russia in the later 1980s and early 1990s in
comparison to the mid-1980s – may be explained quite satisfactorily by
a reduced migratory inclination in times of economic disruption and
heavy competition for resources (Mitchneck and Plane 1995). Other trends
are not so readily accounted for, however. Below, four characteristics
of current migrational activity are examined: the volume and direction
of migration; the socio-demographic composition of migration flows; the
chaotic nature of migration; and the permanence of migration. On the basis
of this, an assessment is made as to whether current phenomena constitute
no more than deviations in the old system due to short-term economic
crisis or, alternatively, constitute a permanent shift in the migration system
of the region as a whole.

Volume and direction of migration

The late Soviet migration system was characterized by a general hesitancy
about migration and a particular reluctance to make long-distance moves.
During the 1970s and 1980s, a relatively small proportion of the total
Soviet population moved inter-regionally; about 5 per cent of the population (compared to 17.5 per cent of the American and 9.6 per cent of the
British population in 1981) made such moves annually and less than
half of those moves were between republics or economic regions
(Mitchneck and Plane 1995: 20). There was also an established directional
flow of the Soviet population out of central Russia eastward towards
Siberia and the Far East, and southward, towards Kazakstan, Central Asia
and the Transcaucasus (Lewis and Rowland 1979).

In contrast by the early 1990s there was a significant increase in the
volume of migration between Russia and the former Soviet republics;
according to the Federal Migration Service, 18 per cent of all migration in
1994 comprised migrations between Russia and the CIS and Baltic states
(a figure which was 7 per cent up on the previous year) (*Informatsionno-
analiticheskii Biulleten'* 1995: 20). This trend has been identified on a
regional level as well; Mitchneck and Plane's study of migration in
Yaroslavl' region between 1989 and 1992 showed that inter-republican
migration increased over the period. Moreover, the movement was one-
way; the proportion of in-migrants to Yaroslavl' region from republics
outside Russia increased from an estimated 12 per cent in 1989 to an

estimated 22 per cent in 1992, while the proportion of out-migrants going to other republics remained stable. The authors thus attribute the growth in inter-republican migration to inward flows of refugees and return migrants (Mitchneck and Plane 1995: 22).

This is confirmed by changes in the direction of migrational flows. Previously stable migrational flows from the central and southern European parts of Russia to the eastern and northern territories are being replaced by the reverse movement (*Informatsionno-analiticheskii Biulleten'* 1995: 20). The flow out of the northern and eastern parts of Russia is a result of socio-economic change in Russia which has led to the collapse of much of the local industry (oil, gas, diamonds, gold, minerals) as well as the loss in meaning of wage differentials and early retirement rights which had traditionally attracted people to these areas. However, there is also a clear tendency in inter-republican migration towards 'ethnic consolidation' (see Tables 6.1 and 6.2).

Table 6.1 suggests evidence of out-migration from the Transcaucasian republics of Azerbaijan and Georgia by the 1960s although this exists alongside a general tendency of the movement of people from Russia to the 'less developed' republics. By the 1970s, however, there was already considerable out-migration from Central Asia and Kazakstan which had come to cover all of the republics of the region by the 1980s.[1] By this time Russia had a net *positive* migration with the other republics, as did the other Slavic republics as well as the highly developed Baltic states which

Table 6.1 Soviet inter-republican net migration (in thousands), 1961–89

Republic	1961–70	1971–80	1981–9
Russia	−1,114	673	1,605
Belarus	−160	−84	12
Moldova	68	−58	−47
Ukraine	530	199	177
Estonia	93	60	47
Latvia	144	104	81
Lithuania	49	68	100
Armenia	144	85	−333
Azerbaijan	−69	−96	−256
Georgia	−94	−162	−62
Kyrgyzstan	130	−99	−140
Tajikistan	120	3	−118
Turkmenistan	10	−9	−55
Uzbekistan	414	150	−591
Kazakstan	414	−562	−779

Source: Codagnone (forthcoming)

Table 6.2 Net migration between Russia and the 'near abroad' (in thousands), 1990–4

Republic	1990	1991	1992	1993	1994
Ukraine	–4.9	–24.7	–12.3	38.5	101.0
Belarus	5.6	–2.0	–4.6	1.2	13.3
Moldova	3.1	4.1	11.1	4.0	7.6
Latvia	3.5	5.2	19.7	19.4	19.3
Lithuania	5.1	4.5	10.2	13.4	5.4
Estonia	2.8	3.6	18.7	10.6	8.2
Georgia	9.5	18.0	29.6	33.8	24.2
Azerbaijan	42.9	17.6	35.1	22.9	19.0
Armenia	3.6	3.3	5.6	6.4	4.6
Uzbekistan	40.2	27.9	65.2	50.7	93.5
Kyrgyzstan	16.1	15.5	41.4	66.4	42.9
Tajikistan	31.7	14.4	47.1	40.9	25.8
Turkmenistan	4.4	4.7	10.9	6.7	13.0
Kazakstan	36.3	25.6	82.4	104.4	234.3

Source: Codagnone (forthcoming)

remained attractive to migrants. If these data are read alongside census data then declines in the absolute number of Russians in the other Soviet republics and the proportion of the population they constituted are evident in the Transcaucasian republics from the 1979 census and in the Central Asian republics from the 1989 census (Zayonchkovskaya, Kocharyan and Vitkovskaya 1993: 198–203). Thus, the process of 'going home' by the Russian and other Slavic populations from the former republics was well established before the manifestation of serious ethnic conflict there.

This trend was significantly strengthened in the post-1989 period. Between 1989 and 1994 3.2 million Russians returned to Russia from the former Soviet republics while 1.4 million moved to other former Soviet republics, indicating a net inflow of 1.8 million (Goskomstat 1995: 422–3). Table 6.2 shows the net migration of Russians from and to the former Soviet republics between 1990 and 1994. The data indicate that by 1993 Russia is receiving rather than sending its population to all former republics of the Soviet Union. While this continues a trend of out-migration in the Transcaucasus and Central Asia (see Table 6.1), there are significant rises in out-migration of Russians from 1992, especially from Kazakstan. Moreover, the sudden rise of out-migration from the Baltic states from 1992 marks a significant break in migration trends (Codagnone forthcoming).

The 'objective' data, therefore, suggest at the very least that something is turning an underlying trend into a torrent and, arguably, causing significant numbers of Russians to move longer distances and in a direction which was not previously typical. In themselves these data do not give too many hints as to why this might be so. Although the movement out from the north and east of Russia lends itself to explanations resting on the lack of economic incentive to stay in an extremely inhospitable environment, movements out of the former republics might be hypothesized to be either economically or politically motivated since during this period political independence coincides with economic decline (in particular decline relative to Russia). In order to draw any conclusion about the nature of the migration under consideration, therefore, these data need to be tested against both other statistical data, which might better indicate the manner in which people leave, and *subjective* data which generate a more accurate picture of the motivational structure of the individual migrant.

Socio-demographic composition of migration flows

The second 'objective' factor which is useful in evaluating current migrational processes is the socio-demographic composition of migrational flows. If it is primarily labour migrations which are being undertaken the migrants might be expected to emanate from the most mobile sections of the population, being male, young, with relatively high levels of education and skills and without dependants. What the data suggest is that while these sections of the population were the first to move, the ethnic, gender and age composition of continued migration indicates that migrants are motivated by more than better economic prospects.

As regards the ethnic composition of current migrational trends, modernization processes might have been expected to have produced in-migration to Russia by the early 1990s as members of the titular nationalities of the former republics sought to apply their increasing education and skills to enhance their employment and living opportunities. However, in fact current in-migration to Russia is dominated by Russians (see Chapter 1). Moreover, even though the 'others' are mainly members of titular nationalities of other states of the 'near abroad', mainly arriving from their *own* country, a number of ethnic groups – Belarusians, Kazaks, Kyrgyz and Turkmen – actually preferred 'their' states to Russia: that is, the number of representatives of these nationalities leaving Russia outweighed those coming in. There are two polar explanations of the domination of Russians in inward migration flows: either a sudden rise in ethnic conflict or discrimination precipitating the 'cleansing' of newly independent states of the representatives of the former imperial power; or the acceleration of a process already under way of the return of these agents of the centre as competition for social privilege (in housing, education and employment) grows alongside the 'development' of the colonial subject. Analysis of the subjective motivational structure of migrants below shows how these two factors are interwoven in current migrations.

In terms of demographic composition, inward migration would be expected to be undertaken by the most mobile sections of the population in the former republics. Indeed, it was, as is reflected in figures indicating the high proportion of in-migrants of working age. Goskomstat figures for 1994 show 24 per cent of all incoming migrants from the former Soviet republics being aged 0–15, 66 per cent being of working age (16–59 for men and 16–54 for women) and 11 per cent being of pensionable age (Goskomstat 1995: 416–17). This compares favourably to the overall age structure of Russian society which in 1995 showed 23 per cent being aged under 16, 57 per cent being of working age and 20 per cent being of pensionable age. However, among *registered* refugees and forced migrants, there appears to be a more 'dependent' population; Federal Migration Service data for those migrants registered in 1994 showed that 29 per cent were under 16, 13 per cent were of pensionable age and 58 per cent were of working age (*Vynuzhdennie Pereselentsy v Rossii* 1995: 40). There are, moreover, indications from interviews that the less mobile sections of the Russian populations may move in a 'second wave'. This is a conscious strategy by many families who send out younger 'scouts' in order to find housing and jobs with the intention of bringing elderly relatives to join them once they had settled. A second explanation lies in the growing economic incentive for the elderly to move. There is an increasing dissatisfaction with the level and regularity of payment of pensions in the former republics and the Russian pension is perceived to be relatively generous and paid regularly.[2] Indeed, in the case of Kazakstan, current attempts to raise the pension age have been read by sections of the Russian population as a direct attempt to encourage them to leave for Russia, and Mitchneck and Plane have already noted a significant relative decline in migration among the younger age group (15–34 year-olds) and a growth in the proportion of migrants at the older end of the working-age population (Mitchneck and Plane 1995: 25).

The gender of migrants has traditionally been an indicator of the nature of migration processes; men have been seen as prime economic (labour) migrants, whereas forced migrations (refugee flows) are associated with the movement of women and children. This thesis has been supported in relation to the migration of Russians from the former Soviet republics by Vitkovskaia's survey of 1,948 potential migrant families in four former Union republics and two autonomous republics of the Russian Federation which suggests that women's migrational activity is – in comparison to men's – 'forced' (*prinuditel'naia*), that is, it results from fears of military and inter-ethnic conflict or ecological catastrophe (Vitkovskaia 1993).[3] It is also supported by research on incoming migrants; in their study of Yaroslavl' region Mitchneck and Plane found that women made up a higher proportion of long-distance migration motivated by political or social conflict (Mitchneck and Plane 1995: 23). According to this line of thinking, not only the dominance, but even the significant presence of women in migrational flows back to Russia would suggest that what is under way is a forced rather than voluntary migration. In fact Federal Migration Service data indicate that women constituted 53 per cent of refugees and forced migrants registered between 1 July 1992 and 1 April 1995 while Goskomstat data suggest that women constituted 48 per cent of all in-migrants from the CIS and Baltic states in 1993 and 47 per cent in 1994 (Goskomstat 1995: 416). This suggests that the proportion of women is indeed higher among forced migrants and refugees than among migrants as a whole, although the former figure equates to the proportion of women in the Russian population as a whole which has been stable at 53 per cent since 1987 (Goskomstat 1995: 29). Furthermore, Mitchneck and Plane found that gender was linked to ethnicity in in-migrants to Yaroslavl' region. While Russian women outnumbered Russian men for in-migration, among non-Russian in-migrants such as Armenians, Azerbaijanis, Uzbeks and Tajiks, men predominated. This, they surmise, indicates economically motivated migration among non-Russian ethnic groups but politically motivated migration among ethnic Russians (Mitchneck and Plane 1995: 24).[4]

In fact, gender-sensitive research shows that in the last decade women have become as prevalent as men in migrational flows (Boyd 1989: 638). The problems with the reasoning underlying continued assumptions about gendered patterns of voluntary and involuntary migration are dealt with at greater length in a separate publication (Pilkington 1997). For the purposes of this study, however, it is the connection Galina Vitkovskaia makes between women's 'forced migration' and their responsibility for their children which is of interest. Vitkovskaia argues that a series of 'push factors' are leading women to incite their families to leave the former republic and that these motivations – especially women's fear of ethnic conflict, fear of the future and fear of discrimination against Russians – result from women's greater responsibility for children (Vitkovskaia 1995). Indeed, while generally the presence of family dependants – children – is considered to be a de-motivating factor in migration decisions, since they must be properly rehoused and provided for in education, in the current migration of Russians from the former Soviet republics to Russia the presence of young children (of nursery/school to military-service age) is a motivating factor in migration decisions. The reasons for this are discussed below with reference to interview data. It would appear that where people leave generally peaceful situations, dependent children are a de-motivating factor but where there is ethnic or social tension they become a reason to migrate.

Chaotic nature of migration

A third major deviation in migration processes from the Soviet period concerns the manner of migration. In the Soviet period migration was highly planned. It was either of a voluntary-obligatory kind – such as those migrations of young people to construction and industrial projects in the north and east – or, if conducted at an individual or family level, migration was undertaken via postings from the place of work after having entered into agreements with local authorities on the exchange of housing. In contrast, today the return of Russians to Russia is a chaotic process. This chaos is indicated by: the dissociation of migration from concrete economic factors ('a job to go to'); and the absence of institutional help in the process of long-distance migration.

Even the most superficial analysis of 'pull factors' for in-migrants to Russia reveals that migrations are not carefully planned economic moves but determined by an overwhelming desire to leave and a dependence upon survival strategies on arrival. Figure 6.1 shows that only a small proportion of migrants interviewed in the author's project had come to Orel region following a firm job offer (either in advance or following a 'forward search party' of family or friends). Indeed, the very willingness of people – predominantly from urban areas – to settle in a rural backwater is in itself indicative of both the desperate nature of the move and a traditional Russian survival strategy: a return to the land, which at least provides subsistence, in times of hardship.

Among respondents in Ul'ianovsk, concrete job offers for at least one member of the family were more commonly encountered: nine respondents moving to the city had such offers before the move. This difference reflects the greater stringency of residence regulations in the city (see Chapter 5). Economic reasoning was also apparent at a more general level; some respondents noted that they had chosen their area of resettlement because of particularly positive economic, geographical or socio-cultural factors. In relation to Ul'ianovsk, for example, factors cited included: good economic prospects, low prices, relative proximity to Moscow and St Petersburg, communist heritage and spirit and a generally pleasant environment. Orel region was also cited as having a reputation for relative prosperity:

> They say you never die of hunger in Orel region . . . the harvest is always good . . . that's why we decided.
>
> (51)

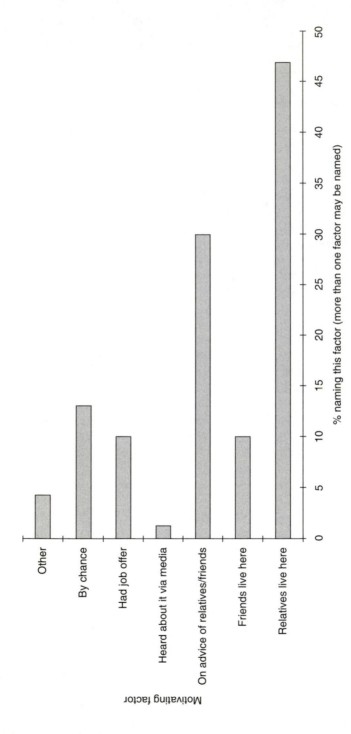

Figure 6.1 Motivations for migration ('pull factors')
Note: No. of respondents = 83, Orel region

The pre-eminence of survival strategy in this respondent's thinking is clear. It is also apparent in the fact that the majority of respondents were attracted to the region by the presence or advice of friends, family or acquaintances (see Figure 6.1), knowing that their presence would provide a support network in the immediate period which would assist them in acquiring residence rights, finding housing and employment, supporting themselves financially and caring for pre-school children. The use of these networks did vary by region, however. Among those settling in Ul'ianovsk it was the presence of relatives, friends or acquaintances in the area who could provide a roof over their heads upon arrival which was significant, while among those settling in Orel region there was a greater tendency to follow neighbours, colleagues or relatives from the former republic of residence – effectively to move as a collective – rather than to move to relatives resident in Russia. This pattern suggests that those who moved to the rural locations of Orel region did so on the promise of permanent housing. Indeed, this factor was cited spontaneously again and again by respondents as the reason for choosing this particular rural location. However, the manner in which it is cited calls into doubt its classification as a genuine 'pull factor':

> I didn't want to come and live here. It just happened like that . . . they sent a telegram that there was a flat here and we packed, sold everything quickly.
>
> (93)

> We didn't care where we went or know where to go . . . most important to us was housing.
>
> (36)

The chaotic nature of migration is confirmed by the lack of information and institutional support received by migrants in making their moves. Respondents were unlikely to have used either the media or government information sources to locate an area for resettlement,[5] and only six of the 195 respondents said they had been directed to their destination by a refugee or migrant organization. During interviews questions asked about what information they had received in the process of making their decision to move and to which institutions they had turned before leaving the former republic and on arrival in Russia revealed that the vast majority of people had received no institutional help at all in planning their move. One in eight of those settling in Orel region (see Figure 6.1) stated that they had arrived in the region completely 'by chance'. From interviews it is evident that this means they had heard of opportunities for housing or employment from chance acquaintances while on scouting missions. As will be shown in

Chapter 7, this reliance on chance networks and hasty decisions often leads to deep dissatisfaction and on-migration into urban centres.

Evidence from respondents suggests that current migrations by Russians from the former republics to Russia are not focused on individual decisions taken with wide knowledge of the environment into which they are moving. On the contrary, the majority, while not 'fleeing' from homes under threats to their lives, feel forced to move and were willing to accept any opportunity which allowed them to 'get out' rather than planning economically or socially advantageous moves. The presence of relatives or friends who can help in the immediate post-move period or verbal promises of farm directors of the provision of housing and employment (at least for one member of the family) were generally sufficient incentive to make a life-shattering move. The relative disregard for the circumstances into which they move places Russian returnees closer to refugees on the refugee–economic migrant continuum than to voluntary labour migrants (Kussbach 1992: 652).

Permanence of migration

The final characteristic of current migrational interchange between Russia and the former Soviet republics which would appear to suggest a major deviation in the migration system is the apparently *uni-directional* nature of migration. Economically motivated migration is characterized by an ebb and flow and circular pattern whereby family members stay behind as recipients of wages earned abroad and there is an expectation of return to the initial place of residence. Table 6.3 shows the number of Russians and members of other nationalities migrating from the Russian Federation to countries of the former Soviet Union. It suggests that the out-migration of both Russians and other ethnic groups from the Russian Federation to the former republics has declined by around two-thirds over the period

Table 6.3 Out-migration from the Russian Federation to the 'near abroad', 1989–94

Year	Russians	All other nationalities
1989	334,503	357,175
1990	291,861	333,915
1991	276,414	310,736
1992	251,893	318,133
1993	175,400	193,715
1994	114,577	117,175

Source: Goskomstat 1995: 423

1989 to 1994.[6] This would suggest that the out-migration of Russians from the former Soviet republics is permanent in nature.

The permanence of Russian out-migration is confirmed by respondents in the author's own study who generally showed a high degree of desire to return to their former place of residence and their talk is characterized by a strong nostalgia for their former lives.[7] However, realistically they felt there was no going back.[8] Asked if she would ever return to Uzbekistan, one Russian woman who had resettled in Orel region said:

> [I would] if everything was like it used to be, like we lived before. I would leave [here]. But the Russian-speaking population has left . . . Of course I long to go back, I want to go and see it, see all the people I knew . . . But then you think, there's nothing there, there's nowhere to go back to. Neither houses nor flats.
>
> (2)

This single statement sums up the three main themes of 'no-return' mentality: a recognition that the clock cannot be turned back to how it was before; a fear of ethnic isolation since other Russians had left; and the material impossibility of starting from scratch again. The last concerned not only the fact that migrants' housing had been sold or occupied by others but, for the majority, there was little possibility of scraping together the money for the return journey. The first concern – that of the potential ethnic isolation of Russians – does not necessarily point to politically rather than economically motivated out-migration but is none the less an indication of the growth of awareness of ethnic issues since previously these people would not have been conscious of such a distinct 'Russian-speaking' community.[9]

Those who maintained a real intention to return were those whose close relatives remained in the former republic. One respondent had even kept his job open in the former place of residence in the hope of returning. For the vast majority, however, the fact that 'everyone else had left' indicated the lack of any network to facilitate return; there would be nobody there to help them find housing and employment and thus to re-establish a former or new life there.[10]

MOTIVATIONS FOR MIGRATION: EVALUATING SUBJECTIVE STATEMENTS

The statistical data presented to date indicate a clear ethnic profile to current migrational anomalies. The data do not – and cannot – answer the question most government officials and academics ask, however: is this movement rooted in ethnic tension as a result of discrimination, and even persecution, of Russians in the 'near abroad' or does it constitute a 'rational' response of the most privileged section of the populations there to rapid economic decline in the post-Soviet period? Not surprisingly, therefore, from a first awareness of these new migrational flows Russian migration experts have conducted surveys among the Russian populations in the former republics to elicit subjective data. The published results of these surveys have suggested that inter-ethnic relations are central to, if not the primary motivation for, migration decisions (Levanov 1993: 36; Boikov 1993: 22–4; Vitkovskaia 1993). Vitkovskaia's survey,[11] for example, suggested that, although evaluations of the inter-ethnic situation vary significantly across the areas of the study (being most negative in Dushanbe and least negative in Kiev), in both Dushanbe and Tashkent about two-thirds of respondents considered that their nationality created difficulties in living in these regions (Vitkovskaia 1993: 13). Public-opinion surveys conducted by the All-Russian Centre for Public Opinion Research over the period 1990–2 among the Russian and indigenous populations of sixteen former Union republics and republics within Russia found concerns about the deterioration in inter-ethnic relations to be only the third greatest worry of Russian populations in the 'near abroad' (cited by 42 per cent of respondents) behind greater concern over everyday economic problems (Gudkov 1994: 177). A strong correlation between feelings of ethnic enmity and a desire to migrate was found, none the less; 40 per cent of those polled declared 'ethnic enmity' to be the reason for their intention to migrate (ibid.: 175).

In the author's own fieldwork a questionnaire was also employed to yield insights into motivation in leaving the former republic; eighty-three people who had migrated from former Soviet republics and resettled in Orel region were asked why they had left their former place of residence.[12] The results are illustrated in Figure 6.2 and also apparently suggest that 'ethnic issues' are more important than economic ones in motivating migration: 38 per cent cited inter-ethnic relations and 27 per cent discrimination against Russians while only 13 per cent noted the general socio-economic situation and 12 per cent a shortage of money.

There are clearly a number of methodological problems in the employment of subjective data to analyse motivations for migration. The quantitative surveys cited above are particularly subject to 'mood' swings. They capture above all the desperation of a dispossessed social group who feel forgotten and abandoned by the Russian government. They are also open to significant influence by a sudden deterioration of relations; specific political debates or conflictual incidents can rapidly alter a group mood and thus distort results. Standardized questions permitting quantitative analysis are also open to very different interpretations with similar answers

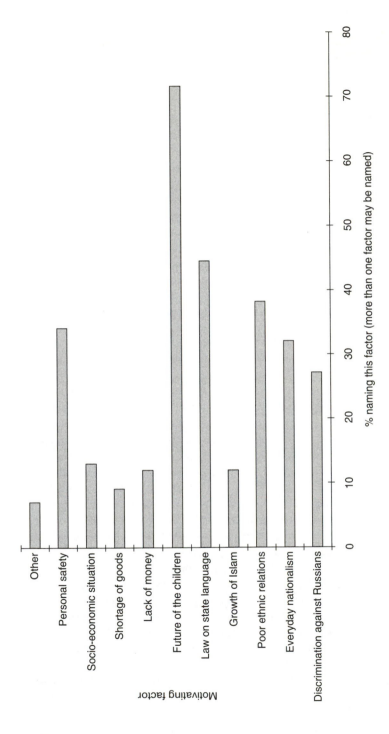

Figure 6.2 Motivations for migration ('push factors')
Note: No. of respondents = 83, Orel region

potentially referring to a wide range of experiences. Respondents stating that they felt their nationality caused them 'difficulties' in life could be referring to a range of experiences from feelings of discomfort through lack of knowledge of the local language to discrimination at work or persecution and ethnically related violence.

Some of these problems were avoided in the author's own research in that the questionnaire was used in interview format and in conjunction with a range of other qualitative research methods. This facilitated clarification of the context of respondents' answers. Respondents were also allowed to state as many reasons as they wished for leaving to avoid falsely singling out a single 'most important' cause in a complex decision-making process. However, other problems arose in my own study as a result of the collection of data from respondents who had already made their migrational move. In particular both the institutional and cultural environment into which they moved may well have encouraged respondents to articulate their experience in the former republic as one in which Russians encountered discrimination. This is due to both the requirement for registration as a forced migrant or refugee of proof of persecution and the suspicions of receiver communities (especially in rural areas) that migrants are those seeking an 'easy life' and who had left the former republics at the first sign of hardship (see Chapter 8). The need to 'justify' the migration may encourage a distorted collective memory among migrant communities which overemphasizes ethnic conflict. The data on motivations are used here, therefore, only in conjunction with the analysis of interviews setting in context issues related to the decision to move. It is clear from these interviews that migrants think about their decision to move in all its complexity – recognizing the interconnectedness of economic and political elements to their decision. Indeed, the determination with which respondents refuted invitations to suggest that interpersonal ethnic relations were the cause of the move was astonishing. Respondents were also careful to differentiate and qualify their experiences in relation to others. Respondents frequently referred to the very different situation of those who had 'fled' their homes (such as refugees from Abkhaziia) or had been driven out by military conflict (such as those from the front-line areas of Tajikistan) and never made glib comparisons. Indeed, as is argued in Chapter 8, there was no positive association attached to the label of refugee to encourage such a self-portrayal. In this sense the post-move study accessed more reflective considerations by migrants as they re-examined their own experiences in relation to those of a much wider group of refugees and forced migrants.

The fact that in surveys respondents tend to under-cite economic reasons for the move – especially if they are asked to name a single 'prime' motive

– while in more general 'talk' about their experience prior to the move interviewees do discuss economic conditions confirms respondents' ability to consider all the motivations involved. There were, in fact, fifteen spontaneous references to economic motivations during interviews including: poor food supplies; wage non-payment; the difference in standards of living between Russia and their republic of residence; general material position; sharp rise in prices; housing difficulties; problems of finding employment and redundancies; low wages; no bread in the shops; and electricity supply stoppages. Dissatisfaction with the ecological situation in the region leading to existing or potential personal health problems was also mentioned by seven respondents as a reason for migration. These respondents came mainly from areas in Kazakstan and Uzbekistan bordering the Aral Sea and from the Shymkent region of Kazakstan which had a highly polluting chemical industry.

The question of the importance of the migration regime itself in shaping 'collective memory' remains open. The very premise of the research undertaken by the author was that the migration regime does impact on the migration system. However, this impact, it is argued, takes place at an institutional level. In terms of affecting individuals' rationalizations of their decision to move, it is unlikely that any crudely distorted image of motivation was given. Only half the respondents had registered with the migration service (and thus had encountered the need to claim direct persecution) and most respondents did not either greatly value or fear the migration service or the status it lent (see Chapter 7). Moreover, there is no real reason to suspect that the researcher was in any way associated in respondents' minds with this or any other state authority to which it was necessary to present this image of themselves.[13]

With all these qualifications in mind, it is argued below that analyses of subjective data related to migration decisions can provide a useful insight into the role of the deterioration in ethnic relations in the former republics in these decisions. This role, it will be argued, is generally speaking not an independent one, but interwoven as a series of ethno-political, ethno-social and ethno-psychological factors.

Ethnic conflict and migration decisions

Despite the high proportion of respondents noting ethnic relations as an important factor in their decision to leave the former republic (see Figure 6.2), a relatively small number of people reported direct persecution or inter-ethnic violence. In a total of 139 analysed interviews, there were twenty-four recounted incidents of inter-ethnic violence or threats directed towards the respondent personally or to those close to them.[14]

Discrimination on ethnic grounds or nationalism was reported to be the prime motivation for leaving the country of residence by an additional five respondents. The reports of violence and discrimination came from individuals who had left Tajikistan, Uzbekistan, Kyrgyzstan, Kazakstan, Azerbaijan and Moldova. The most extreme actual and threatened violence was reported from Azerbaijan (by those of both Armenian and Russian nationality) where ethnically motivated violence was experienced by respondents in a manner akin to 'ethnic cleansing'. One Russian woman – married to an Armenian – described how she left Baku in October 1992:

> you work with people and they suddenly turn round and say things behind your back . . . in Baku they said, 'You are an Armenian and you should suffer for your people'. They started talking about my passport, 'You are Russian, why have you got an Armenian surname, change your passport' . . . I was pregnant at the time . . . Nobody attacked us but they attacked my mother-in-law and my uncle. They beat him up.
>
> (177)

The Russian-speaking population also became caught up in internecine conflict in Tajikistan. A 20 year-old woman from Dushanbe who had left the city in September 1992 described why:

> They started to threaten me, saying I was Russian so go, go home to Russia . . . they came and told us we had twenty-four hours to clear out.
>
> (157)

The practice of armed groups threatening individuals and families with violence or death if they did not leave within a given time was also reported by Russians having left Chechnia; one young doctor who had left a small town outside Groznii in June 1993 had been forced to leave the family flat and flee to Krasnodar with her brother while her parents were on holiday and had not managed to re-establish contact with them since.

Ethnic motivations for migration to Russia need not be exclusively negative in nature; respondents might have been 'pulled' to Russia following the collapse of the Soviet Union since Russia constitutes their 'historical homeland' and resolves problems of ethnic discomfort being experienced in their current place of residence. Some evidence of a desire to be 'among one's own' was evident in motivational patterns as one female respondent who had arrived from Karakalpakstan explained:

> my sister lives here . . . And when we had seen what it was like here we decided, we wanted to be closer to Russians.
>
> (4)

Others were clearly nearer to being the 'anticipatory' refugees referred to in migration literature (Richmond 1993: 11) in that they felt moving now was the best way to avoid having to flee in the future. Migrants articulated this via statements of 'we knew what was going to come', relating the revelation to news of events in another city or republic which indicated a potential deterioration of ethnic relations in their own area. One such family who had moved from Kapchagai in Kazakstan in 1992 said they had done so:

> so that there wouldn't be any problems later, because when all is said and done Kazaks are Kazaks and Russians are Russians. That's what we think.
>
> (97)

This couple had the kind of 'frontier' mentality that undoubtedbly their parents' generation had also had when they had made their move to the Soviet periphery in the first place; they were confident about the contribution they could make to Russian society and certain of their connection to that land. A more common sentiment was a certain diffidence about the return 'home' as expressed by a 50 year-old teacher returning from Uzbekistan:

> Russians are naturally being pushed out of work. And the majority of Russians there have been left without work. So we had nowhere else to go, we had to come to Russia.
>
> (194)

The exceptional nature of those citing ethnic hostility alone as the reason for migration is confirmed by survey data from the All-Russian Centre for Public Opinion Research. Polls over the period 1990–2 showed that such motivations were found primarily among respondents from regions with high levels of tension (Moldova, Kyrgyzstan and Tajikistan) and among respondents who had a relatively short period of residence in the former republic, who had little or no knowledge of the local language, culture and traditions and who experienced a high degree of isolation in their everyday life (often having worked for Union-subordinated enterprises, as economic managers, government officials or servicemen) (Gudkov 1994: 181). Gudkov's profile of the young, highly qualified specialist having met a sudden collapse in opportunities open to him/her as a new political elite promoted members of the titular nationality fits precisely the couple cited above (97) who articulated more clearly than any other respondents the inability to accept the loss of cultural superiority previously ascribed to Russians in the former republics.

Ethno-political factors

In most reported cases of ethnic conflict, therefore, respondents maintained that friends, neighbours, work colleagues or other known people of the titular nationality had not 'turned' against the Russian-speaking population. On the contrary, they stressed the mixed nature of their working collectives and neighbourhoods and the lack of animosity at an interpersonal level. One Tatar returnee from Tashkent noted:

> We all worked together and we never felt that he was an Uzbek, I was a Russian or he was a Tatar . . . many of my friends were sorry that we were leaving.
>
> (160)

The ethnic tension experienced rather had been 'whipped up' by those who had a vested interest in so doing. In this sense respondents clearly related ethnic conflict not to inherent ethnic difference but to political interests associated with it. One woman who had settled in Orel region from Kazakstan spoke for many when she said:

> Whose fault is it? Those at the top . . . they have a meeting, they sat down and decided, they did not think about who would suffer as a result. Those at the bottom are the ones who suffer. Not one of those at the top suffered.
>
> (133)

The language of economic speculation – the scourge of post-Soviet life – is employed to describe the artificial manipulation which respondents blamed for ethnic tension:

> I think that it was just individual nationalist elements, those it would benefit, who artificially inflamed it in order to gain some political dividends on the crest of this nationalism. As for the rest it is the fault of the government for not stopping it in time.
>
> (167)

> They wanted this, those who overthrew everything, they wanted it . . . They have ripped us off . . . and appropriated everything for themselves. That is what it boils down to. And they divided up the power in order to do this. They overturned everything . . . all these former secretaries, former directors . . . What was our strength? It was our friendship. But now this friendship is gone. There is no moral foundation to the state and that is why all this happened.
>
> (108)

The old state officials are not the only 'they' to blame for the ethnic conflict afflicting the former republics, however. In respondents' talk there is also an anonymized 'they' representing members of the titular nationality who also incite trouble. These people are often referred to as 'out-of-towners', those from the 'villages' or 'mountains', young hotheads or other 'losers' who might be mobilized by those at the top to fight their battles for them. Thus, the ethnic discomfort felt personally by respondents had often occurred in public places,[15] where they had been exposed to these 'other' (as opposed to 'our') members of the titular nationality who translated nationalist sentiments sanctioned at the state level into crude anti-Russian slogans and jibes. This kind of 'everyday' (*bitovoi*) nationalism was frequently reported (see Figure 6.2) and is illustrated by this Russian woman who had left Bishkek, Kyrgyzstan, in May 1992:

> There were constant reproaches . . . wherever you went you constantly heard 'Russian, go back to Russia' . . . if there was a hold-up in the supply of bread, they would shout, 'Russians, go back to Russia, eat there . . . you are eating our bread here'.
>
> (192)

Ethno-social factors

Respondents felt that the conjunction of ethnic and political interests was making Russians – or, more accurately, members of the non-titular nationality – effectively second-class citizens in the newly independent state. This may, in some cases, be sufficient to encourage people to migrate. If the relatively low migratory intention of Russians in the Baltic states – in two of which this second-class status has been written into citizenship laws – is compared with the high migratory intention of Russians in the Central Asian states, where citizenship is offered to all residents, it would seem that migration is precipitated by ethno-*social* factors. What are these?

Vitkovskaia notes that 'competition for employment is one of the hidden springs of inter-ethnic conflicts' (Vitkovskaia 1993: 22) and in my own study respondents in Orel region were deeply concerned that their future socio-professional prospects were being jeopardized. This is evident in concern about 'the future of the children' and the adoption of the state language law (see Figure 6.2), both of which interweave ethnic and socio-economic concerns.

The adoption of the language of the titular nationality as the official state language in place of Russian[16] creates ethnic discomfort for Russians, the majority of whom had pitifully poor knowledge of it. It also provides the legal basis upon which to prioritize native speakers and for this reason was perceived as an expression of the intention of the new governments to oust Russians from professional spheres. Thus economic and social-status prospects become inextricably bound to ethnicity and motivations for leaving.

To a certain extent the professionalization of the local population – especially in Central Asia – had been squeezing Russians out from the 1970s (see Table 6.1 above).[17] However, in other former republics such as Lithuania – where the urbanization of the titular nationality was not an issue – the connection between difficulties in finding employment and the need to know the Lithuanian language was more obvious. Moreover, respondents in the author's study made clear and spontaneous reference to the introduction of the language of the titular nationality as the state language and its detrimental effect either upon their own employment or the prospects of education and employment for their children. A middle-aged graduate from Kyrgyzstan noted:

> Kyrgyz was made the state language . . . [and] a gradual squeezing out of management began. Where there were Russians they began to be replaced with those who knew the state langauge. At our age you can't learn the state language.

(192)

The almost instantaneous impact of this was noted by a Russian welder who had left Uzbekistan in 1991:

> A rumour went round that at the electric power station the documentation, the plans, had all arrived in Uzbek . . . And the lads began to pack up, they started to leave in whole brigades. They settled up and left.

(126)

As is evident from Figure 6.2, however, by far the most frequently cited motivation for leaving the former republic is 'the future of the children' (cited by 72 per cent of respondents). Indeed, such was the prevalence of this phrase in initial interviews that it was explored further in repeat interviews. This testing revealed that the term referred to a number of concerns. The first, and most tangible, was a concern for the physical safety of children. This is expressed by a female returnee from a small town in Uzbekistan who had left in 1991:

> We were most concerned about the children . . . before we left there were cases of children disappearing . . . we left because of that . . . We didn't even let them go out to the shops.

(195)

Bullying on ethnic grounds at school was noted and many parents of Russian children said they had feared that their sons and daughters were vulnerable to physical or sexual attacks on ethnic grounds. Without doubt the most frequent concern, however, was that over the future educational prospects for children, particularly the guarantee of teaching in Russian and future access to Russian higher education. The most frequently repeated motif was that they had moved because Russian schools had been closed, as one female respondent from Shymkent, Kazakstan, who left in 1991 suggested:

> we came because they closed our school, that's why we came here . . . At the time that was the only reason. Only because they closed the school.
>
> (51)

Separating the truth from the moral panic in the debate over the closure of Russian-language schools is difficult. There clearly is a strong belief that Russian schools were being deliberately closed and many respondents referred to specific closures of their local schools. On the other hand, figures provided by the governments of the former republics suggest that provision in Russian language is far from inadequate; in Kazakstan at the beginning of 1993 only 36 per cent of general secondary schools conducted teaching in Kazak while 38 per cent taught in Russian (*Informatsionno-analiticheskii Biulleten'* 1995: 59). Moreover, anecdotal evidence suggests that an initially active programme of the transfer of schools to Kazak has been significantly slowed and that – due to the inadequacy of teaching materials in Kazak – many concerned Kazak parents are switching their children to Russian-language schools.[18]

A second complaint is that the lack of Russian-language school tuition meant that there would be no possibility of entrance to higher education either in Russia – where Russian language was needed – or in the newly independent state where knowledge of the state language was prioritized and corruption ensured that only 'theirs' got in. While such concerns about access to education in the mother tongue of an ethnic minority are legitimate, there is a tone of cultural superiority in some of the statements mirroring the flat denial of the need for the interviewees themselves to learn the state language. As one Russian woman from Uzbekistan said:

> he [my son] was speaking in Uzbek. He will sink if they talk in Uzbek, they will forget their mother tongue. And where will they go after school?
>
> (20)

Socio-economic and ethnic motivations are intertwined in fears that the prospects of respondents' children in terms of socio-economic mobility were actually significantly poorer than their parents'. The articulated concern about 'the future of the children' is thus a metaphor for a more general fear of the future borne of their own social and cultural displacement in the newly independent states; a concern which for many is sadly not resolved by migration (see Chapter 8).

Ethno-psychological factors

> It simply began as a chain – one left, a second left and so everyone had to leave.
>
> (118)

Migration networks have not only a pragmatic but also a psychological function and there were twenty spontaneous references during interviews to what might be called 'ethno-psychological' factors in migration decisions. A sense of impending isolation developed out of watching other Russians leave and their houses and jobs being taken by incomers of the titular nationality. Concerns were in some sense still pragmatic; a small Russian community reduced the chances of provision of schooling and other cultural facilities in Russian. Moreover, the formation of networks of people moving to the same place in Russia significantly reduced the 'cost' of the migration decision; these networks provide short-term adaptive assistance, such as housing, money, information (about employment and general survival strategies) and emotional support (Gurak and Caces 1992: 154). However, the articulation of individuals' concerns revealed a fear of ethnic isolation experienced primarily as a vulnerability in public places. This is evident in the following statement by a young Russian who had left Dushanbe, Tajikistan, in 1994:

> [before] there were still Russians . . . I lived in a district which had always been Russian, then I began to notice that there were fewer and fewer, fewer and fewer, then the last young people left, I noticed in summer. There were only pensioners left, nobody else, very few Russians. When you got on a trolleybus you could count them on the fingers of one hand.
>
> (143)

CONCLUSION

Interpreting the amalgam of objective and subjective data presented is not an easy task. Listening to the testimonies of respondents as they describe the devastating effect that the collapse of the Soviet Union had on their lives, causing them to abandon all that they had worked for and move into what many felt was a living hell, the researcher cannot help but draw the conclusion that these decisions were not taken lightly and were not rationally conceived for financial gain. Even the quantitative data collected via survey methods which should 'objectify' statements lead Vitkovskaia to suggest that the majority of migrants coming to Russia from the former Soviet Union are 'forced migrants'; the proportion which might be considered 'forced' ranged from 85 per cent in Dushanbe and Tashkent to 38 per cent in Ukraine (Vitkovskaia 1993: 28, 117). There is no real way of quantifying the qualitative data generated by the current author's fieldwork but a crude count of the number of times respondents mentioned what might be categorized as 'push factors' and 'pull factors' in their motivation for leaving shows that the push outweighs the pull by almost 9:1.[19]

What has been argued in this chapter, however, is that to conclude in this way is inadequate, not only because of the methodological issues raised above, but also because the division between voluntary (economic) and involuntary (political, ethnic) migrations is a constructed dichotomy utilized primarily for institutional purposes.[20] In fact the qualitative data from this project suggest that while migrants feel that 'ethnicity' (nationality) plays a prominent role in their decisions to leave the former republic, this cannot be equated with a sharp deterioration in inter-ethnic relations at all levels. Rather these relations have deteriorated at specific levels (state and anonymous public) and have had an impact not only on individuals' sense of security but also on how they see their long-term economic future in the newly independent states. Thus, a minority of respondents had 'fled' their homes while the vast majority articulated their motivations for migration in a way which clearly illustrated that ethnic issues were inextricably entwined with socio-economic and political dissatisfactions.

Rather than manipulating data into the categories provided by the migration regime, therefore, the migration regime itself should become an object of study in motivations for migration. As is clear from the discussion above, on the one hand, the migration regimes of the former republics have encouraged – or failed to discourage – non-titular ethnic groups to stay via citizenship and language laws introduced in the process of nation-state building. The significance of the local migration regime can be measured by changes in out-migration linked to alterations in aspects of this regime. For example, following the recognition in 1993 by President Akaev of Kyrgyzstan of the negative economic consequences of the mass emigration of the Russian population from Kyrgyzstan and the announcement of measures to encourage them to stay – including the discussion of the upgrading of the status of Russian to that of second official language[21] – the number of migrants arriving in Russia from Kyrgyzstan in 1994 fell in contrast to the previous year by almost 32 per cent. At the same time, the established links with Russia and the openness of the migration regime to them has encouraged people to migrate to Russia. In 1994 just under 92 per cent of those who left Kazakstan moved to Russia despite the fact that only 57 per cent were ethnic Russians (*Informatsionno- analiticheskii Biulleten'* 1995: 54). Moreover, the insistence that Russians will have to learn the state language threatens to maintain, if not accelerate, the out-flow.[22] The migration regime also affects the final destination in Russia of the migrants; the open favour given by some national migration regimes – such as Australia, the USA and Canada (Gurak and Caces 1992: 157) – to those who have either family or other 'sponsors' to help them in resettlement is repeated on a less formal basis in Russia via differential regional migration regimes (see Chapter 5).

The initial openness of the immigration regime, however, brings with it expectations among migrants. The gap between these expectations and the realities of their actual reception are discussed in relation to their socio-economic adaptation in Chapter 7 and cultural adaptation in Chapter 8.

7 Surviving the drop
Social and economic adaptation

For the majority of the population of the former Soviet Union, the post-Soviet period has been one in which they have suffered a severe drop in living standards. This drop has been caused by a fall in real incomes,[1] frequent and long wage arrears, unemployment, short-time working, temporary lay-offs and enforced 'holiday', and inflation. The social and economic difficulties faced by refugees and forced migrants settling in Russia during and after the collapse of the Soviet Union are thus far from peculiar. However, they have been intensified by: the loss of housing, property and savings; the relocation for many from urban to rural areas which exacerbates de-skilling processes;[2] and the loss of extended family and acquaintance networks which are central to survival strategies in post-Soviet Russia. Moreover, material hardship is made more difficult to bear by the cultural discomfort experienced upon return to Russia and, in some instances, hostility from local residents who may associate the arrival of refugees and forced migrants with the decline in their own living standard. This chapter draws predominantly on data from the author's own field-work[3] to explore: obstacles to the socio-economic integration of forced migrants and refugees; and the strategies adopted by migrants to survive the socio-economic dislocation they experience in both the short and the long term. Throughout the chapter, the difference in experience among different sections of the migrant community will be highlighted. In particular the experiences of men and women will be contrasted and the peculiar problems faced by those settling in rural locations will be explored.

MEASURING THE 'DROP'

It was argued in Chapter 6 that migrants leaving the former republics do not generally expect their economic situation to improve, at least not in the short term. Upon arrival the expected drop in living standard is indeed realized; Figure 7.1 shows that almost three-quarters of respondents had

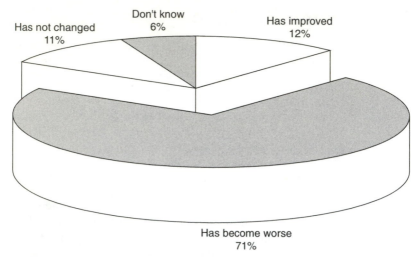

Figure 7.1 Impact of migration on standard of living
Note: No. of respondents = 134, Orel and Ul'ianovsk

suffered a fall in their standard of living. Nevertheless, the majority are not prepared for the feelings of desperation and helplessness which they experience in their new lives in Russia. The following quote from a 32 year-old Russian woman from Uzbekistan who had resettled in a village in Orel region speaks for many:

> What about us? Good lord, what does it matter about us? We are finished, we have had our day ... The only point of us going on is for the sake of the children ... I regret it ... if everything had stayed as it was there, I would never have left ... I never thought I would live in a rural place and that my children would be like this ... the only thing now is the children, it's for their sake that you live and think.
>
> (20)

To what extent the experience of forced migrants and refugees is objectively worse than other sections of the Russian population is open to debate. However, it is worth noting that the heightened perception of drop in living standard among forced migrants might have an objective as well as subjective basis. When forced migrants evaluate the drop in living standard they have experienced their points of comparison are with their lives in the former republic *before* the collapse of the Soviet Union. The displacement they undergo, therefore, is not only one of place, but also of time; they find themselves catapulted into the post-Soviet era and are ill-prepared for the new modes of economic practice and information flows which are associated with the new Russia. This is because economic change has taken place more slowly in the former republics from which these respondents had come, making the more ruthless economic environment awaiting them in Russia appear unduly hostile, and because their socio-professional status – and the accompanying housing and employment opportunities – had been heightened in the former republic by the historically rooted privilege attached to their ethnic origin. The situation for refugees and forced migrants in finding employment and housing – the two most basic requirements for socio-economic integration into the new community – is described below to explain the source of their disillusionment.

Employment

Refugees and forced migrants do appear to suffer disproportionately from unemployment in Russia. A Federal Migration Service survey of refugees and forced migrants in eight regions of the Russian Federation[4] showed that the proportion of unemployed among the refugee community was significantly higher than average.[5] It found 29 per cent of refugees and forced migrants out of work compared to 13.7 per cent of the Russian population as a whole.[6] Of the respondents who were not employed, 7 per cent were officially registered as unemployed (*Informatsionno-analiticheskii Biulleten'* 1995: 31).

The data from the survey conducted by the Federal Migration Service do not indicate the differential availability of work across the regions they sampled. However, an earlier survey by Vitkovskaia shows significant variation. Her survey included urban and rural areas in Moscow, Tver' and Orel regions and indicated that unemployment among refugees and forced migrants was highest in Moscow region (68 per cent) and lowest in Orel region (5 per cent) (Vitkovskaia 1993: 64).[7] Vitkovskaia explains these variations by the fact that in Moscow the respondents were exclusively refugees who had fled their homes in extreme circumstances while in Orel there was a greater proportion of non-extreme and even voluntary migrants.[8] The second finding of Vitkovskaia's survey was that unemployment was higher in urban than rural areas; comparing the experience of refugees and forced migrants in Tver' region, Vitkovskaia found that unemployment stood at 19 per cent among forced migrants and refugees in the urban centres of Tver' region but was only at 11 per cent in the region's villages.

It is, of course, not entirely appropriate to compare such large, quantitative surveys with the qualitative fieldwork conducted by the author; the latter makes no claims to representativeness. Nevertheless, given the overlap of at least one region – Orel – of Vitkovskaia's survey with the study described here, counterposing the results may be illustrative of some of the changing issues relevant to employment opportunities. Overall, among my respondents the rate of unemployment was 13 per cent, which compares to an official rate of registered unemployed at the end of 1994 of around 2 per cent[9] and an estimated 7.1 per cent of the total population unemployed with a further 6.4 per cent on administrative leave or short-time (*Russian Economic Trends* 1995: 87).[10] Thus, Vitkovskaia's claim that refugees and forced migrants are more vulnerable to unemployment than the population in general was confirmed. However, the suggestion that forced migrants and refugees in urban areas suffered more from unemployment than those in rural areas was not repeated among my respondents; on the contrary, 17 per cent of respondents in the villages of Orel region were unemployed whereas only 4 per cent of those in Ul'ianovsk city could not find work. This difference is most plausibly explained by the time-lag between the two studies; as respondents themselves commented, those who had moved into Orel region first (1989–91) had been able to find work quite easily, but by 1994 lay-offs on the farms were widespread and residents had already begun to compete for jobs, particularly in female-dominated areas of work such as administrative positions and nursery schools.

Post-Soviet Russian society – economists assert – has a suspiciously low unemployment rate. It has 'achieved' this by a cocktail of measures to cushion the impact of marketization. However, this does not mean the Russian workforce has been left unaffected by the economic reform; in fact there has been a widespread shift of professional personnel into insecure employment in petty-trading and the – often informal – service sector and to accept employment not commensurate with their qualifications.

The refugee and forced-migrant community is no exception to the tendency towards this form of de-skilling in the Soviet economy. The Federal Migration Service survey referred to above showed that returnees from the former republics were likely to move from mental to manual work; before the move 44 per cent of those surveyed had primarily mental work and 48 per cent had primarily manual work, whereas after the move 53 per cent had primarily manual and only 32 per cent had primarily mental work. Respondents also tended to move from industrial to agricultural employment; before the move 25 per cent were employed in industry, afterwards only 13 per cent, while before the move 4 per cent worked in agriculture, compared to 11 per cent after the move (*Informatsionno-analiticheskii Biulleten'* 1995: 31).

In reality this professional downgrading means high levels of dissatisfaction with their work in particular and the move in general. The most frequent complaints are: the work is dirty and heavy; the work available does not correspond to qualifications; wages are low; farm managers show a lack of understanding in finding lighter work for women and in allowing flexible hours to fit in with child-care. The impact of de-professionalization on migrants' sense of self-worth is immense and has negative consequences for integration into the receiver society. Signs of serious depression were evident among a number of respondents. One woman who was visiting her sister in the village explained the latter's obvious distress when talking about her situation:

> She is an accountant by training . . . she worked in the state bank for five years. But now she works on a building site, where else can she get a job?
>
> (115)

Another woman talked of the way professional de-skilling had destroyed her husband's life:

> He is employed as a simple manual worker here, a plumber; there is nothing in the area of his professional training for him here, of course. It is as if his whole life has been destroyed.
>
> (112)

Although both men and women experience unemployment and de-skilling, that experience is clearly gendered. Galina Vitkovskaia found that in Tver' region 9 per cent of men compared to 21 per cent of women were unable to find employment. However, in the rural locations of her survey in Orel region her findings are reversed; only 2 per cent of women compared to 6 per cent of men could not find work (Vitkovskaia 1993: 64). The author's own study in 1994 found that of the 195 respondents in Ul'ianovsk and Orel region, 17 per cent of women and 9 per cent of men seeking work could not find it. However, when the regional variation is added to the gender breakdown, then the findings are rather different from Vitkovskaia's. Figure 7.2 illustrates the particular problem of female rural unemployment identified in the author's study; 21 per cent of women respondents in rural areas of Orel region could not find work while, at the other end of the spectrum, among male respondents having resettled in Ul'ianovsk city, there was nobody without work.

The pocket of female rural unemployment among refugees and forced migrants is explained, it is suggested here, by a number of factors. First, education levels among respondents were higher among women than men; 23 per cent of women (compared to 16 per cent of men) were graduates while 38 per cent of women and 33 per cent of men had secondary specialist education. In normal circumstances higher levels of education

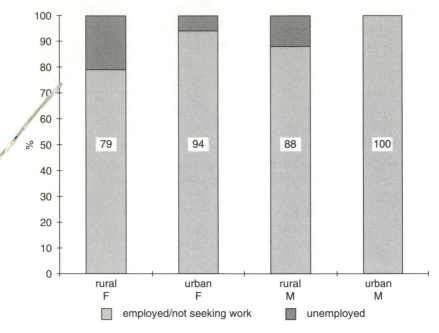

Figure 7.2 Unemployment by gender and region
Note: No. of respondents = 195, Orel and Ul'ianovsk

– especially the supposedly vocational secondary specialist eduction – should equip women better in the labour market. When this is super-imposed on to the urban to rural move, however, it appears that women are trained in narrow professional niches for which there are no outlets in rural areas. This is reflected in women's talk by reference to the fact that:

> There are no jobs . . . he says that we don't need teachers . . . They are not taken on . . . He says, go and work on the threshing floor . . . So I went and worked there for a few days, but it is impossible there. They lift sacks of 70 kg. I am not capable of lifting that . . . But he says there is no other kind of work.

(114)

Thus women are prone to a greater mismatch of skills to available jobs and a subsequent de-skilling.[11] Comparing professional qualifications (or usual professional practice) with current employment, Figures 7.3 and 7.4 indicate the different relocations of male and female respondents in my study in the labour market after migration to Russia. Male forced migrants, it would appear, are much more likely to find employment in the same job (almost one-third) (see Figure 7.3). Women, in contrast, find it very

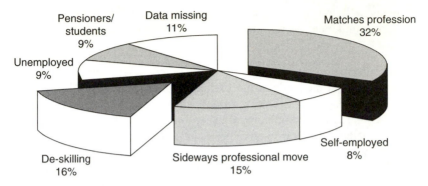

Figure 7.3 Current employment of male respondents relative to previous profession
Note: No. of respondents = 75, Orel and Ul'ianovsk

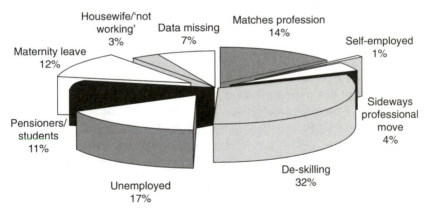

Figure 7.4 Current employment of female respondents relative to previous profession
Note: No. of respondents = 120, Orel and Ul'ianovsk

difficult to continue in their old profession (just 14 per cent were working in the same kind of job) (see Figure 7.4). The acute problem of mismatch of skills is confirmed by both Vitkovskaia and Kosmarskaya who note that men (especially those with engineering qualifications) are more likely to find work in the new place of residence akin to their urban profession, whereas the social distance between women's pre- and post-migration occupations is much greater (Kosmarskaya 1995: 156; Vitkovskaia 1995). Many women said that it was far easier for men to gain employment on the farm than for women:

the work here is mainly for men, men's work, the only thing [for us] is
to be a milkmaid, work with livestock and that's all.

(18)

A second reason for the peculiar problem of female, rural unemployment,
therefore, is that the kinds of profession in which men were trained were
more easily adaptable to the new labour environment. Male respondents in
my study were, for example, more likely to cite more than one profession
(9 per cent did so) than women (3 per cent). The male respondents' professions were also less exclusively urban based. The three most common
professions among men were welder, electrician or mechanic and driver
or chauffeur, all of which could find direct outlets in rural locations. In
contrast the most common professions among women were economist
or accountant, teachers (from lecturers to nursery-school teachers) and
medical workers (doctors, pharmacists and nurses). A limited number
of accountants and teachers were required on farms but there was intense
competition for such positions since these were also the kinds of profession
local young women sought. Those trained in the medical professions, on the
other hand, were almost unemployable in their original lines of work.[12]

While the problems of de-skilling and unemployment are particularly
acute for women resettling in rural areas,[13] they are far from unique to
them. Female refugees and forced migrants who had settled in Ul'ianovsk
complained of direct discrimination on the part of employers,[14] who, they
said, would always take male employees over female ones because 'men
don't take sick leave to look after their children'. Those who had found
work complained that it was heavy, factory work to which they were
unaccustomed, while many others (especially older women) took work as
cleaners or hostel caretakers in order to secure tied accommodation. In
Ul'ianovsk six women among those interviewed had taken this option,
including a graduate economist, an accountant and a pharmacist. One
respondent explained this choice:

> Nobody would take me in the capacity for which I was trained . . . [So]
> I went to work as a caretaker and I have been working as a caretaker for
> two years now . . . I want to leave but I am afraid to, it is very difficult
> to find work at the moment . . . It is possible to find someone to take you
> on as an accountant but only if you train to use computers first. But
> these courses are very expensive.

(178)

Many other respondents had taken jobs in factories or other workplaces
where accommodation was offered in hostels. Thus Vitkovskaia's finding
that women resettling in towns tend on the whole to be more satisfied with

their new work than men may well reflect above all the primacy of the problem of housing over employment for forced migrants resettling in urban areas, rather than any positive feelings about that employment; their prime concern was securing a roof over their children's heads. However, Vitkovskaia's finding that women forced migrants working in urban areas – whatever their work – are more satisfied than women in rural areas is, without doubt, accurate (Vitkovskaia 1993: 65–6).

Employment prospects for refugees and forced migrants are also apparently affected by age. Vitkovskaia suggests that young people and those close to retirement age are the most vulnerable to unemployment (Vitkovskaia 1993: 64). Since my study did not sample its respondents it would be of spurious value to test her finding against my own. Certainly there was a general 'belief' that it was more difficult for those close to retirement age to find work, although among those of this age in my study,[15] there was actually a slightly less than average tendency to be unemployed. Young people in the study, however, were more likely to be unemployed.[16] However, it should be borne in mind that the total number of respondents of this age group was just twenty-one. My study, on the contrary, painted the typical portrait of the unemployed in the image of a woman in her mid-thirties with two or more children.

Long-term prospects for employment may not be as bad as they appear currently. A comparable study of the return of French settlers from Algeria in 1962 showed that while in the short term they suffered disproportionate unemployment – peaking at 20 per cent in December 1962 – this fell to 6 per cent within the following year and 4 per cent a year after that (Layard, Blanchard, Dornbusch and Krugman 1992: 47). However, in seeking an optimistic scenario we must not forget the very different general economic context prevailing in the two countries at the time; a healthy economy with declining population would without doubt not only absorb but benefit from the return of Russians whereas the economic crisis prevailing in post-Soviet Russia means little more than extra strain. Moreover, there appears to be very little political will in Russia to tackle the issue of the successful integration into employment of refugees and forced migrants. Neither the Federal Migration Service nor the Federal Employment Service has provided any positive programme of retraining and utilization of the significant skills and resources of Russian-speaking forced migrants. The government has sought rather to utilize the sheer physical resources of returnees to repopulate poorly developed northern and eastern regions of the country and the depopulated rural regions of central Russia in a crude attempt to minimize potential social conflict ensuing from repatriation (see Chapter 4). This lack of foresight is likely to encourage a new migratory push of deeply dissatisfied returnees out of the villages to which they moved with some initial optimism to the more hospitable towns and cities of European Russia.

Housing: dream cottages?

It is the failure to resolve their housing problems satisfactorily upon return to Russia which is the most distressing aspect of life for the majority of refugees and forced migrants. The Federal Migration Service survey cited above found that only 22 per cent of families had found 'proper' housing (that is more than temporary accommodation) within the first year of resettlement and 60 per cent of those who had been in Russia for more than a year had not resolved the problem (30 per cent were still living with relatives or friends and 30 per cent had found only temporary housing) (*Informatsionno-analiticheskii Biulleten'* 1995: 28). This situation was regionally highly differentiated; 57 per cent had found permanent housing in Pskov region, but only 9 per cent in Belgorod region.

In my own study data on housing conditions before and after the move were collected from 134 respondents (51 in Ul'ianovsk and 83 in Orel region). The overall picture is illustrated in Figure 7.5 which shows that respondents had generally exchanged a good housing situation (having permanent housing in their own house or state flat) for much less secure housing arrangements (single rooms in hostels, rented rooms and farm-owned houses).

In Ul'ianovsk city the tendency was for the move from own house or state flat (96 per cent of respondents) to rooms in hostels (56 per cent). Overcrowding in hostel accommodation was often acute and wholly unsuited for family life. Families generally ate and slept in a single room (during interviewing the largest encountered in such circumstances was a family of seven) and shared kitchen and bathroom facilities with a number of other families. Some families feared being evicted even from this accommodation, however, if they ceased to work for the factory which owned it. Of those interviewed, 29 per cent had obtained state flats but they were almost unanimously dissatisfied with the accommodation; it was generally much smaller and in worse repair than their previous housing. Those who had received flats were primarily refugees from Baku who had been allocated housing in Ul'ianovsk between 1989 and 1992 by central authorities trying to clear them from temporary accommodation in sanatoria and hotels in the Moscow region. Among those who had managed to find flats there was also a higher tendency to share the flat with parents which increased domestic stress. One person was found to be homeless and moved between acquaintances willing to put her up temporarily. As was noted in Chapter 5, the right of forced migrants and

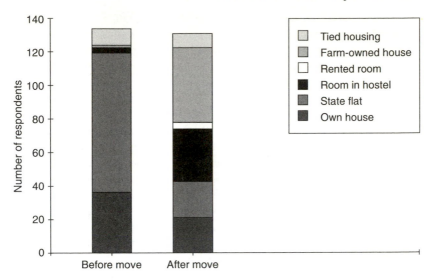

Figure 7.5 Housing before and after migration
Note: No. of respondents = 134, Orel and Ul'ianovsk

refugees to be placed on priority-housing lists appeared to be recognized by some parts of the regional migration service but not by others. In any case, as was noted by one migration worker, even the priority-housing list moved so slowly that anyone other than single and disabled pensioners and large families had little hope of being rehoused by the state in the foreseeable future (see Chapter 5).

In Orel region the general tendency was a move from privately owned houses or state flats in the former republic (86 per cent of people) into farm-owned housing (54 per cent of respondents in Orel region). Contending with poor standards of housing was particularly painful for those having moved to the villages, however, since major sacrifices had been made in moving to a rural area in terms of social mobility, employment opportunity and education in order to ensure a decent immediate living environment. As was noted in Chapter 6, the availability of housing had been the prime motivation for migrants in choosing to settle in a rural area and respondents talked about having 'fallen in love' with the cottages they had seen on one farm.

Housing was a major cause of dispute and stress in the rural areas where fieldwork was conducted. One source of this stress was the battle to privatize housing which led to bitter disputes with farm managers. Migrants complained that they had been prevented from privatizing housing on the grounds that they had not lived there long enough and that the houses had been constructed with Federal Migration Service money and thus must remain for temporary accommodation and were exempt from privatization. In the main fieldwork base, migrants were allowed to buy their houses from the farm but at a sum well beyond the means of most of their occupants. The money could be paid over a two-year period, but the purchasers had to agree to work on the farm for at least ten years, before which time they could not sell the house except back to the farm. Given the general dissatisfaction with rural life among migrants (see Chapter 8) this was a major disincentive. One family's attempt to win the right to privatize their home via the courts had reportedly failed in 1995.[17] In a second rural fieldwork base migrants were allowed to privatize but were charged 200 to 300 per cent more than local residents.

A linked source of dissatisfaction was that houses had to be bought from the farm at high prices despite the fact that many migrants had virtually built them themselves. Migrants had been attracted to the region by the availability of complete houses of the new 'cottage' type and an apparent ongoing building programme. However, by the time many had arrived all these houses had been taken and they were forced to live in the farm hostel, corrugated iron wagons (*vagonchiki*) and, in one case, a cow shed, while they built their own houses. This was a considerable struggle since the majority had no formal construction training and no money to purchase building materials. Progress was thus very slow and involved protracted battles to obtain building materials from the farm director and to be connected to piped water and gas. Far from moving into completed houses, therefore, families often occupied shoddily constructed and semi-plastered houses with no heating or running water. Not surprisingly, they felt deceived and in July 1995 one forced migrant said he intended to take the farm director to court over his failure to fulfil the 'agreement' signed with incomers to supply them with 50 per cent of the cost of building materials needed to construct the houses.

Life in permanent domestic chaos had a particularly negative impact on women's lives. Many women suffered from a sense of failure at having lost their former homes and being unable to create a pleasant home environment for their families in the new residence. This loss of self-worth was intensified by the fact that they had given up any hope of achieving personal professional fulfilment by moving to the village (see above).[18]

A final source of dispute was the relationship between housing and employment. Some migrants sought to resolve their employment problems by looking for work in nearby urban centres where there was a wider range of employment opportunities and higher wages. However, farm directors immediately doubled or tripled rent payments on housing and raised nursery-school charges for anyone not employed on the farm. Moreover, if both parents ceased to work on the farm, they were threatened with eviction from their houses. This was on the grounds that the houses actually belonged to the farm, which contradicts the argument noted above that normal privatization was not possible since Federal Migration Service money had been used to construct the housing. Attempts by migrants to resolve these contradictions by recourse to the legal service were confounded by their lack of access to any of the necessary documents concerned with the status of housing and what they considered to be a biased legal system which always supported those in power. In July 1994 at least four families in the main fieldwork base were locked in battle against eviction from their homes. Not surprisingly, migrants frequently expressed feelings of powerlessness; they had effectively become hostages in their 'dream cottages'.

SURVIVAL STRATEGIES

[T]hey say that there is something for refugees . . . for all poor families, but I am not looking because they snubbed me once and I try not to humiliate myself, I'll manage on my own . . . We'll survive.

(178)

Despite the severe socio-economic difficulties faced by refugees and forced migrants upon arrival in Russia and the bitterness they feel at the devastation to their lives caused by the move, respondents did not allow themselves to become victims but strove continuously to improve their lives in both the short and long term. The success with which they have managed to integrate into the new socio-economic environment is dependent on many factors including the site of their resettlement, age, gender, education and training and the support networks available to them. On the basis of qualitative data it is impossible to generalize about the factors facilitating socio-economic integration, and the project instead focused upon identifying the strategies adopted by respondents to facilitate that integration. These strategies include: the tactical use of state support; entrepreneurial initiative; political and legal organization; and on-migration.

State assistance: bubble gum for the children

Few returnees are positive about the way in which they are received back by the state. They complain of the amount of bureaucracy and paperwork required both before leaving and in the process of resettlement, and about the absence, at the federal level, of legislation that would really help them. At the same time, new legislation detrimental to the interests of migrants is passed without thought to them.[19] Most hurtful, however, was the perceived general disinterest in the problems of migrants among all state institutions.

Refugees (from the 'near abroad') tend to evaluate Russian government policy more positively than forced migrants. This is partially because they have often received concrete help (evacuation, refuge, food, housing) in extreme situations, and partially because as non-Russian citizens they have generally been less inclined to 'expect' Russia to help. However, only a tiny proportion of out-migration from the former republics was officially 'organized' by the state; by 1992 only 50,000 or 5 per cent of forced migrants had been 'evacuated' (Vitkovskaia 1993: 82).

Quantitative indicators suggest that the majority of forced migrants and refugees receive very little material help from the state either in the form of a cash benefit or help with the cost of purchasing or building housing for themselves. Table 7.1 shows the proportion of people in the author's two fieldwork areas who had received some kind of cash benefit and/or a loan for the purchase or building of housing for themselves.[20] Evaluations of help received by respondents during in-depth interviews are even more revealing. One-off cash benefits were universally considered laughable; typical statements were that they were enough to buy the kids chewing gum, or for a packet of cigarettes. More positively evaluated were other forms of 'help in kind' received mainly by those settling in rural areas. Such help included the provision of 'rations' of meat, milk and sugar from the farm.[21] Some forced migrants said that for the first two to three years they had not been asked to pay for services such as electricity or water. Many migrants remained confused about their rights, however, and did not differentiate between benefits received due to forced-migrant status, those given to anyone settling in a rural area from a city, and those due to pensioner or large-family status.

Whatever the statistics, forced migrants and refugees clearly feel that they have received little help and are highly sceptical about the migration service. Their attitudes are reminiscent of those of Russian refugees in

Table 7.1 Proportion of refugees and forced migrants receiving state assistance in Orel and Ul'ianovsk regions

	Percentage receiving state assistance	
Kind of help received	Orel	Ul'ianovsk
One-off cash benefit	31	14
Loan to build housing	4	0

Note: No. of respondents = 134, Orel and Ul'ianovsk

Europe in the 1920s who referred to their refugee documentation cards, the Nansen passports,[22] as 'nonsense passports' (Chinyaeva 1995: 150). Where help is appreciated – most conspicuously in the form of housing – it has come not from local authorities or state bodies but from local employers. As a result there is an increasing tendency not to register, as the experience of others is passed on. Among the eighty-three respondents completing questionnaires in Orel in 1994, 52 per cent had registered with the TMS while in Ul'ianovsk the tighter residency controls meant the figure was somewhat higher – around 70 per cent had registered. Nevertheless, scepticism about the value of registration is high and migrants view the migration service as just another bureaucratic organization from which little can be expected, and many noted that you might well spend more on travel and payment for documents in order to obtain the status than the size of the benefit, if any, received after status had been granted.

Given the tight economic constraints under which the Federal Migration Service and its regional branches are working, it is perhaps understandable that it has been unable to ease the social and economic integration of such a large number of refugees and forced migrants significantly. What is more disturbing, however, is that the service is seen by many to hinder that process as a result of its brutal bureaucratism and humiliating attitude. Of course, this should not be universalized; some respondents find TMS workers to have a sympathetic ear and feel a deep attachment to the people who become the first in Russia to help them. However, analysis of interviews suggests common experience in both regions as well as some problems specific to each.

In Orel region criticism focused on the sense of helplessness in the face of a united bureaucracy; a number of respondents felt the TMS was in league with the farm director, the local authorities and the local courts rather than on their side. This was particularly evident (and painfully felt) in relation to housing where disputes over privatization were frequent (see above). Moreover, despite the region's reputation for a positive attitude to incomers, the migration service in Orel itself does not escape criticism. The director of a migrant commercial association set up in 1995 complained that he had been given a 'cold and bureaucratic reception' by Orel TMS (Shved 1996: 57).

Ul'ianovsk respondents, in contrast, complained of the refusal, or inability, of migration service workers to provide any real help despite the fact that this had been promised either before departure from the former republic or in Moscow. They were also more likely to report humiliating treatment, conflict with individual district administrations (including those responsible for migrants) and refusal to register them. A 53-year-old woman who arrived from Uzbekistan at the beginning of 1993 described her experience of assistance to forced migrants thus:

> When I arrived I went round all the offices, and in one place I was even asked, 'What do you need a flat for? You'll be dead soon.' We went to the migration service, they looked at us and did not even record us in the book. They said Ul'ianovsk does not give anything to refugees.
>
> (162)

An evacuee from Baku in 1992 who had been sent to Ul'ianovsk from a temporary reception centre in Moscow also experienced more hostility than sympathy:

> They don't treat us very well to be honest . . . We couldn't get a job anywhere when we first came . . . We asked so often for help . . . the children did not even have warm boots . . . but they did not give me anything, they said that we have enough of our own poor . . . you will just have to manage yourselves . . . they said that, that we have enough of our own.
>
> (178)

Despite the extreme scepticism among forced migrants about material and psychological support from the state and its agencies, migrants used friends and acquaintances to establish what might or might not be the benefits of dealing with state institutions, including the migration service, to assist their employment and housing prospects. One respondent claimed that forced-migrant status had helped them gain admission to higher education, while another had decided to register because she had heard that gas pipelines would be laid free of charge to those houses where forced-migrant or refuge families were resident. As was noted in Chapter 3, some migrants appear to have effectively subverted the system by registering in more than one region, and amendments to legislation had to be introduced to prevent this.

Entrepreneurial initiatives

As a consequence of economic collapse in post-Soviet Russia, the Russian population has increasingly supplemented wage incomes by entrepreneurial activities. These range from setting up private businesses to selling personal possessions on the street to survive. Refugees and forced migrants are no exception to this rule and Vitkovskaia's finding that 45 per cent of her respondents in Orel region would like to have their own business (Vitkovskaia 1993: 68) suggests a high entrepreneurial initiative among this group. Among my respondents a number wished to become independent farmers while others expressed ideas about setting up their own business either on the farm (especially in providing services and consumer products to villagers) or in the town:

> I hope to organize a firm here, or rather two firms. A firm which will train . . . [pilots] for the whole of Russia, and a second which will produce . . . sausage and cheese . . . I am 98 per cent certain that we will succeed . . .
>
> (150)

However, in practice, these desires had been fulfilled in very few cases. In Orel region respondents related this to the obstacles put in their way by farm directors. There were complaints about not being able to take on their own private farming; in one place land had been divided up during the period between the migrants agreeing with the farm director to come and their actual arrival, and thus the migrants were forced to work as farm labourers for the new private farmers. Others complained of blank refusals to grant permission to set up commercial enterprises on the farm which would have provided much needed services to the locals. In relation to the latter migrants were particularly keen to use farm produce to make and sell their own bread, milk and cheese, even alcohol, instead of buying it in from the towns (whence supplies were erratic and expensive). Individual initiatives then were confined to the selling of surplus potatoes and other vegetables from allotments in the towns and taking up waged work in nearby towns. On return to one village in 1995, it was also reported that a number of families had managed to pay the first instalment of 500,000 roubles towards the privatization of their houses in the autumn of 1994. This, they hoped, would secure their long-term future.

In Ul'ianovsk, respondents had found it difficult to work in an environment in which they had been deprived of the contacts via which they would normally seek to establish business deals. It was also clear that they found the new economic environment unfamiliar; at least one respondent was unsure why his attempts to set up his own business were not proving successful. All those interviewed who were seeking to establish themselves as self-employed business people were men and generally uncomfortable about talking about their failure.

There is a wider gender dimension to the question of self-employment. As is clear from Figures 7.3 and 7.4, a significantly greater proportion of men than women appear to move into self-employment or business. Vitkovskaia would explain this with reference to an apparent tendency for women to be less keen to enter into entrepreneurial activity. However, from the analysis of in-depth interviews with forced migrants in both rural and urban areas of fieldwork, it would appear that this apparent gender difference may reflect gendered modes of articulation rather than any fundamental difference in outlook and experience between the sexes; women who are out of waged employment talk about being, at least temporarily, 'at home' while men in this situation refer to themselves as 'self-employed'. Many women were taking longer maternity leave than they would have done in 'normal circumstances' in order to protect their work record or because it was financially disadvantageous to work. The latter was the result of a combination of the sudden rise in nursery-school fees, extremely low wages in rural areas and the loss of extended family networks previously facilitating child-care. Such women occupy their time by working on their allotments, either to feed the family or to sell produce at markets, preserving food and making clothes (sometimes for sale).[23] However, they would describe themselves as 'on maternity leave' or 'not working at the moment', since they are conscious of the temporary, 'survival' nature of the option and would prefer 'a proper job'. Men in urban areas involved in similar survival strategies, however, would be more likely to describe their path as 'having gone into business' even though this business often involved only petty trade, or the process of trying to establish some kind of intermediary selling business, and in practice meant they were predominantly at home and actually undertook a good deal of the domestic burden.[24] One woman explained what other people would call her husband's unemployment thus:

> He is not working in his professional area at the moment, we have a small-holding . . . we keep bees . . . but he does not have a problem with work. He could live . . . and work in any city.
>
> (137)

Indeed, far from being resistant to entrepreneurial activity, female respondents clearly identified the need to use women's service skills on collective farms where no such services were available. As one female forced migrant who could only find temporary labouring work on a farm in Orel region noted:

> I have always had one thought, to start up my own business of some kind, to open some kind of services complex . . . Why should they come in from the town when we have everything virtually on the spot – hairdressers and dress-makers; I myself, for example, love baking, love handling dough.
>
> (113)

However, women settling in rural areas have little chance of achieving their aims; the 'double burden' of the cities is transformed into a 'triple burden' of work, children/home and the allotment.

Collective action

The individual court actions against the farm director referred to above were the first sign of a growing confidence in the power of forced migrants and refugees as a group. Although they were individual initiatives, they were widely supported by the whole migrant community and the results were followed closely by other migrants with a view to pursuing further claims. In the main fieldwork base migrants even joined together to defend their rights. In autumn 1994 (directly after the end of fieldwork) one migrant to the village,[25] set up a civic 'union' which he referred to as 'in defence of human rights'. Locals, however, saw it as an oppositional organization of migrants, and its primary purpose appeared to be to remove the current director of the farm whom many migrants saw as the chief obstacle to their successful resettlement. Subsequently the founder of this union was nominated to stand against the current farm director in re-elections to the post. However, it was claimed, intervention from the local council (under the orders of the governor of Orel region not to let the director be replaced) ensured his survival. Thereafter, it was said, those involved in the union were removed from their jobs and a policy was conducted of giving all new houses which became vacant and the best jobs to locals.

There are, of course, both positive and negative elements to this experience which are reflected in the split mood among forced migrants and refugees. When asked on whom their future depended, respondents were fairly evenly split between suggesting that migrants themselves are powerless and can expect no help from the state to suggestions that it is individuals who must take the situation into their own hands.

At a less organized level, as they become more settled, migrants are able increasingly to bring over their extended families and, at the time of the fieldwork, many were in the process of bringing over parents who could help with domestic work and child care. In the meantime, or for those cases where this extended family was absent, other migrants came to fill this role and migrants prided themselves on helping each other out much more than was the practice among the local community (see Chapter 8). In Ul'ianovsk, networks of migrants from the same city (*zemliaki*) were common and friendships had been forged around these ties.

Moving on . . .

Few people seriously considered return to the former republic as a strategy
of escape from their current difficulties. Of fifty-four statements directly
concerning whether they would return to the former republic, only four
indicated seriously thinking about this or planning such a move (see
Chapter 6). Of seventy-five direct statements concerning potential plans to
move on from their current residence, the majority – forty-two – said they
would stay.[26] Although sometimes this was related to positive statements
– the fulfilment of a dream of living 'on the land', or satisfaction with
Ul'ianovsk's central location – for most this was a pragmatic decision
borne of the belief that they would not find anything better anywhere else,
that 'Russia is the same everywhere' and the stark reality that they had
neither money nor energy to uproot again. Some respondents expressed an
overwhelming desire to *stop* moving, to make the best of things and put
down roots again. Twelve respondents said they wanted to move either into
an urban area or (among Ul'ianovsk respondents) into a bigger city while
another three said they would move if they were able to move to specific
cities (Moscow, Leningrad (*sic*) or Tver'). Seven said they would move
anywhere they could simply to get out of where they were now or anywhere as long as the conditions were better. All of these were from the
rural settlements of Orel region and during the period of fieldwork two
families moved to other regions of Russia and another two did so shortly
after. Reports back to the village were that their feelings after the move
were as if 'the nightmare had come to an end'.

Six people indicated a desire coupled with some possibility of moving
to the west (three to Germany, one to the USA, one to Canada and one did
not state a preferred destination) while another wanted to move back to
Armenia.

When asked about general plans for the future, concerns are usually
expressed in relation to the children, revealing a resignation often about
their own future, but a desire to improve conditions for their children.
These concerns generally related to fears that their children would not
receive a good education and thus as parents they would effectively pass
on their own de-skilling and produce a decline in social status across
generations. Two respondents summed this up thus:

> The children who study here will not be able to get in [to higher
> education] anywhere. They will grow up to be tractor drivers and milk-
> maids again . . . I don't want my child to be a tractor driver.

(17)

If we stay here, there will be no future for our children. This is what frightens us more than anything, that there will be no future for them, nor for us.

(29)

CONCLUSION

The weak social and economic integration of forced migrants and refugees in post-Soviet Russia does not inherently signal a 'problem' group whose dissatisfaction is likely to drive them towards extreme political solutions; indeed, Rimashevskaia suggests that 80 per cent of the Russian population as a whole is as yet not 'adapted' to the new economic environment (Rimashevskaia 1996). However, social and economic integration is without doubt problematized for migrants by a number of factors.

First, they generally do not choose their place of resettlement (see Chapter 6). Although, in the short term they use networks of family, acquaintances and contacts from the 'home country' to cushion integration (providing material help with accommodation, employment and child-care), this may not be sufficient to secure a long-term future.

Second, state-support programmes are inadequate and focus on encouraging refugees and forced migrants to settle in those parts of the country considered to be advantageous to the country as a whole. However, this does little to address the real problems where migrants have actually settled; problems which are widely recognized to be those of poverty, the impossibility of finding employment, difficulties in adapting to a new place, and, most of all, housing (Popova and Tekoniemi 1996: 45). Indeed, the failure to act is likely to store up worse problems in the future. Run-down areas of central Russia might have been a positive place to settle in the immediate post-Soviet period but there is evidence of growing unemployment and dissatisfaction in these areas and the desire among those who had initially resettled there to move on. Indeed, even in the relatively prosperous Ul'ianovsk, cutbacks in working hours in the city's major factories from the end of 1995 had exacerbated existing employment problems.

Third, as the socio-demographic profile of migrants changes, it is likely that those who arrive will be less well off (*Informatsionno-analiticheskii Biulleten'* 1995: 34–5) and thus the proportion needing urgent state support will grow.

Fourth, the inability of migrants to resolve their long-term housing crisis is a serious and growing problem. Such is the apparent lack of hope among migrants that a group of refugees has reportedly established a squatter camp in the deserted villages within the 30 km radius that constitutes the Chernobyl zone of radioactive contamination (Popova and Tekoniemi

1996: 45). Such a situation oversteps the boundary of the acceptable reliance by the state on individual 'survival strategies' to overcome the problems of socio-economic adaptation borne of displacement and borders on a wilful neglect of its people.

8 'Us and them'
Crossing the cultural border to post-Soviet Russia

A striking absence in the media debate about Russian-speaking forced migrants returning to Russia is the culture shock they experience upon return.[1] This chapter charts the boundaries of the 'us' and 'them' identities forged between migrant and receiver communities. It examines the culture shock experienced upon return to Russia and the importance of memory of the former place of residence in fuelling a common collective identity among these self-professed 'other Russians'. In this sense it challenges widespread beliefs that common ethnicity precludes any problem of cultural adaptation upon return to Russia for Russian-speaking migrants from the former republics. The chapter also considers the perspective of the receiver community. Drawing on a small-scale survey in Ul'ianovsk region and interviews with non-migrant residents in Orel region, common stereotypes about refugees and forced migrants and their consequences for integration into the new community are also explored.

CONSTRUCTING THE MIGRANT 'WE'

When asked to state with whom they *identified* during an interview-based questionnaire, Russian-speaking forced migrants in Orel region indicated that above all they identified with each other; 40 per cent noted an identification with 'other similar migrants' – by far the single largest category. More authentic (but less easily quantifiable) markers of group identity would be those categories of inclusion ('us') employed by respondents spontaneously in the course of interviews.

Analysis of transcripts suggests that the most frequently employed categories were indeed displacement-based identities, primarily that of 'migrants' (*pereselentsy*), as well as its Anglicized variant '*migranty*'. Occasionally pejorative terms used by locals to describe migrants '*immigranty*' or '*emigranty*' are adopted by the migrants themselves. The most extreme of the displacement self-identifications 'refugees' (*bezhentsy*) was used by few and signalled flight from fighting or ethnic persecution.[2] In no instance did 'refugee' act as a positive collective identity, however, and it was rejected by many for falsely 'victimizing' those it affected and conjuring up images of poverty and disease which degraded and dehumanized them.

Culturally based identities were also commonly used. This was especially true of migrants into rural settlements of Orel region where the terms 'townies' (*gorozhane* or *gorodskie*) were used. The most frequently encountered term, however, was that of 'newcomers' (*priezhie*); a term borrowed from the local population's description of the migrants and denoting anyone coming from outside.[3] In contrast, ethnically inclusive regional identities were particularly strong in Ul'ianovsk.[4] These identities – particularly common among those from Baku (*Bakintsy*) and from Dushanbe (*Dushanbintsy*) – were consolidated by networks of mutual help and support created in the process of leaving and settling in the new place of residence and appeared to be ethnically inclusive.[5]

Ethnic or racial identities were expressed only when migrants were consciously distinguishing themselves from local, native populations in the former place of residence. For migrants having left Central Asian republics the term 'Europeans' or 'European population' might be employed to distinguish themselves. More widely and frequently, however, the term 'Russian-speaking population' was used.[6] The ethnically exclusive term 'Russians' (*russkie*) was used on occasion as was 'Slavic population' and 'Russians on the periphery'. 'Russian citizen' (*rossiianin*) was employed spontaneously by only one respondent as a term of self-identification.[7] The significance of the resistance to civic Russian identity is explored in greater detail in Chapter 9.

Having determined that there is an 'us' to which forced migrants and refugees refer, the interviews were analysed using 'us' and 'them' and 'here' and 'there' binaries drawn from interviews to determine the boundaries of this identity and the characteristics ascribed to 'self' and 'other'. The findings of this analysis are summarized in Figure 8.1. The analysis shows that the collective 'us' for forced migrants is forged through distinguishing self from 'them' (*oni*) where 'they' are the native population in the former republic ('them there') *and* locals in the new place of residence in Russia ('them here').

The 'other' identified in the former place of residence was generally an ethnically determined 'other'; 'they' referred to nationality (the Kyrgyz, the Uzbeks, etc.). The only common general term was *natsionaly* (or the more colloquial *natsmeny*) which indicated those of the titular nationality although the term 'Muslims' was used on occasion and the racially loaded 'blacks' (*chernie*) by two respondents. In ascribing characteristics to the

'Them' (here)	'Them' (there)	'Us'
• simple	• kind, friendly	
• unhappy	• hospitable	
• downtrodden	• respect for women, elders and parents	
• drunkards		
• thieves	• don't know own language	
• nasty		
	• like to be boss	

'There'	'Here'
• respect (especially for women, elders)	• lack of respect
• better educated, brought up	• swearing
• hospitality	• cold, harsh climate
• good weather, fruit and vegetables all year	• dirty
• multi-ethnic environment	• drunkenness
• affluent lifestyle, big house/dacha	• savage
• everything was our own	• life is hard
• many friends and relatives	• exploitative
• mix more, more leisure and rest time	• lack of prospects
• friendliness and kindness	• everyone for selves
	• on our own

Figure 8.1 The cultural construction of migrant identity

titular nationality, respondents differentiated between village and urban residents (the latter were described sometimes as 'russified'), and between older and younger generations (the latter being seen as more aggressively oriented). The characteristics ascribed to 'them there' are indicated in the top-left quadrant of Figure 8.1.[8] The bottom-left quadrant lists characteristics ascribed to the cultural world 'there' more widely,[9] and when contrasted with the description of 'here', it is clear that returning Russians feel far from 'at home' in the new Russia. It might, of course, be anticipated that the culture clash for those resettling in rural areas as opposed to urban ones would be greater. For this reason only attributes ascribed by respondents from both regions are included in the bottom-right quadrant of Figure 8.1.[10] Finally, a surprising 'them, here' is identified in the top-left quadrant of the Figure 8.1. This 'other' was referred to most commonly in both areas of fieldwork as 'the locals' (*mestnie*). In Orel locals were also frequently referred to as 'villagers' (*derevenskie, kolkhozniki, sel'chane*) or 'those from here' (*zdeshnie*). Although the confrontation with rural culture – for the reasons discussed below – makes integration much more problematic for respondents in the Orel region, there appears to be enough in common in the labelling of the 'other' in Orel region and in Ul'ianovsk to suggest that the significant 'other' is Russians (*rossiiane*) in general and not merely rural residents. One respondent spelled this out:

> People here are very envious, completely ignorant. When I came, I thought it was just the village here, but it would appear that it's like this everywhere.
>
> (101)

While the top-right quadrant in Figure 8.1 has been left blank, it will be argued below that the sense of self of forced migrants is more than the positive outcome generated by the meeting of two negatives. The positive sense of 'we' and its components are discussed below while the significance of the boundaries drawn between 'self' and 'other' indicated in the rest of Figure 8.1 is explored in detail in Chapter 9.

Shared current problems

Collective identity among forced migrants and refugees is most obviously rooted in their shared current problems and their empathy for each other's situation.

> We have different headaches . . . how to feed the family, how to sort ourselves out better, the locals don't have to worry about that . . . most

of those who have arrived . . . have landed on a barren place, they have had to start from scratch.

(141)

The bond is not just practical, but emotional:

We share a common pain, that we did not come of our own free will, but had our roots torn up, that is what unites us. As I said, we can tell each other at a distance. This pain is a single pain felt by everyone.

(5)

Greater collectivity

Perhaps precisely because of the difficulty of the problems they face and the lack of 'roots' in their new places of residence, migrants come to play for each other the role of the family, kin and friendship networks they have left behind. Thus respondents almost unanimously talked of the greater collectivity among migrants than among locals.

Even the locals . . . say that the emigrants look out for one another.

(1)

Recently a little boy drowned here, all the migrants went running to help in whatever way they could. They all took whatever they had [to the funeral] . . . But they [the locals] wait until they are invited. They themselves say . . . that we are more friendly.

(10)

However, it would be wrong to idealize this collectivity. Collective spirit is much more prominent in the villages (where such networks are essential to the bearing of the additional burdens of rural life) than the cities, where respondents noted rifts in the migrant community. This was not unknown in the villages either; some respondents found that friendships they had brought with them from their urban residences had not survived the pressures of decreased anonymity in the village. Many complained of 'gossiping' and that their 'confidences' had been betrayed. Any rosy vision of tightly knit migrant communities, therefore, is significant primarily as a collective myth which helps protect individual families from the deep sense of isolation experienced. This finding is confirmed by those working closely with compact settlements of refugees and forced migrants in Russia where, it is claimed, a worsening in relations with the local authorities generally begins with a 'betrayal' from within the migrant community (Grafova 1995b).

'Soviet work ethic'

A recurrent theme of self-identification might loosely be labelled a common 'Soviet work ethic'. It is rooted in a long-standing belief that it was the 'brightest and best' who had been sent to the non-Russian republics to raise the cultural and economic level of the backward parts of the Soviet Union. In this sense it refers back to the 'leading by example' ethos of Bolshevik ideology. The experience of migration back to Russia, however, has provided a second focus of comparison: locals in Russia who are seen as drunkards, lay-abouts and as having failed to improve their standard of living through hard work.

> Local people do not understand us, we are very serious people, we work. Local residents, Ul'ianovsk residents, they . . . don't know how to work, that's why they don't like us, because we are too good.
>
> (150)

Migrants see themselves not only as harder but *better* workers. They identify significant differences in the culture of work they had brought with them from the former republic and local work practices. Thus they criticize locals for swearing, drinking and gossiping at work and, where their new colleagues were found to be satisfactory, this was often explained by the high proportion of other migrants in the work collective:

> I work in the animal husbandry section. There are lots of newcomers [*priezhie*], it is more friendly. Where there are a lot of newcomers, it is more friendly . . . They swear less.
>
> (27)

The greatest – and most oppressive – cultural difference which emerges from respondents' talk, however, concerns the culture of management. This was a particular issue among those having resettled in rural areas. Migrants complained of the lack of respect evident towards them as workers; this was symbolized by the use of the familiar form of address to them by bosses (*na ty*). But they also complained of injustice, favouritism towards locals and arbitrariness with regard to management decisions, especially punitive acts such as the docking of wages for apparent misdemeanours which were often not committed, or committed by another. Above all migrants resented the petty despotism of collective-farm managers which worked from the principle that unless shouted at, employees would not work:

> We have had clashes with the boss[11] . . . He so easily lets fly. He will not have a quiet word with you but immediately starts swearing. He doesn't understand people . . . He immediately docks your pay or bonuses . . . it

takes away your will to work . . . He comes and starts shouting and telling you not to bother to come to work tomorrow. It wears you out.

(14)

it was not the practice that the director ran around checking, that if he did not check up then they wouldn't do it . . . If the director said do it then it had to be done.

(133)

These remarks are from migrants settled on different farms, so the issue was more than the problem of a single strong character. Some migrants did temper criticism with either positive remarks about the farm director – such as that you had to be strict and that he had good contacts and was keeping the farm going when around everything was collapsing – or negative remarks about the general culture of the countryside which had necessitated such crude managerial relations. For most, however, the lack of respect shown to them as productive members of a work collective came as a daily reminder of the loss of their self-worth.

Even migrants who had moved to the city of Ul'ianovsk noted a more authoritarian managerial approach which deprived workers of any sense that they were respected and expected to have ideas and initiatives of their own:

Here the work ethos is completely differently . . . here they are used to thinking, if he's the director, that's it . . . but at home that's not the case – the director is the director but a person is still a person. Relations are more simple, good-natured, but here they are used to . . . going round with their heads bowed.

(146)

To what extent this work identity is rooted in imperial consciousness, modernization ideology, social class or professional ethos is an issue requiring further consideration and may usefully become the subject of comparative research with other communities who have undergone or are in the process of repatriation.

Higher cultural level

The image of themselves as more dedicated workers constitutes one element of a wider superiority complex among migrants *vis-à-vis* the local Russian population which expresses itself in everyday cultural practice. Migrants consistently described locals as rude, disrespectful (especially of their elders), linguistically impoverished, drunken and lazy (see Figure 8.1), while:

we have a different intellect and a different cultural level.

(35)

Our standard of living there was a lot richer and we are generally more cultured people . . . we always tried to live better. But here they are just out to earn a few bob and drink it. That is savage to us.

(92)

Such was the extent of spontaneous reference to drunkenness and swearing as a cultural difference between local and incoming communities that this theme was taken up in repeat interviews. From this further exploration it became clear that concerns about drinking were more than evidence of a puritanical streak among a set of respondents who had come from more restrictive eastern cultures. Respondents were concerned with the impact of alcohol use on their families, and women, in particular, expressed fears that their husbands would start drinking – indeed, they already had in some cases – under peer pressure from local men.[12] A further concern relates to the role alcohol plays in Russian village communities as an informal currency. This is expressed by a young female respondent in Orel region who had moved to Russia from Kyrgyzstan:

They drink . . . as a norm. You can buy anything for a bottle, they don't know any other price . . . here women living on their own, when they ask for help with the cattle or the allotment, they must have a bottle, nobody ever takes money . . . so you learn how to make moonshine [*samogon*].

(194)

This is not just a difference between urban and rural cultures. The above statement is, in fact, made by a respondent who had moved from a rural area in Kyrgyzstan and the complaints about drunkenness and swearing were repeated by respondents who had moved to Ul'ianovsk. What is interesting is that the above speaker is indicating the different significance of alcohol in her new environment; it takes on a crucial role in the social and cultural system of favours and assistance. If the newcomers do not join in – start making and drinking *samogon* – then they are left with only the migrant community to fall back on and this consolidates the migrant 'we'.

The other major theme in migrants' talk about the lack of culture in their new place of abode relates to the absence of 'upbringing' (*vospitanie*). The chief site of this absence is the lack of respect shown by locals to women and elders in society. Migrants expressed their disgust at this through the retelling of stories. Most concerned everyday stories of young people failing – even refusing – to stand up for old people and women on the bus to and from the district centre, of throwing away bread and of swearing in front of women. Other stories consisted of rarer examples of extreme disrespect for the vulnerable; a little girl had recently been run over at the bus station in the district centre as passengers engaged in the daily stampede to get on the last bus out to the farms. In all cases, however, the stories express the impression among incomers that they had arrived in the 'wild west', an uncivilized land inhabited by those cut off from normal human behaviour:

> it is called upbringing, culture . . . culture is culture. And if you bring your child up so that he knows that this is bread and it must be looked after, that you have to respect your elders, then he will grow up into a human being.
>
> (110)

The implications of this apparent inversion of the migrants' own sense of cultural superiority – which, after all, was based on the story of Russians 'civilizing' the east – is explored in greater depth in the following chapter. Certainly part of the explanation for the apparent cultural chasm between locals and incomers is the move from urban – even capital city – environments into rural areas or provincial cities. Newcomers into rural areas in Orel region feel superior and interpret hostility towards them as based on the famous Russian peasant jealousy of those who do well for themselves:

> We are all from cities and are a level above them. And they sense this . . . and intentionally or not they develop . . . a feeling of inadequacy.
>
> (37)

This cultural superiority was often symbolized by the use of language; migrants claimed that locals' accents and turns of phrase indicated an impoverished cultural environment. One respondent spelled this out:

> I, for example, would never say I 'went down the town' ['*poekhal u gorod*'], it should be 'I went to town' ['*ia poekhal v gorod*']. There's the difference; [they say] 'down Livny' ['*u Livny*']. They have a kind of mixture of Belarusian, and Polish and Russian. They have mixed them all up and you can't understand them.
>
> (24)

The struggle over the definition of authentic Russianness which this quotation indicates is returned to in Chapter 9.

'US' AND 'THEM': RELATIONS WITH THE LOCAL COMMUNITY

The adaptation process between locals and migrants is two-way; it is not only the incoming community which must 'cope' with the culture shock of their new place of residence, but the receiving community must learn to live with the newcomers. While this is true, the consequences of being excluded – of remaining an 'outsider' for the migrant – and of not accepting a newcomer as 'one of us' are not commensurate; the migrant clearly has much more to lose.

This has implications for research methodology and the validity of the research findings. The 'outsider' is more likely to be aware of this status than those who put her or him on the outside and this is reflected in locals' talk by an apparent indifference and denial of any 'problem'. Only extensive and holistic anthropological investigation would satisfactorily answer questions about the cultural adaptation process being undertaken among the receiver community; something well beyond the scope of this study. In the rural field base members of the receiver community were interviewed and field observations recorded in the same way as with the migrant community.[13] However, only a handful of formal interviews were conducted and even these had reduced validity since the researcher was already identified by the local community as 'one of them' (the first two months had been spent interviewing migrants exclusively). The quality of interview – and subsequent textual analysis – therefore, is significantly lower than that of interviews with migrants. Moreover, in the urban area, the lack of personal contact with migrants by much of the population meant that in-depth interviews would have been an inappropriate methodological tool to uncover feelings. Instead, a small-scale, but representative, survey was conducted in Ul'ianovsk region to help paint a broad-brush picture of the weight given to refugee and forced-migrant issues and the general mood of the local population with regard to them (see introduction to Part II of the book for details).

The story told by refugees and forced migrants about their reception is discussed next, before the opinions of the receiver communities are assessed.

'Migrants, immigrants, emigrants . . . however you say it, it means outsiders'

Notwithstanding their own sense of 'difference' described above, migrants claimed that they were labelled as 'outsiders' by the local community and interpreted the labels as resentment of their arrival. The terms most frequently used to describe migrants in rural areas are 'newcomers' or 'strangers' (*priezhie*) which is a standard word for anyone coming into the village from outside. However, other terms such as 'immigrants' (*immigranty*), 'emigrants' (*emigranty*), 'migrants' (*migranty* and *pereselentsy*), 'refugees' (*bezhentsy*) referred more specifically to the origins of these incomers.

> Of course it grates to hear the word 'emigrants' . . . They don't know the meaning of the word simply . . . They [want to] show their superiority, that they are boss here and that we are nobody. So they say 'they have swarmed down' . . . We are outsiders [*chuzhie*]. We are simply outsiders.
>
> (43)

The term here 'swarmed down' renders a much neater term in Russian – *ponaekhali* or *poprinaekhali*[14] – which respondents repeatedly presented as the way locals talked about their arrival. The significance here, obviously, is the implication of a sudden and mass arrival with all the threats to collective security and cultural integrity that this implies.

The metaphor for invasion is consolidated by a further linguistic mechanism: the reference to (Russian) migrants according to the republic from which they had come, for example, as 'Kazaks', 'Kyrgyz', and so on:[15]

> Here . . . we are simply Kyrgyz, they call us Kyrgyz, and the others are called Kazaks.
>
> (93)

It was this which migrants found most hurtful, since it denied their Russianness and thus any sense of having returned 'home':

> You hear 'migrants' constantly . . . 'immigrants' . . . They've swarmed down on us and changed everything. That they lived well before and now they live badly . . . What are we guilty of, why is it our fault that we are here? . . . They do not accept us as Russians.
>
> (20)

Moreover, refugees and forced migrants are clearly being positioned in a standard racist discourse as the foreigner who threatens the social and economic well-being of the nation. This is articulated by a refugee from Baku, of mixed Russian and Armenian origin, who had resettled in Ul'ianovsk:

> we are not treated well, all the time we are called 'blacks' . . . 'foreigners' . . . They don't like us. Many say, 'You have taken our flats'. Very many complain, 'You have swarmed down on us, taken our jobs, our flats, because of you life is tough here now.'
>
> (178)

Not surprisingly, perhaps, it was refugees and forced migrants of non-Russian ethnic origin who were singled out in this way in the urban fieldwork base. Other respondents in Ul'ianovsk were cautiously positive about relations with the local community,[16] and some noted an 'indifference' among the local community suggesting the more anonymous relations of the urban environment.

In contrast in the villages there was much more opportunity for daily conflict as people came into direct contact with each other more frequently, and a third of all statements by respondents in Orel region about relations with the local community characterized them as generally hostile or concerned actual conflictual incidents (such as fights or serious arguments). A further 43 per cent of statements qualified a positive evaluation of relations by reference to the fact that others had problems, that there had been problems in the past, that one heard things said, and that some individuals were hostile but one couldn't tar all with the same brush. The sites of conflicts with locals were generally shops, schools and public transport; the very same places as in the former republics:

> You go into a shop here [and you hear], 'Look at them swarming down [*Vot ponaekhali*].' That's what they are all like . . . 'You're not one of us' and that's it. They say, 'You will work a bit here and then leave, but we have to live here' . . . They don't get on with people easily . . . They don't like the fact that we have come.
>
> (46)

> I have a son at school. Not long ago he came home upset and said, 'Mum they are calling us "immigrants"' . . . Once the teacher said, 'You have swarmed down here, you are getting your thieving fingers everywhere.'
>
> (116)

This is not to say that relations are always felt to be negative; some respondents (almost a third in Ul'ianovsk and almost a fifth in Orel region) made positive statements about the way in which they had been received by the local communities. References to the kindness and generosity of the local people were most frequently heard from refugees such as this respondent from Abkhaziia who had settled in an Orel village:

> Local people helped us . . . They gave us milk and potatoes . . . they are sorry that this [fate] befell our family . . . I am very grateful to people . . . they sympathize, the people here, because they lived through the war themselves and they are very sympathetic, especially towards the children.
>
> (124)

It is also worth noting that some respondents understood the concerns of the locals, empathizing with their feelings at seeing forced migrants and refugees jump the queues in housing and understanding why they might associate shortages of food and deteriorations in their own standards of living with the arrival of forced migrants and refugees.

> If you have two full rats in a cage they won't touch each other, right? The problem here is that the local residents, some of them, live very poorly . . . very poorly . . . When you have two hungry rats, one will eat the other . . . When we came – it was only 1990 – the situation wasn't like it is today. I don't remember hearing us being called 'newcomers' [*priezhie*]. We did not try to stand out and no one marked us out. I think it is only a result of common difficulties, we all have it bad.
>
> (78)

By 1994, however, it was clear from the testimonies of refugees and forced migrants that they *were* marked out and that their 'otherness' was not something which was celebrated by the local population but classed them as outsiders who were potentially or actually threatening in socio-economic and cultural terms.

The receiver community: 'no problem'?

Members of the local communities in both Orel and Ul'ianovsk regions paint a far rosier picture of relations with the migrant community than that presented above. This picture emerges from two separate sources of research: a small-scale representative survey conducted across the population in Ul'ianovsk region;[17] and interviews with local residents in one of the rural fieldwork bases in Orel region.[18] The results of this research are examined below to assess: the extent to which receiver communities perceive migrants to be a 'problem' in social, economic and cultural terms; the ability of local communities to empathize and sympathize with the plight of the newcomers; and the likelihood of relations deteriorating into open conflict.

Problem, what problem?

The Ul'ianovsk survey clearly showed that refugees and migrants are not considered a source of serious social tension; only 15 per cent of those surveyed included the influx of refugees and forced migrants among the five most acute problems facing the region chosen from a list of fourteen 'social problems'.[19] This is almost certainly a result of the lack of visibility of forced migrants and refugees in urban environments.[20] When asked more directly what impact the arrival of refugees and forced migrants might have on the region, however, there was clearly an awareness that existing competition for housing and employment would be heightened (see Figure 8.2).

Evidence from interviews in one of the rural fieldwork sites in Orel region is more ambiguous. Some local residents felt that, if anything, the migrants were breathing new life into the local economy and culture devastated by depopulation and rural poverty:

> They are working, they are carrying on our collective farm, there is nobody else left to work . . . so it's good that they all came here . . . The young people have left, we are all old.[21]

However, those still employed on the farm were more aware of the threat the newcomers posed to the traditional ways in which things had been done on the farm. One local teacher expressed the fears of farm workers about the ability of the farm director to sack people at will – if they did not turn up for work after a heavy drinking session on a holiday – since there was always a secondary pool of labour to turn to. A male farm worker expressed the threat very tangibly:

> they [the migrants] come and go, come and go, you can't make head nor tail of if . . . [even though] there is not enough work for our own here.

The feeling of being labelled as 'other' described by migrant respondents above appears to have more basis in rural than urban settlements. In Ul'ianovsk region those surveyed generally considered Russian-speaking migrants and refugees to be 'one of us' (*svoi*) (28 per cent) or to become so once they had lived there for a while (34 per cent); in contrast only 13 per cent considered migrants to be 'outsiders' (*chuzhie*) or only temporary residents of the region. This does not mean that no cultural difference is recognized at all: 29 per cent of those surveyed perceived migrants from the former republics to be representatives of a different culture and traditions. There was a greater awareness of this cultural difference among rural respondents, however, confirming reports of migrants themselves which suggested that people 'dissolve' into the city more easily.

Interviews with village locals in Orel region also indicated perceptions of cultural difference. Interestingly, rural residents tended to turn the forced migrants' cultural superiority on its head. This is especially true of the local 'intelligentsia' – primarily the village schoolteachers – who clearly resented suggestions made by migrants that standards in rural schools were poor:

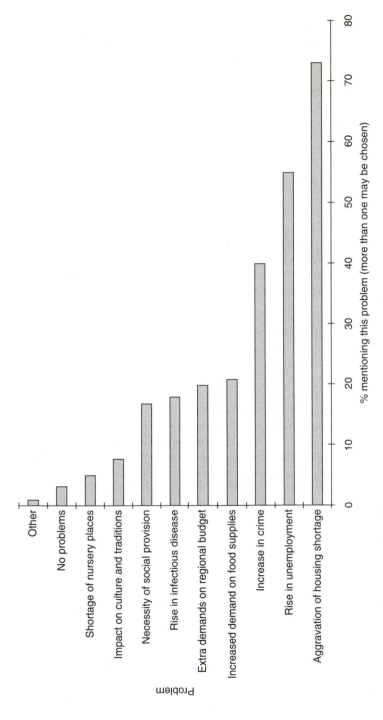

Figure 8.2 Problems associated with the arrival of migrants from the former USSR
Note: No. surveyed = 370, Ul'ianovsk

They come and they all [think they] know everything, but when you come into contact with them and dig a bit deeper, nobody knows anything . . . And you think, if they were getting fives there, when you're lucky to find anything to give a three for here . . . It is the south there after all . . .

Locals also claimed that, far from speaking a 'standard' Russian, forced migrants had Central Asian accents and intonation, were ignorant about traditional Russian customs and festivals and had negatively affected local work ethics by encouraging the purloining of farm materials and tools. Thus, in sharp contrast to the migrant story recounted above, in which migrants raise the cultural level of the rural community into which they move, locals consider the arrival of migrants to have lowered the general level of cultural communication in the village. The newcomers are portrayed as city types who do not bother to get to know their neighbours, who do not greet each other as they pass and do not join in traditional festival celebrations. In short they are not 'bad', simply ignorant about rural life:

As people they are not bad . . . They are just city people, they don't even understand, they don't even want to tend their plots . . . they don't know what to do.

Understanding the newcomers: sympathy or empathy?

In analysing the degree to which local communities sympathize and empathize with newcomers, it is essential first to disaggregate the category of refugees and forced migrants. In the understanding of respondents in the Ul'ianovsk survey, refugees were those who had been forced to 'flee' their former place of residence due to military or inter-ethnic conflict, because they had to save their own or their family's lives or because of other extreme circumstances. In contrast, forced migrants were seen to have left because of the general political situation, for personal reasons, because of the economic situation or as a result of natural or ecological disasters. Forced migrants, therefore, were perceived as having had some time at least to gather together their belongings and were generally not seen to be victims of military conflict. Neither group was considered by many to have moved in search of an easy life, however.

The association of refugeedom with a more extreme displacement experience, however, has an ambiguous impact on the emotional reaction evoked. The Ul'ianovsk survey found that whereas urban residents react to the word 'refugee' with understanding, rural residents do so with pity but also 'irritation' and 'disgust'. Indeed, for all respondents in Ul'ianovsk – urban and rural – greater 'understanding' was expressed for forced migrants than refugees (36 per cent for refugees, 48 per cent for migrants).

One possible explanation of this rather surprising finding is that locals' own experience was too far removed from that of refugees to empathize. In contrast a large proportion of Russians now have some member of the family or friend who has experienced some kind of 'forced migration'. Of those surveyed in Ul'ianovsk 27 per cent had relatives, friends and acquaintances who had come to the region from the former republics of the USSR or 'hot spots' within the Russian Federation.[22] Another explanation is that refugees are, in legal terms, non-Russians and thus conceived of as 'foreigners'. Finally, the term 'refugee' is linked historically and culturally to anxieties among the 'civilian' population about disease, social breakdown, crime and poverty (Gatrell 1996: 7) which may reduce public sympathy.

Among rural residents interviewed in Orel region, there was also a mixed response. For those interviewed the reference point for evaluating refugee and forced-migrant behaviour was not so much acquaintances in the same position, but their own experience during the Second World War when they had fled the farm from occupying forces. To some extent this evokes empathy:

> I feel sorry for them, we ourselves were evacuated . . . it's not as if they leave of their own accord . . . there was a war there as well.

However, the same respondent felt that, in comparison to what she herself had suffered, today's refugees 'live like kings'. Another respondent even implicated current refugees in their own fate, accusing them of being afraid to take the consequences of their earlier arrogance:

> There are those who were forced to come, and there are those who came because they were stupid . . . They got scared when they didn't need to be . . . they were too sure of themselves, did not behave as they should have done and then they got scared that they would be made to pay for it.

The negative attitude among locals in the Orel region is an interesting phenomenon.[23] It might be explained by the experience of older residents during the occupation which leads them to minimize the problems faced by forced migrants whom they see as being relatively well off and receiving preferential treatment. It might also reflect a wider problem of cultural communication in such Central Russian regions, however; the depopulation over the last three decades has left these areas populated by those who were unable to leave and who have consequently led largely parochial lives and find it difficult to interact with strangers. To seek any particular hostility towards forced migrants may be a mistake.

Competition for resources and potential conflict

Although relatively few cases of direct conflict between migrants and locals were reported by the respondents in the author's study, nevertheless, it is clear that competition for housing and resources does create tensions. Figure 8.2 indicates that the local population in Ul'ianovsk region was concerned that the arrival of migrants into the region might exacerbate housing problems (73 per cent), unemployment (55 per cent) and food shortages (21 per cent). Local migration workers in the city confirmed that there was no serious tension between the migrant and local populations as yet, but competition for meagre resources in the future might provoke resentment from locals. Indeed, there is already evidence that the Russian population does not see the justification for special assistance being afforded refugees and forced migrants. A nationwide Russian survey in December 1992 asked people for their views on what kind of state assistance should be afforded to refugees in: finding work; state benefits; and housing provision. Although the majority favoured providing assistance in finding employment (58 per cent) and state benefits (56 per cent) only 29 per cent favoured assisting refugees with housing while more – 33 per cent – were against it (Boikov 1993: 26). These results indicate a clear resistance among the Russian population to viewing forced migrants and refugees as a socially disadvantaged group whose needs were greater than their own.

Whether these potential tensions will develop into serious conflict depends on a variety of factors. A key one is certainly the ethnic composition of the migrant group as well as the existing ethnic make-up of the region into which they move. As growing tension in the southern regions of Russia (especially Stavropol' and Krasnodar territories), where there has been a high influx of non-Russian refugees and forced migrants, indicates, the chances of conflict are much greater where incomers and locals are ethnically different (Boikov 1993: 27). The additional strain placed on these regions due to the Chechen conflict over and above the constant stream of refugees and forced migrants received from the Transcaucasus since 1990 has led local residents in Stavropol' to fear the sparking of inter-ethnic conflict (Efimova 1994: 199; Open Society Institute 1996c: 2).

As reported in Chapter 5, the solution to this problem so far has been for individual regions with potentially difficult problems to set immigration quotas. Indeed, there now appears to be a growing mood in Russian public opinion for Russia as a whole to set stricter immigration criteria. A survey conducted across thirteen regions of Russia in December 1992 found that 36 per cent of the population favoured the acceptance of all citizens of all republics of the former Soviet Union regardless of their nationality, while

51 per cent favoured accepting only Russian citizens (*rossiiane*) and 11 per cent said nobody from the former republics should be accepted at all (Boikov and Levanov 1993b: 45). Moreover, 65 per cent of those surveyed stated that refugees should eventually be returned to their previous residence (Boikov 1993: 25). The survey conducted in Ul'ianovsk in 1994 for the purposes of this research showed an even more conservative approach: only 20 per cent of those surveyed thought that all refugees and forced migrants should be accepted, while 37 per cent thought that only those who had relatives in the region should be accepted and 5 per cent thought that nobody should be accepted.

The second crucial factor which will incite or prohibit tension is the future economic climate since, even where tension is not already high, the two communities compete directly for jobs and housing. This is as true of the villages as the cities since any initial capacity for housing and employment in depopulated rural areas has been quickly exhausted. Indeed, in rural areas the tension between local and migrant communities appears to be intensified by the cultural gap between them, mixed with a distinct failure of communication. This is not irresolvable, but it takes effort. As one, self-critical, forced migrant from Kyrgyzstan who had settled in a village in Orel region commented:

> How can you not make friends? We came to live here. We have to find a way to live with the people . . . Right or wrong, sometimes you just bite your tongue, just listen, you have to do it their way . . . they are just people like us. And you make friends and reconcile yourself.
>
> (189)

Finally, the argument advanced by many in favour of the promotion of compact settlements of refugees and forced migrants (see Chapter 4) should be considered. It is certainly true that in the short term cultural isolation for the returnees is minimized by settlement in a community comprising others with comparable experience, who may even be friends or acquaintances from the former place of residence. However, in practice compact settlements have often led to an intensification of the socio-economic hardships of resettlement. These settlements are formed in areas where there is little or no social infrastructure which means extremely poor initial living conditions with people often living in temporary housing, usually corrugated iron portakabins (*vagonchiki*) while houses are built. In the 'Zov' settlement in Lipetsk region migrants lived in such *vagonchiki* in an empty field for three years. For eighteen months of this period they were without electricity and are still without running water (Grafova 1995b). In the 'Novosel' settlement 250 migrants still live in temporary wooden shacks they built themselves, have no running water, no access to medical help and virtually no employment (Owen 1995a). This takes its toll on family life and relationships, resulting in disputes and break-ups which make the living conditions even harder to bear.

Moreover, the evidence suggests that local hostility is not avoided by such a mode of settlement. On the contrary, many of the well-known compact settlements have suffered continual harassment on the part of the local authorities. The most graphic recent case of such obstruction has been that of the 'Zov' compact settlement where the district administration withdrew land given to the organization for the construction of thirty-six houses and refused to allow the granting of any further residence permits for settlement there as part of a long-running battle to persuade the migrants not to settle in one compact settlement but to disperse across several different villages. In a number of cases – including the one of 'Zov' – accusations of tax evasion have been levelled against migrant associations as reasons for their closure or freezing of their assets (Grafova 1995b).[24]

Compact settlements have also met resistance by local residents who have found it difficult to accept their new neighbours (Rotar' 1993; Sokolov 1994: 69). A key stumbling block is reported to be the envy of the success of migrants by local residents (Zhdakaev 1994) and in particular of the attractive houses – referred to as 'cottages' (*kottedzhi*) – which the migrants build themselves (Grafova 1995b).

CONCLUSION

It has been suggested in this chapter that the process of the cultural adaptation of forced migrants in Russia is more problematic than might be anticipated from the scant attention paid to it in the Russian media and academic literature. This adaptation process, it has been suggested, is particularly difficult for those whose move from the former republics is simultaneously a move from an urban to a rural living environment. Of the 195 respondents in my study, 74 per cent had settled in rural areas and of these only 26 per cent were known to have formerly lived in a rural area or small town.[25] However, evidence from interviews with forced migrants presented in this chapter suggests that there is enough common experience with those fifty-one respondents moving to a city environment to suggest that respondents perceive not only a rural–urban lifestyle difference but a cultural difference from Russians who have been born and brought up in Russia. They consider themselves and are considered to be, quite simply, 'other Russians'.

There is evidence to suggest that this otherness – the distinct 'we' of Russians outside Russia – may be partially forged before leaving the former place of residence. Lebedeva's research among Russian migrants in the Transcaucasus reveals the same kind of distinction between 'us' (Russians in the Transcaucasus) and 'them' (Russians in Russia) (Lebedeva 1993: 66). However, the wide diversity of Russian communities in the 'near abroad' suggests that this common identity is unlikely to exist everywhere and for everyone, and, as will be discussed in Chapter 9, there was little consciousness of a Russian community abroad as a whole before the collapse of the Soviet Union.

Nor can one attribute the 'otherness' of forced migrants solely to a labelling process by the receiver community. The fact that in most localities the incomers are Russians or Russian-speakers minimizes the perception of the incomers as an alien 'other' threatening the cultural identity of the local population. Although, to a degree, migrants are perceived as a potential threat – as is clear from sentiments expressed about the competition for jobs and resentment over perceived priority given to migrants in housing – the nationwide awareness of general economic decline and difficulty means that local populations do not attribute the deterioration in their own living standards entirely to 'immigration'.

The cultural 'closeness' of migrant and receiver communities thus reduces the potential for conflict and the tendency to turn the migrant into the 'cultural other' (Huysmans 1995: 61). However, it does not eradicate totally the cultural difference perceived to exist between the two communities, and receiver communities clearly identify refugees and forced migrants as a distinct social group or community. This was true even in Ul'ianovsk where forced migrants were largely 'invisible', and this tendency towards 'silencing' the difference between refugees is – according to Huysmans – one characteristic of the securitization of the migrant (ibid.). However, the discourse of 'integration' which so often accompanies 'immigration' is disrupted in post-Soviet Russia since the arrival of a distinct sub-group, bringing with it its own narratives of Russianness, defies the writing of this group into post-Soviet Russian society via a process of one-way cultural homogenization. In Chapter 9, it will be argued that the distinctive 'we' of Russian-speaking forced migrants emerges out of the experience of the displacement process itself and that it has generated narratives of Russianness which compete with existing notions of national identity in a period in which the relationship between state and nation in Russia is in permanent motion.

9 The 'other' Russians

Displacement and national-identity formation among forced migrants

The 'otherness' of Russians returning from the former Soviet republics – as perceived by both the migrants themselves and the receiver community – cannot be equated to that embedded in a securitized immigration debate found in other European countries today; 'other' Russians remain, after all, 'other' *Russians*. This does not close the debate about displacement and national identity, however, but rather opens a new chapter in it, since the presence of another Russianness raises fundamental questions about the relationship between ethnicity, territory, nation and identity in post-Soviet Russia.

'OTHER' RUSSIANS: A FIFTH COLUMN?

Chapters 6, 7 and 8 have portrayed returning Russians as a group who feel forced out of their homes by anti-Russian sentiments, who have experienced serious socio-economic, cultural and psychological dislocation in their resettlement and who have been met with indifference by the state and often hostility by local communities. This, it might appear, provides ample foundation for the fears expressed by Russian political commentators that Russian-speaking forced migrants will become the ballast for a resurgent Russian nationalism (Abdulatipov 1994; Rotar' 1993; Safarov 1994; Toshchenko 1994). Indeed, refugees and members of a dominant group experiencing decline in power and prestige – which Russians abroad certainly are – are counted among those who may suffer an 'identity crisis' in the modern world and react by seeking the security of authoritarian conformity which is closely linked to adherence to fascist-type ideologies (Richmond 1994: 21). Moreover, recent experience in Europe has led to growing concern over the 'resurgence of ethnicity' (Rex 1995: 33) and the explosion of nationalism in Europe following the collapse of the Soviet 'Empire'. As Rex notes, although much of the academic focus has been on resurgent nationalisms of previously subordinated nations, in fact the collapse of imperial and multinational systems leads also to the emergence of irredentist – though equally 'nationalist' – movements around settlers of the former dominant nation (ibid.: 28). Thus, a study of returnees (former 'colonizers') might be expected to uncover widespread support for oppositional political movements calling for greater protection of Russians in the 'near abroad', or even the reforging of the Russian state around its ethnic representatives rather than its current administrative borders. Indeed, primafacie evidence from the voting patterns of Russians in the near abroad suggests that such a correlation exists. There was much talk of a strong pro-Zhirinovskii[1] vote among Russian citizens abroad in the December 1993 elections and first analyses of voting patterns in the 1995 parliamentary elections suggest that the Congress of Russian Communities took a much larger proportion of the vote among Russians in the 'near abroad' than it did overall, coming second only to the Communist Party (Parrish 1995b).

Before empirical data from interviews with Russian returnees are applied to the question of their views on nation and state, however, the theoretical basis for the 'rise of nationalism' thesis requires unpacking. This is necessary because operational theories of 'collapse of empire' and 'rise of nationalism' so often applied to the former Soviet Union and Eastern Europe are premised on a deeper theoretical assumption about the primordial roots of nationality.[2] This is not to suggest that they are applied only to the former Soviet bloc; Grosby argues that the very persistence of notions such as 'homeland' and 'fatherland' indicates that an important element of the modern world outlook is the linking of individual identity to a territorially bounded collective identity via a perceived biological connectedness (Grosby 1995: 151). However, given Soviet ideology's apparent rejection of nationalism for internationalism, the suggestion that the civic identity fostered by communism was never able to overcome the more deeply embedded moral and cultural codes of ethno-nationalism (Schopflin 1995) has particular significance. In the context of the reconfiguration of post-Soviet Russian national identity, the primordiality thesis can be seen most strikingly in the application of the term 'historical homeland' (*istoricheskaia rodina*) to describe the Russia to which forced migrants are returning; this notion clearly ties national collective consciousness to a bounded territory as well as rooting the present sense of nation in its historical content.

While primordial notions of national identity have a legitimate place in the theoretical debate over nation, national identity and nationalism, it is essential that their current revival is not naturalized but understood as one strand of a complex theoretical tapestry. Moreover, the advancement of the primordiality thesis is currently being undertaken as a conscious challenge to modernist and postmodernist emphases on the newness and political functionality of nations. The essential connection between blood, land and state is the most fundamental challenge to claims that 'nations' are imaginary constructs brought about through the invention of unifying myths (Smith 1995).

Postmodern conceptions of nation have been a particular target for criticism. Postmodernists are accused of overemphasizing the significance of cultural construction and ignoring the roots of nations in real social processes (urbanization, mass education, uneven capitalism) and thereby reducing the 'nation' to no more than a text for deconstruction (ibid.: 9). A second criticism has been the overemphasis of the role of 'other' over 'self' in the formation of national identity (Shils 1995: 107) which, when taken to the extreme, according to Parekh, falsely reduces identity to difference (Parekh 1995a: 256).

The study of the collapse of the Soviet Union is fertile ground for the revival of primordial notions of nation; there is no clearer example of a modernist construction of a unifying inter-national myth being swept away under the weight of the tide of nationalisms borne of primordial notions of ethnic ties and historical claims to territories. Given these apparent substantive flaws in modernist understandings of nation, the only alternative to the revival of primordial theses appears to be to accept postmodernist accounts of the origins of national identity. Yet these are often abstract and highly theoretical and thus appear inappropriate when applied to the very real, active and often violent field of nation-building in the post-Soviet space.

The temptation to join the backlash to postmodernist thinking is resisted in the discussion which follows. The central pillar of postmodern explanations of nationality – that national identities are narratives produced in the process of the cultural interaction of individuals and state institutions and are thus multiple and constantly changing – is retained but tested in the field as an attempt is made to reveal the concrete processes of the formation of these narratives and the full spectrum of their possible political outcomes. A textual analysis of transcribed interviews with Russian-speaking forced migrants is employed to trace the boundaries of the 'imagined community' of the Russian nation as perceived by forced migrants and the narratives of nation which are constructed. It will be suggested that although there is considerable evidence of imperial consciousness among Russian-speaking forced migrants which might be channelled into support for the reconstitution of nation around ethnos rather than state in the image of neo-imperialism, there is also evidence of a narrative of Russianness distinct from, and a challenge to, both neo-imperialist and civic, federalist constructions of the post-Soviet Russian nation. Possible political outcomes, it is suggested, are thus multiple.

NARRATIVES OF NATION: AN 'IMPERIAL MINORITY'

Figure 8.1 indicates that forced-migrant identity is rooted, partially at least, in imperial consciousness; there is a clear cultural superiority expressed both *vis-à-vis* the locals in the rural and provincial areas of Russia to which they had returned (see Chapter 8) and the titular nationality of the former republic.

As was noted in Chapter 8 this superiority is founded in the myth of the brightest and best of the Russian people being sent out to the former republics to 'raise' them to the level of Russia. 'Civilization' is thus brought by Russians, symbolized by the fact that:

> The Russians taught them [the Tajiks] to make jam, to preserve fruit for the winter, they couldn't do anything. They were very backward, savage, a savage people.
>
> (43)

If the Russians go – it is implied – the 'natives' will revive their uncivilized ways:

> There will only be Kazaks left . . . They are very dirty, Lord. We had some Kazaks living near us . . . they had cockroaches and everything . . . they were dirty . . . And what will happen if all our neighbours are Kazaks? . . . They have villages [*auli*] and if they have got used to living in filth in the village, then they will live in filth here.
>
> (47)

This differentiation between town and village dwellers is characteristic of Russians' talk about the titular nationality in the former republics. Urban 'natives' are described as 'russified' (121) and thereby civilized, while the villagers are not only dirty, but stupid enough to allow themselves to be manipulated by nationalist agitators (143) without realizing that they cannot survive without their big Russian brother:

> The Kazaks are not all bad, among them there are good people who understand that the Russians leaving . . . [means] the brains are leaving, the brains are leaving . . . there will be nobody to teach the students.
>
> (155)

The widespread belief that the newly independent states will not survive if the Russians leave is linked also to the collective adherence to a 'Soviet work ethic' described in Chapter 8. Representatives of the titular nationalities in the former republics are seen as being capable of working only in commerce ('speculation') and incapable of doing real work, that is *producing*:

> Who worked? Only the Russians worked. They [the Tajiks] are not
> capable of anything. Only to be shopkeepers or work in cafés . . . to
> water down the vodka. They are masters at short-changing . . . but
> physical work . . . that's not for them.
>
> (43)

The other common complaint is that those of the titular nationality 'love
management positions' but, when it comes to hard graft, are dependent on
the Russian workforce. This belief is rooted in the negative experience of
the Soviet national cadres policy which – like positive discrimination in all
societies – is largely resented by those who lose out:

> The people in Kirgiziia [*sic*] just like those in Central Asia, they all love
> management positions, although they don't like to work themselves . . .
> A position came up in the nursery school and they told me straight that
> if I had been of the titular nationality . . . if I had been a Kyrgyz, then I
> would have been appointed the manager. But since I wasn't a Kyrgyz,
> they found one . . . one who was not even trained.
>
> (191; 192)

Emil' Payin (head of the inter-ethnic relations department of the Russian
presidential apparatus) recognizes the juxtaposition of imperial past and
consciousness and current subordinate position of the Russians abroad, and
the difficulties of adapting to this, in his term 'imperial minority' to
describe the position of Russians in the 'near abroad' (Payin 1994: 22–5).
The content of this label is articulated by a female doctor who had resettled
in Ul'ianovsk from Tashkent:

> the state splitting off had a psychological and emotional effect on us, we
> began to feel different people . . . We began to feel our inadequacy, a
> kind of inferiority, and this all began to oppress us.
>
> (160)

Another respondent, also from Uzbekistan, but having settled in a village
in Orel region, put the dilemma about leaving more concisely, saying it
boiled down to the question of whether 'one could stand being an inferior
person' (121).

NARRATIVES OF NATION: 'OTHER' RUSSIANS

It was argued in Chapter 8 that Russian-speaking forced migrants have a
collective identity which differentiates them from local Russians. The
implications of this for the articulation of national identification are
apparent from Table 9.1 which shows the rejection among Russian-

Table 9.1 Self-identification of forced migrants in Orel region

Whom I would include as 'one of us'	Percent
Russians (russkie)	**25**
The 'Soviet people'	30
Russian citizens (*rossiiane*)	12
People of the same age or generation	6
People of the same profession or kind of occupation	6
Russians (*russkie*) from . . . (former republic)	27
People of the same income bracket	2
Other similar migrants	**40**
Only my family and relatives	20
Nobody, I get by on my own	1
Other	10

Note: No. of respondents = 83, Orel

speaking forced migrants of any sense of civic Russian identity. When asked to state their nationality during the completion of questionnaires, 89 per cent of respondents in Orel region declared themselves to be of Russian nationality. However, when the same people were asked with whom they *identified*, only 12 per cent of respondents included Russian civic identity (*rossiianin*) in their response, while significantly more were comfortable with Soviet identity (30 per cent).[3] Among the Russian populations in the former republics the preference for Soviet identity is even higher; the All-Russian Centre for Public Opinion Research found that only in the Baltic states did the Russian population identify themselves as citizens of the new states while on average 81 per cent of respondents declared 'their' country to be the USSR and not the republic in which they lived (Gudkov 1994: 179).

While the attachment to all-union structures – not least for the purposes of protection – is understandable among a population struggling to come to terms with a new 'minority' status, the persistent preference of 'Soviet' over 'Russian' identity among Russian returnees to Russia is a deeper enigma. In-depth interviews may help explain the identification processes under way. Respondents persistently ascribe the negative characteristics of 'them' (local Russians) (see Figure 8.1) to Russian citizens (*rossiiane, rossiiskie, rossiianka*) as a whole. In this way positive Russianness is associated with their previous lives – and is thus read as *Soviet* – while the *rossiianin* stands for all that is negative in their current environments:

> by nationality I am Russian but I consider myself Soviet . . . I don't consider myself a '*rossiianka*' . . . the locals . . . they are pure '*rossiiskie*' people . . . a Russian [*russkii*] it seems to me should be a good, kind,

considerate, hospitable person, a cultured, educated person, but a '*rossiiskii*' – that is about getting drunk, not going to work, all that . . . all the bad characteristics.

(119)

The cultural superiority expressed by returning Russians is strongly reminiscent of other returning colonizers and suggests that a new 'civilizing mission' could evolve as the political resolution of the displacement experienced by those returning to Russia. As one forced migrant who had settled in Orel region noted:

> there is no civilization here, no order, nothing. They [local Russians] don't want to change their life *themselves*.

(20; my emphasis)

The implication here is that a 'strong hand' is needed to impose this order. If there is a resurgence of an aggressive Russianness among returnees, however, it will almost certainly be at least partially borne of a defensiveness as they fight their corner from the peripheral position ascribed to them in their new communities. The suspicions and scapegoating suffered by forced migrants at the hands of the local community have been described in Chapter 8. Here it is worth emphasizing two ways in which Russian-speaking forced migrants appear to be being written into post-Soviet Russian society which are likely to encourage such a defensive reassertion of Russianness.

The first relates to the effective exclusion of forced migrants from the common ethnic and civic community via the challenge made to their Russianness. Respondents frequently recited stories of how it had been assumed that they were Kyrgyz, for example, if they said they came from Kyrgyzstan. This, it was suggested, deprived people of their civic voice:

> The same Russians don't accept us as Russians . . . We have no rights at all here.

(1)

The second label to merit further attention is that of 'emigrant'. As reported in Chapter 8 this term was widely used to talk about forced migrants by the local population – especially in the Orel region. To some extent migrants noted that this was largely explicable by locals' ignorance of the real meaning of such a loan-word; they were not differentiating between the words 'migrants', 'immigrants' and 'emigrants'. However, others saw a clear link to the negative undertones of former 'emigrants' of the Soviet period who were labelled traitors to the motherland for leaving the country. Indeed, migrants returning to Russia reported accusations that they had 'sold out' Russia by failing to stay and defend her interests:

Many of them say that we are traitors, they even say we are traitors. That there is war there and yet we abandoned everything and left. [They say] why didn't you stand up like all Russians, and 'give them one', as they say? What are you like, just abandoning everything and leaving, cowards and so on.

(44)

This kind of talk cannot but encourage counter-claims among forced migrants that they in fact represent a 'more authentic' and proud Russianness which has been lost in Russia itself. Indeed, such claims to be the bearers of the 'true cultural values' of Russia have been documented by Chinyaeva with regard to Russian emigrés in Central Europe in the 1920s (Chinyaeva 1995: 149).

NARRATIVES OF NATION: CULTURAL HYBRIDITY

The rejection of Russian civic identity together with evidence of the potential for regressive, nationalist reworkings of the experience of displacement among Russian-speaking forced migrants would appear to support the claims noted above that Russians returning from the 'near abroad' are a potential ballast for neo-nationalist movements. However, the textual analysis of interviews with forced migrants suggests that there is a pattern of national identification among them which challenges existing, monolithic narratives of Russianness. Four areas in which this pattern appears are outlined below and a case is made for viewing the essence of collective identity as being rooted in 'cultural hybridity',[4] rather than imperial consciousness.

'Other Russians'

Although we are Russians [*russkie*], we are not the same kind of Russians that live here.

(1)

One reason why the top-right quadrant of Figure 8.1 remains blank is that in differentiating themselves from local Russians forced migrants ascribe to 'self' those positive characteristics attributed to the peoples of the republic of former residence (top-left quadrant of Figure 8.1). Indeed, many respondents openly acknowledged this, saying that they had assimilated much from the peoples they had lived with:

We arrived like that . . . the east is like that. We were taught like that there. The Uzbeks, the Tajiks, they are all like that. For them the main thing is the family . . . that is why we have got more in common with the newcomers [*priezhie*] than with the locals. There is a big difference between us and them.

(20)

The idea that Russians living outside Russia take on a kind of hybrid character through the assimilation of national characteristics of those with whom they are living is confirmed by Lebedeva's study of Russians in the Transcaucasus. Russians who had settled in Azerbaijan, for example, were found to claim that they were 'something in between Azerbaijanis and Russians' (Lebedeva 1993: 102).

Given the cultural superiority expressed above, it is tempting to read the distances felt by Russians returning to Russia as a variation on the theme of 'returning colonizers', but the nature of forced migrants' self-professed 'otherness' problematizes any suggestion that 'imperial consciousness' can fully describe the identities forming among forced migrants. The 'forced' or, at least, state-driven initial migration of the present Russian-speaking population to the former republics is also a factor here; Russians, it is often claimed, were equal victims of 'socialist imperialism'. Moreover, Russian-speaking forced migrants may be unique in their experience of displacement which sees them not only displaced, as refugees and migrants are worldwide, but simultaneously confronted with the realities of the 'imagined community'. In fact one should say 'imagined communities' since the issue is further complicated by the explosion of two myths of nation: the first, the 'Soviet people' which was revealed to be an artificial construct; the second, 'Russia as historical homeland' which was exposed as a cultural backwater rather than metropole.

'*U nas tam . . .* '

That returning to Russia is an experience fraught with confrontation and contestation rather than a smooth journey 'home' is evident in the peculiar distortion of us/them, here/there boundaries found among forced-migrant respondents. While one would normally expect to find among ethnic Russians in Russia the connections 'us-here' and 'them-there', Russian forced migrants frequently cross-grid, talking about 'at home there' (*u nas tam*), and 'them here' (*oni – tut*). Although impossible to list all articulations of this (it is a general speech pattern) the following statements make clear the impossibility of assuming the presence of even the fundamentals of Russian identity: common language and shared home.

> *Our* Tajiks are very hospitable, our republic is called little Switzerland, it is very beautiful.

(9; my emphasis)

... we don't even understand the Russians. When we arrived the first time, we could not understand the Russians, how they speak, the language. We could not understand. *They* don't understand us, and we them.

(31; my emphasis)

Empire or international?

Despite familiar colonial statements about the 'civilizing mission' of Russians in the former republics described above, the statements of Russian-speaking forced migrants are tempered with a yearning for the multinational environment they have left behind and a strong belief in the negative nature of a mononational culture. This was most evident in a recurrent theme in respondents' talk; the claim that people in the former republic were 'kinder' (*dobree*) than in Russia. Repeatedly respondents asserted that there were academically proven theories that what they saw as the 'more civilized' nature of the former republic was a direct result of the multinational nature of the society:

A nation can't live on its own. You need some kind of mix . . . because each nationality differs from others somehow. One might be lower in culture, another higher. One in hospitality . . . Each nation takes something from another . . . and the result is something better, because each takes the best from the other nation . . . But alone, for example, the Russian nation, what can they get from one another?

(44)

There it was better, people there were better . . . probably a multi-national population is better.

(28)

Such statements far outweighed the alternative conclusion that one might expect migrants to draw from their experience; that the collapse of the Soviet Union proved that it was an unnatural state of affairs for representatives of any nation to live outside its territorial borders. Indeed, while the 'Soviet people' (*sovetskii narod*) may have proved unworthy as a description of 'a new historical community of people', for Russians in the former republics it was not an empty ideological shell but a lived reality, and an ethnically exclusive sense of Russianness is uncommon among forced migrants. This, it is argued here, lowers the likelihood of an extreme nationalist political outcome from their experience of displacement.

Blood, earth and native land

> Maybe we were brought up like that more, we did not absorb a pure Russian culture which came from the earth but more an international culture and because of this . . . relations between people and towards life are a bit different.
>
> (139)

'Soviet' identity continues to be attractive to forced migrants (see Table 9.1) since it allows for the resolution of the disjuncture between ethnos and territory experienced upon displacement. This disruption is evident in migrants' statements relating to 'native land' (*rodina*) and appears to be resolved in favour of 'earth' rather than 'blood'. Of the seventy-nine respondents in the Orel region answering the question whether they considered their move to Russia as a return to their native land, only twenty-six (one-third) said they did while two-thirds expressly said they did not consider it a return to the *rodina*:

> I was born there, lived there. Of course it is hard. You yearn . . . for your native land. And that native land is there, there where you were born, in spirit you never leave.
>
> (189)

This uprooting is experienced differently but always painfully. For some the awareness of the split between blood and earth leads to a challenging of their sense of national belonging and a recognition of their 'hybridity':

> Our native land is Kazakstan and here we are not accepted as Russians, we are not Russians.
>
> (5)

For others, however, displacement leads to a bitter sense of loss of belonging anywhere:

> We haven't got one [*rodina*]. We are aliens there and we are aliens here . . . the children were born there in Uzbekistan. We haven't got a native land!
>
> (125)

Statements made by forced migrants concerning their 'native land' are complex and contradictory. While theorists of the postmodern would suggest that our contemporary world of diaspora, mass population movement and transcultural flows naturally problematizes the notion of native land (Gupta and Ferguson 1992: 10), this does not fully explain the sentiments expressed by respondents. For Russian-speaking forced migrants, there was no problem of envisaging what constituted a native land;[5] it was clearly symbolized by 'where I was born', 'where the children were born' and 'where my parents are buried'. The problem was rather a sudden disembodiment of that native land. The 'imagined community' (Russia) had been severed from the physical native land (former republic) leaving migrants displaced.[6] This displacement – evident in the 'choosing' of one native land over the other or in a sense of having lost any native land – however, provides a serious challenge to primordial notions of nationality; blood and earth do not necessarily have to be fused for territory to have significance.

CONCLUSION

Post-Soviet Russia is faced with a non-coincidence of state and nation which ethno-nationalists are reluctant to accept.[7] The Russian-speaking populations in the 'near abroad' are living symbols of this split and, consequently, increasingly have become the focus of intense political debate. Most of this debate has concerned the situation of 'them' (Russian diaspora) 'there' (the 'near abroad') reflecting the security and foreign-policy aspects of the phenomenon of the 'compatriots' abroad which has fascinated outside observers. In contrast the research described in this book has explored the cultural parameters of the 'otherness' of the 'other Russians' after their resettlement in Russia and it has been argued that such 'otherness' forms in the process of the displacement itself. Such a cultural perspective does not negate the possible *political* significance of Russian-speaking populations, it rather resists arguments which rest on the essentializing of the connection between Russians in the near abroad and their 'historical homeland' and, moreover, the (nationalist) political projects which might be seen to accompany it. As Bikhu Parekh has argued on the basis of the study of the Indian diaspora's experience, the idea that the ancestral place of origin is really still 'home' constitutes an untenable ethnic view of the state at a theoretical level while at a practical level many Indians have returned to a country in which they are no longer comfortable (Parekh 1994: 101). Thus, it will be argued, in conclusion, that there is no reason why ethnic Russians should *necessarily* return to Russia nor why they should form part of a resurgent anti-democratic or nationalist move-ment if they do. Indeed, there is not one but a number of possible political outcomes of forced migration for post-Soviet Russia.

First, migrant identity may prove transitory. The high negative content of migrant identity noted above means that, in some cases, it will be replaced rapidly by other social identities. This is already evident among cohesive professional groups (such as doctors and academics), who quickly re-find their niche in a new city, and among the younger generation. Those advising the president, at least, confidently predict no *ethnic* tension to result from the return of forced migrants, anticipating at most some minor *social* tension as migrants increasingly compete with locals for housing and employment (Mukomel' 1995a).

Second, migrant identity may prove a progressive, democratic political force. The socio-cultural profile of the forced migrant community would certainly suggest that, had they been resident in Russia, these people would be a natural constituency for democratic forces, thus in this sense the loss of refugees and forced migrants to the nationalists would be a double loss for the Yeltsin government. The evidence from voting in the first round of the 1996 presidential elections suggests that the Russians abroad are, as yet, not lost; only Russian voters in Latvia (65 per cent) and Estonia (63 per cent) voted overwhelmingly for Ziuganov while in other former republics Yeltsin generally won. In Almaty, the capital of Kazakstan, for example, 50 per cent of Russians were reported as having voted for Yeltsin, 16 per cent for Ziuganov and 13 per cent for Lebed' (Morvant 1996d).

As was indicated in Chapter 7, under certain circumstances migrant identity may be strengthened and express itself in collective action. Although political resistance is not generally a common characteristic of socially vulnerable sections of the community, in this sense forced migrants are a very peculiar group; they constitute a socially disadvantaged group with extremely high socio-cultural capital at their disposal. Indeed, some respondents involved in the research described here already had come to see their problems not only in terms of personal tragedy, but as evidence of the state's failure to fulfil its obligations, its willingness to sacrifice them for its own purposes and its apparent readiness to use them as 'hostages'. Yet the democrats remain reluctant to bite the bullet of counteracting the nationalist attempts to win over the migrants. Grafova claims Boris Fiodorov had told her organization that with 150 million 'Russians' and 2.5 million forced migrants, it wasn't 'politically advantageous' (Owen 1995b). Not only does this show lack of political foresight on the part of the democrats, but also a view of forced migrants as 'not really Russians'.

Thus the increasing organization of nationalists around forced-migrant issues continues unchallenged and migrant identity may coalesce into a nationalist political stance. In this reading the experience of forced migration – feeling driven out of one's 'native land' on ethnic grounds – may give rise to a defensively aggressive sense of nation. As one returnee from Moldova noted:

I am a Russian [*russkii*], not a Russian citizen [*rossiianin*] because . . . I lived on the border . . . On the border of the division of nations.

Russians [*rossiiane*] who live here don't understand that . . . Only now are they beginning to sense that other nationalities exist, they have not understood this yet. I understood this a long time ago . . . and thanks to this, there on the national periphery, I became more Russian than the Russians here.

(136)

Moreover, the cultural superiority of Russian-speaking forced migrants could still find future expression in the form of a new 'civilizing mission' in Russia alongside support for a greater commitment to the 'defence' of Russians in the 'near abroad'.

Although the political implications of forced migration may be far from clear as yet, studying narratives of nation among Russian-speaking forced migrants raises important questions about the 'naturalness' of the primordial notion of national identity. As Parekh argues, national identity does not refer to 'a mysterious national soul, substance or spirit' passed down through blood and earth, but to 'the way a polity is constituted' (Parekh 1995a: 263). It thus contains disparate, even contradictory, elements and is constantly evolving in reaction to changing circumstances. Russia is not unique in having rival conceptions of its own collective identity, therefore, and, it has been argued here, the 'otherness' of the returning Russians merely makes visible the unfixedness of national identity. Forced migrants as a social group express this contradictoriness particularly acutely since their marginal positioning on the borderlands of nations means they inhabit that space where the boundaries between 'ourselves' and 'others' have become destabilized and unfixed (Gupta and Ferguson 1992: 20). This is perhaps most straightforwardly and succinctly expressed by one 34 year-old returnee from Bishkek who had settled in Orel region:

Here we are not Russians [*russkie*], we are Kyrgyz. In Kirgiziia [*sic*] we were Russians but in Russia we are not Russians.

(92)

In political terms, the narrative of nation articulated by Russian-speaking forced migrants challenges the nationalist idea of nation as 'a homogeneous cultural unit' formed on a common territory and linked by blood ties (Parekh 1995b: 32). The cultural hybridity of Russian-speaking forced migrants, moreover, suggests an 'other' narrative of Russianness which disrupts the unifying myth of the modern nation. But this need not condemn Russia to the chaos of 'difference', for, as Bhabha argues, the recognition of such hybridity may provide the space to raise the real questions about nation, citizenship and national belonging necessary to allow us to avoid the 'politics of polarity' and emerge as 'the others of our selves' (Bhabha 1994a: 37–9). This is more than wishful thinking; it is a pattern of identification already visible in forced-migrant communities.

10 Conclusion
Migration without boundaries?

Many of those who constitute these new communities of interest, such as refugees, underclasses, diasporic – by their very nature many of these people often don't have access to their own representation. And I think their experiences, and their voices must be heard in their own words in order to make us rethink what we understand by nation, national belonging, or national culture: to question nation, to question citizenship, to question community. It's never adequate to say their voices must be heard as voices, because none of their voices are just innocent voices, their voices are mediated through the dialogue they have with the questioner, through their own sense of what it means to represent themselves, through their own ideologies, so they are also framed voices, if you like, and produced voices. But in just that sense they are testimonies of the construction of a changing identity, of a changing polity, of a changing transnational community.

(Bhabha 1994b: 199)

This book has tried to present to the reader the voices of those displaced by the collapse of the Soviet Union, whose very presence in post-Soviet Russia causes us to question and rethink for ourselves the notions of community, nation and citizenship. No grand conclusions can be drawn from the essentially exploratory empirical research described in the book and in their place a call is made for current migratory processes in the former Soviet space to be read within the wider context of global, national and regional migration regimes. This is because, as Bhabha suggests, migrants' voices are not 'innocent' but 'framed' in the discourses of migration which shape their experience and position them in a changing world. At the same time their voices challenge the institutional boundaries of global and national migration regimes and the restrictive academic boundaries of both migration studies and post-Soviet studies. These boundaries restricting access to the cultural nomadism which globalization supposedly promises in the twenty-first century are exposed in this final chapter.

THE MIGRATION REGIME: BEATING THE WEST AT ITS OWN GAME

The international migration regime, which Russia is entering for the first time, is undergoing fundamental change. In Europe, in particular, refugees are increasingly considered a security rather than a humanitarian issue (Widgren 1994: 45). Indeed, some would argue that the old, humanitarian, international refugee system based on the Office of the UN High Commissioner for Refugees was itself a product of Cold War politics as the granting of asylum to those fleeing Soviet bloc countries successfully meshed political interest and humanitarian concerns (Jessen-Petersen 1994: 1–2). Its legacy, however, was that western governments found themselves awkwardly trying to shut the doors on those fleeing violence and economic collapse from former Yugoslavia, in particular, and Eastern Europe more generally (Fielding 1995: 44).

The change in discourse has meant a steady growth in the role of European institutions defining policy in relation to refugees and migrants and the sidelining of the original, essentially humanitarian, institutions of the international refugee system. As Widgren notes, there are currently about fifteen multilateral forums dealing with migration problems in Europe, as compared with five in the mid-1980s (Widgren 1994: 45–7). These intergovernmental groupings are currently setting the agenda for policy development on migration in Europe (ibid.: 55), an agenda headed by the forging of a joint border area from west to east, establishing joint long-term objectives for immigration policies and the development of comprehensive security strategies and a collective response to refugee movements. In short, the new policy-movers in Europe are concerned primarily to secure Western Europe from a potential new influx of unwanted immigrants composed not only of citizens of the former Soviet Union but also of so-called 'transit migrants' from third countries.

European legislation has been oriented, therefore, towards securing a 'buffer zone' around Western Europe. However, one person's 'buffer' is another's 'migrant problem'. Indeed, the clearest shift in the migration system in Europe in recent years is not any influx into Western Europe from the east but rather significant intra-regional movements in Eastern and Central Europe; according to the OECD, since the early 1990s many Central and Eastern European countries, including Russia, have had greater immigration than emigration rates (OECD 1995: 58).

Not surprisingly, this is a state of affairs which, increasingly, is resented by the Russian government; the latter claims that the refugee problem faced by Russia is significantly aggravated by transit migrants whose aim is to reach the west. Indeed, there is a serious criticism to be addressed here by the international community. While international organizations frequently refer to the need to prevent massive east–west migration by solving 'root causes' – economic, social and political instability in the former Soviet Union (see, for example, Kussbach 1992: 665) – they have done little to address those problems or assist with wider displacement issues in the region.

Given the nature of Russia's past, the absence of nationally conceived 'grand schemes' for the resettlement of millions of actual and potential returnees might appear to be a positive step towards the relinquishing of governmental control over individuals' freedom of movement. In practice, however, it is the economic not democratic climate which is driving the policy of 'helping migrants to help themselves' and it is all too easy for those in the democratic camp in Russia to condone the failings of government policy by reference to the general economic crisis and the impossibility of any effective and coherent policy towards this group, who are, after all, only one of many sections of the community requiring serious social attention in post-Soviet Russia. Moreover, as the Federal Migration Service increasingly off-loads its welfare responsibilities on to even more under-resourced non-governmental organizations, there is a danger that the FMS will become primarily a policing organization, acting in the interests of the state to keep out unwanted immigrants and to encourage the Russians in the 'near abroad' to remain where they are. This danger is heightened by the current politicization of the question of 'compatriots abroad' which is closely entwined with the reconfiguration of the identity of the Russian nation-state; in such circumstances the 'securitization' of migration (among other issues) is facilitated (Huysmans 1995: 63).

Accepting that there is unlikely to be either a sudden decrease in the numbers of in-migrants to Russia in the near future or any increase in resources made available to ease their resettlement process, nevertheless, both federal and regional-level institutions of the Russian migration regime could work more effectively.

Almost all commentators are agreed that the improvement and *active implementation* of inter-state agreements on the rights of potential and actual migrants is of the highest importance.[1] Such agreements should be founded on the objective of facilitating real choice for those facing the dilemma of determining precisely where their cultural and civic self-identification lie. Measures which might improve this area of legislation and practice include: the simplification of the acquisition of citizenship; an improvement in the flow of information to potential migrants before departure;[2] the regulation of property rights and facilitation of housing transfer; the preservation of pension guarantees, insurance and share-holding rights; the conclusion of an agreement on inter-state norms on individual rights which would prevent the discrimination against ethnic minority groups which is leading to mass exodus; and the establishment, none the less, of a set of norms in the event of the necessity of mass flight or evacuation, ensuring that receiver nations provide a common set of rights, welfare provision and support.[3] A recently published report by the Centre for Ethnopolitical and Regional Studies in Moscow recommends the formation of an Office of the CIS Commissioner for Refugees and Forced Migrants to coordinate measures relating to those displaced in the region at an inter-state level (Mukomel and Payin 1996: 39–44).

Such measures would not only allow migrants to leave with more dignity and less physical and mental trauma, but would mean that they arrived in a far better position to help themselves and thus constituted a lesser burden on the meagre resources of the Russian federal and regional authorities upon arrival. Migration service workers at the regional level express concern that migrants are often given wrong information before they leave the former republics, leading to false expectations when they arrive. This particularly concerns the experience of many migrants who had been told by embassies that they would be provided with housing in Russia if they abandoned their existing housing; a promise which was impossible to fulfil. Perhaps more importantly still, the conflicting messages about the acquisition of Russian citizenship from the authorities in the former republic and of those in the Russian Federation effectively put migrants in a double bind. In the former republic migrants are advised not to obtain Russian citizenship before departure as this can lead to problems with the sale of housing and the transporting of personal property. However, upon arrival in Russia, processing citizenship claims can take six to nine months,[4] and without citizenship it is increasingly difficult to obtain work, since all non-citizens are considered 'foreign labour' for which enterprises have to pay a levy.

While not all refugees and forced migrants are in a position to plan ahead and regulate their own migration, many families have a degree of control and are eager to ensure that they do not have to turn to the state for help on arrival. To date, however, they have been prevented from managing their migration successfully by a combination of economic and political factors in the former republic. They have also been hindered by legislation penalizing rational attempts to pre-plan their momentous move; registration of forced migrants is only accepted when the whole family has arrived – thus, one member cannot go ahead in order to secure work and housing before the rest of the family arrives. This effectively encourages migrants to act in the worst interests of their family and the receiver community.[5]

Federal-level support for those arriving in Russia could also be improved. While the very real problem of minimal budget allocations given to the migration service is recognized, existing money could be reoriented and outside investment stimulated in ways which would benefit the whole community and not appear to privilege refugees and forced migrants. These might involve: the use of tax breaks, employment schemes, state orders and stimulation of private orders from migrant association producers; the better provision for retraining and redeployment of forced migrants and refugees; the recognition of the role of NGOs and an improvement of coordination and cooperation between the FMS and non-governmental organizations; and a principled refusal to play 'the nationalist card' in relation to migration policy. The thrust of these suggestions must be towards the widening rather than narrowing of opportunities both in terms of choosing resettlement locations and the employment available to refugees and forced migrants in their new places of residence. Hence, the current state orientation towards a blind encouragement of movement to the Russian Far East and depopulated rural areas – which has so far caused considerable resentment on the part of both forced migrants and receiver communities and constitutes an inefficient deployment of skills – must be rethought.

Regional and local policies towards refugees and forced migrants must be carefully balanced between addressing the real problems faced by migrant communities while avoiding raising the profile of forced migrants and refugees in a way which might serve to increase resentment and concern among the local population. On the one hand, the potentially positive aspects of migration need to be emphasized, while on the other, sensible attention to economic and cultural difficulties faced by refugees and forced migrants might help stimulate further NGO input into resolving these problems. With regard to the differentiation of policy at the regional level, while concern over large concentrations of migrants in individual regions of the country (such as Stavropol' and Krasnodar territories) is understandable, it must be recognized that current, heavy-handed measures to prevent further immigration may be proving counter-productive and fuelling inter-ethnic tension. Perhaps most importantly, however, the Federal Migration Service must seek to prevent legal violations at local level which effectively limit the human rights of refugees and forced migrants. This refers, of course, primarily to violations of forced migrants' right to freedom of movement via the introduction of limits on the number of migrants admitted, the requirement of local residence permits, and restrictions on buying and selling of housing.

At the same time the hostile administrative and resource environment which often hinders the work of committed and diligent individuals in regional migration services must be recognized and tackled. Regional migration service staff note a number of organizational problems inhibiting their work, most serious of which are inadequate staffing, the absence of training, poor provision of equipment and information technology (Chelnokov 1994; *Informatsionno-analiticheskii Biulleten'* 1995: 15).[6] The most frustrating problem faced by migration service workers, however, is the apparently insurmountable resource crisis which prevents the implementation of migration programmes. Particular problems are faced by regions not designated as obliged to implement a mass reception of refugees (and thus not prioritized for funding) and as a result of unexpected crisis situations (Chechnia and, to a lesser extent, Sakhalin). Under-resourcing brings a sense of disempowerment to migration service workers. The low resourcing of benefits, and especially the unrealistic level of housing loans, the irregularity of supply of budget allocations from Moscow, the absence of housing-priority allocation for migrants and the lack of power to demand places in enterprise-owned hostels mean that migration service workers are unable to provide what they consider to be effective help to refugees and forced migrants. Regional-level migration service workers, disillusioned by their inability to provide any real help to clients, may well allow all social assistance functions to pass to equally poorly resourced and over-burdened NGOs.

Finally, despite the criticisms of the international regime above, Russia should continue to abide by the provisions of the 1951 UN Convention and Protocol. To this end the Federal Migration Service should prioritize adherence to the principle of non-*refoulement* which should be strictly observed, regardless of the country of origin, or the country of transit, of asylum-seekers, and the draft amendments to the law on refugees proposing restriction in the refugee regime should be abandoned (Korkeakivi 1996: 27). Indeed, as was suggested in Chapter 3, the legislative environment created for the Russian migration regime is generally a positive one. Initial problems in its implementation were largely due to the fact that the 1993 laws did not have a proper implementation mechanism, as a result of which *ad hoc* implementation occurred via instructions produced at federal and local level which often went against the spirit of the legislation. The growing input of NGOs at the policy-making level is a further positive step and, if accompanied by active and constructive critique from international organizations, could provide a further impulse towards the improvement of the general environment for those migrating into Russia.

INNOCENTS ABROAD? TRANSGRESSING ACADEMIC BOUNDARIES

As the international migration system changes, so the migration regime at a global level is being remoulded. However, the latter currently appears to be reacting to shifts in the migration system by fixing, even more rigidly, the academically defined categories of migration experience. As a result, the ever stricter differentiation between 'voluntary' and 'involuntary' migrants, between 'refugees' and 'economic migrants' is increasingly determining national migration regimes, including that of post-Soviet Russia. This tendency, however, flies in the face of actual migratory experience, characterized by a growth in flight of large groups of people as a result of ethnic violence, environmental catastrophe and famine related to civil war and political manipulation. This has meant that differences between 'refugees' and other migrants are becoming increasingly blurred and emphasized largely in order to justify political attempts to reduce assistance to all migrants, including refugees (Jessen-Petersen 1994: 1; Black 1993: 5). It is essential, therefore, that the inappropriateness of these categories is exposed, not only at the theoretical, macro level, but also through regionally embedded empirical work.

The arguments for the transgression of the academic boundaries of migration studies were rehearsed in Chapter 1 and will not be repeated here. The second half of this book presented the testimonies of migrants on the territory of the former Soviet Union who have, themselves, experienced a migration in which ethnic, political, social and economic motivations are woven together. This experience suggests not only the need to halt the legislative tendency to tighten distinctions between voluntary and involuntary migrants but also the necessity of rethinking 'push' and 'pull' models of migration more generally. The latter require empirical work of both a quantitative and qualitative kind, but also keen attention to the role of the migration regimes of both sender and receiver societies in order to generate a more integrated understanding of the forces governing a particular migration system.

Such work – which is only just beginning – will facilitate a more sophisticated understanding of the migration system of the former Soviet space than can be offered currently either by modernization or 'collapse of empire' models. While the former overemphasize continuity, the latter focus too heavily on political impulses for migration. Both, moreover, draw exclusively on quantitative measures of movement into the 'periphery' by Russians and their subsequent withdrawal. Attention to the actual agents and cultural context of migration in the former Soviet Union allows the researcher to measure migration in rather different ways and chart the movement of migrants across not only political but also social and cultural boundaries.

Identifying, and crossing, these boundaries with the migrants whose experience was studied reveals a startling picture of 'voluntary' migrants making significant and long-term social 'downshifts' and ethnic Russians failing to identify with the 'mother Russia' to whom they return. The testimonies of migrants, framed as they are in the researcher's expectant confirmation of existing academic categories, in fact challenge such classifications. Moreover, these challenges are not sanitized academic ones but subjectively ordered and articulated; the experience of displacement is shaping new identities in Russia. It is in this sense that the 'other' Russians are far from 'innocent'; their voices speak to the new Russia, and the world beyond, in different tongues and from different political agendas, but in a way which challenges us to reconsider the nature of community, nation and citizenship. It is imperative that these voices are not distorted as they are filtered through the institutional and academic boundaries constructed to interpret and manage the experience of displacement whence they have a tendency to emerge apparently speaking not to a transnational future, but an imperialist past.

Notes

PART I THE FORMATION OF THE RUSSIAN MIGRATION REGIME

1 Did they jump or were they pushed?

1 The term 'former Soviet Union' is used to refer to the now extinct political entity of the Soviet Union comprising fifteen republics including the Russian Federation (then RSFSR). The terms 'former Soviet republics' and 'newly independent states' refer to the independent states formed by those former republics after the collapse of the Soviet Union and are preferred to the term 'Commonwealth of Independent States' (CIS) since the latter excludes the former Baltic republics (Latvia, Lithuania and Estonia). The terms 'Russia' and 'Russian Federation' are used interchangeably to describe the independent Russian state formed after the collapse of the USSR.

2 This should be provided by a publication in press at the time of writing, see Demko, Zayonchkovskaya, Pontius and Ioffe (eds) (forthcoming).

3 The term 'Russian-speaking' (*russkoiazychnii*) population refers to all non-titular nationalities in the former Soviet republics and is thus not interchangeable with the term 'ethnic Russians'. Indeed, it is a matter of dispute that this term is often used to refer to non-Slavic minorities such as the Uzbeks in Kazakstan whose cultural affinity may be closer to the titular nationality than to Russia.

4 When the Soviet Union collapsed, the number of refugees was estimated at between 700,000 and 1 million people. This constituted about 0.3 per cent of the total population and was thus no greater than the international average at that time (Zayonchkovskaya, Kocharyan and Vitkovskaya 1993: 204). By 1996, the UNHCR had identified 164 territorial disputes 'based on ethnic issues' in the former Soviet Union and estimated that there were 9 million forced migrants on the territory of the former Soviet Union. In other words one in every thirty citizens of the former USSR had changed their *country* of residence since 1989.

5 As far as possible data are given for 1994 since this is the year of the fieldwork described in the second part of the book and thus provides the most accurate background picture for the reader. It is also the most recent year for which official demographic data are published by Goskomstat, although more recent

statistics are available from the Federal Migration Service and are used where relevant.

6 'Ethnic Russians' is used here to refer to those people whose officially registered nationality is 'Russian' although this will inevitably include people of mixed ethnic origin or of non-Russian ethnic origin who have chosen Russian nationality.

7 'Titular nationality' refers to members of the ethnic group whose name is given to the state (for example, Armenians in Armenia, Uzbeks in Uzbekistan). Given the ethnic diversity of most regions, this term is not synonymous with 'indigenous population'.

8 The legal distinction between these categories is explored in detail in Chapter 3. Here it suffices to note that those returnees recognized by the Federal Migration Service in the Russian Federation to have been forced to leave their former place of residence due to persecution or violence on the grounds of their race, nationality, religion, language, social group affiliation or political conviction are granted the status of 'refugee' if they are non-Russian citizens and of 'forced migrant' if they hold Russian citizenship.

9 It is almost impossible to calculate the full scale of the problem since data on the number of forced migrants and refugees in the country are notoriously unreliable. There is a persistent underestimation of numbers due to the fact that the Federal Migration Service records only the number of officially registered forced migrants and refugees even though a relatively small proportion of those arriving actually receives official status (Marnie and Slater 1993: 48). The extent of the underestimation is equally difficult to quantify but estimates for 1994 (when there were 1.1 million arrivees, but only 254,000 registrants) suggest that only about 25 per cent of arrivees are included in Federal Migration Service figures. The picture is further muddied by the fact that until the beginning of 1994 refugees and forced migrants were counted together while, even after that date, the Federal Migration Service continues to publish data in a way which collapses the two categories. Discrepancies between the Federal Migration Service and the Ministry of Internal Affairs (MVD) also cause confusion as the MVD persistently produces higher estimates of the numbers of forced migrants and refugees (Kovalev 1994: 3). The process of registration and criteria for qualification for status are discussed at length in Chapters 3 and 4.

10 Transcaucasia is used to refer to the former Soviet republics of Georgia, Azerbaijan and Armenia.

11 Central Asia refers to the republics of Tajikistan, Uzbekistan, Kyrgyzstan and Turkmenistan. The republic of Kazakstan is referred to separately.

12 The Federal Migration Service estimates 2–5 million while the Ministry of Labour suggests 3–4 million.

13 This figure is cited in information provided for the parliamentary debate on cooperation between government agencies, legislative bodies and non-governmental organizations in the resettlement of refugees and forced migrants which took place in Moscow on 23 April 1996.

14 This is calculated on the premise that it is first- and second-generation Russians from those former Soviet republics which manifest a relatively large cultural distance from Russia – Turkmenistan, Kyrgyzstan, Tajikistan, Azerbaijan, Uzbekistan and Kazakstan – who are likely to leave.

15 The term Baltic states refers to the newly independent states of Latvia, Lithuania and Estonia.

16 The legislative amendments documenting this are discussed in Chapter 3.

17 Exceptions here are Lebedeva (1993) – although she is studying migrants from Russia to the Transcaucasus, not vice versa – and Vitkovskaia (1993), although the latter uses survey methods which, arguably, do not adequately address these socio-psychological questions.

18 In migration studies, this has been traditionally provided by 'systems approaches' which concern themselves with both the micro (individual, family, household) and macro (national and international social, political and economic structures) in order to explain migratory decisions and patterns. Systems approaches explain migratory flows by exploring the linkages between societies and the flows of information, goods and services which often influence flows of people; these constitute migration systems. While explanations of migration may thus be essentially structural, the focus in research is on individuals and groups of migrants and the networks which develop and sustain migrational interchange between sender and receiver societies (Goss and Lindquist 1995: 326; Boyd 1989).

19 These conditions were applied at the analysis stage to weed out inappropriate subjects.

20 Displaced persons crossing *international* borders are defined by the global migration regime as 'refugees'.

21 This does not mean that Russia has a 'national identity crisis' but that the post-imperial condition of Russia has necessitated a redefinition of 'Russianness'.

2 Redrawing a nation's borders

1 A formal content analysis of the discussion of the issue of refugees and forced migrants was conducted on all issues (783 in total) of seven central (five daily and two weekly) and three local newspapers over the period 15 June– 15 November 1994. The central newspapers were: *Nezavisimaia Gazeta*, *Segodnia*, *Novaia Ezhednevnaia Gazeta*, *Izvestiia*, *Komsomol'skaia Pravda* (all of which are published five times a week), *Obshchaia Gazeta* and *Argumenty i Fakty* (both weeklies). The local papers were all from the Ul'ianovsk region: *Ul'ianovskaia Pravda* (published four times a week), *Narodnaia Gazeta* and *Simbirskii Kur'er* (both published three times a week). The central papers were chosen as middle-of-the road quality papers representing a range of non-extremist positions. Six broad categories were used for analysis:

1 General characteristics (frequency of articles on migration, amount of space devoted to migration, broad theme of articles, primary or secondary nature of the theme of migration, aspect of migration primarily considered, level of generality of the information given, journalistic genre and the geopolitical location of subject).

2 Factors influencing migration.

3 Factors influencing adaptation.

4 Social agents discussed.

5 The structure of migrational flows.

6 Authors and political slant (background of authors, aim of article (factual, critique), attitude of author to issue, tone of article, labelling of migrants).

In addition, an ongoing review of the Russian press including the local press of Orel region and of western and Russian academic literature on the issue of forced migration was conducted and a bibliographical database constructed.

2　The overwhelming majority (81 per cent) of articles emanated from central daily newspapers while central weekly papers devote the highest proportion of their space to migration issues. Most attention to the issue was given by *Obshchaia Gazeta* (0.96 per cent) followed by *Argumenty i Fakty* (0.43 per cent) (that is the weekly central papers). Daily central papers gave from 0.22 per cent to 0.37 per cent of space to the issue while the least was given by local papers – from 0.005 per cent to 0.2 per cent. Both these indicators reinforce the finding that the press considers the issue to be one of high politics as opposed to a social issue affecting the everyday lives of Russian citizens.

3　The content analysis of the press conducted in 1994 revealed that 3.2 per cent of articles were authored by forced migrants or refugees themselves.

4　There were 118,690 forced migrants and refugees registered by the Federal Migration Service of Russia from Central Asia during 1994 and a further 63,533 from Kazakstan. In contrast just 9,903 forced migrants and refugees from the Baltic states were registered by the Federal Migration Service in 1994.

5　*Komsomol'skaia Pravda* appears particularly hostile; references are exclusively to the negative attitudes at all levels to Russians.

6　The extreme situation in Tajikistan makes it an exception here; personal-tragedy stories dominate discussion of migration out of Tajikistan.

7　Shakhrai left government after the December 1995 parliamentary elections but remains a member of the parliament.

8　The Russian Far East is currently perceived to be under threat from illegal Chinese immigration.

9　The term '*mankurt*' is a neologism invented by Kyrgyz writer Chingiz Aitmatov to describe Central Asian prisoner-slaves who have been deprived of their memory via a brutal torture process which restricts the skull under a skull-cap. The aim is to create docile slaves who, stripped of their ability to remember, become totally subservient to their masters (Levin 1994: 18). The term has been coined in contemporary Central Asia to indicate people who have lost their ethnic ties and have no desire to rediscover their cultural roots.

10　A disproportionate amount of attention is given to military personnel, however: 61 per cent of articles are about the military while other professional groups are mentioned far less frequently; 9 per cent of articles mention teachers, 4 per cent mention doctors and academics, 6 per cent mention the creative intelligentsia and 4 per cent mention manual workers.

11　This is consistent with the greater propensity towards the biographical genre of article in local papers which characterized 31 per cent of articles as opposed to just 3 per cent of those in the central daily papers.

12　This includes stress suffered by migrants and difficulties of interaction with the receiver community.

13　This includes adaptation to new national traditions and habits, longing for the 'native land' (*rodina*), problems of language and accent, and of alienation and isolation.

14　The social-status problem is exaggerated by the fact that refugees and forced migrants are generally highly qualified urban people but are usually offered resettlement and employment in rural areas where there is a lack of correspondence between qualifications and jobs available (Toshchenko 1994).

15 This term may come to be reappropriated into government parlance, however, as is discussed in Chapter 3.

16 Significantly, Vishnevskii stresses the multi-ethnic nature of the colonization process. By the eighteenth century, he argues, the number of great and small Russian colonizers was beginning to exhaust itself, encouraging the Russian government to turn to encouraging settlement by the Southern Slavs (Serbs, Bulgarians) from the then Turkish and Austrian lands, Greeks and Armenians from the Crimea and Germans (Vishnevskii 1994: 179). The final wave of colonization, associated with the externally driven modernization in the Soviet period, was also multi-ethnic; although mainly Russians and Ukrainians, they brought with them other Russian-speakers such as Belarusians, Tatars, Jews and Armenians some of whom came involuntarily as members of repressed and deported peoples (ibid.).

17 He notes a similar tendency in perceptions of the *pieds-noirs* returning from Algeria and suggests that the experience of other countries shows that, in fact, radical political leanings among refugees are exhausted as soon as the majority have successfully adapted to their new lives (Okulov 1994: 14).

18 The content analysis did not include expressly nationalist papers.

19 The ratio of positive to negative articles does vary across newspapers, however. The most negative was *Obshchaia Gazeta* with a ratio of 1:15 while the most positive were *Argumenty i Fakty* and two of the regional papers studied, *Ul'ianovskaia Pravda* and *Narodnaia Gazeta*, all of which were 1:1.

20 Financial support for a publication – *Pereselencheskaia Gazeta* – produced by and for migrants themselves was also promised.

3 The legislative framework

1 The most widely used definition is that of the 1951 United Nations Convention on Refugees, amended by the New York Protocol of 1967, which identifies refugees as people who are 'outside their own country, owing to a well-founded fear of persecution, for reasons of race, religion, nationality, membership of a particular social group or political opinion' (Black 1993: 7).

2 Soviet legislation of 1981 did provide for the granting of asylum to foreign citizens who had been persecuted for defending the interests of the working people or the cause of peace, for participation in the revolutionary or national-liberation movement, and for progressive socio-political, scientific or other creative activity (Tunkin, Boguslavsky and Gridin 1985: 64).

3 The first official document to refer to the 'forced migrant' was the resolution of the USSR Council of Ministers of 7 April 1990 'On measures to assist citizens forced to leave the Azerbaijan and Armenian republics' drawn up to deal with the consequences of ethnic conflict in these two republics (and in particular the pogroms of Baku and Sumgait) supplemented by further resolutions in June and November 1990 specifically referring to 'refugees' (June) and 'refugees and forced migrants' (November) arriving in the Russian Federation (Susokolov 1994: 187).

4 Despite criticisms of its hasty formulation, this legislation was not quick to be drawn up. The first version of a law on refugees had been prepared under the Soviet system (by December 1989) and a draft 'Principles of USSR and Republic legislation on protecting the rights of USSR citizens who have been

forced to leave their places of permanent residence' was drawn up defining minimum amounts of guarantees and compensation, providing for the creation of a state migration service and specifying the responsibility of the Union and the republics (Livshin 1991). Following the collapse of the Soviet Union the Russian parliament was in no great hurry to pass the law and it took another year of haggling before the two laws were passed (Schwartz 1993: 242).

5 The amended law adopted in December 1995 omits the phrases 'or intends to' and 'or other circumstances significantly restricting human rights'. The implications of this are discussed below.

6 Other signatories among former Soviet republics were Armenia, Azerbaijan, Kyrgyzstan and Tajikistan (Mukomel 1996: 148).

7 The focus is the Law on Forced Migrants since the empirical work described in the second part of the book was conducted primarily with forced migrants rather than refugees.

8 In 1993 the Orel Territorial Migration Service and the Ul'ianovsk Territorial Migration Service were using a document signed by Tat'iana Regent on 2 June 1992 entitled 'On the territories from which migrants may be recognized as refugees or forced migrants' which provided for the granting of status to applicants from the regions of: Moldova; Azerbaijan (or rather those who had left in connection with the events of January 1990 in Baku, others were not automatically eligible); Georgia (if leaving in connection with the South Osetian conflict); and Tajikistan. This list is confirmed by Vitkovskaia who adds Chechnia (a Russian Federation republic) to the list (Vitkovskaia 1993: 3). In 1994 the head of the Ul'ianovsk Territorial Migration Service noted that Moldova and Georgia were no longer included as regions for automatic registration but that Uzbekistan had been added (Belozertsev 1994). Status was also to be granted automatically to groups of migrants who had formed associations to help resettlement in their new place of residence and which had been registered with the local authorities.

9 Kovalev resigned from his post as head of the presidential Human Rights Commission on 23 January 1996 and declared his intention also to leave the presidential council citing concerns over the retreat from democracy of the Yeltsin regime (Morvant 1996b).

10 Refugees have fewer rights in this respect, being allowed a choice of place of permanent residence from those offered by the Federal Migration Service or to live with relatives (with their agreement) ('O bezhentsakh' 1993: 717). However, the law on refugees also states here that 'refugees enjoy all the rights of a citizen of the Russian Federation unless otherwise provided for by RF legislation' (ibid.: 716).

11 Sobchak failed to be re-elected as mayor of St Petersburg on 2 June 1996.

12 Despite the fact that officially no such de-registration ('*vypiska*') should be necessary the Federal Migration Service continued to demand official stamps in the passports of refugees and forced migrants certifying that their residence permit has been annulled for their former house or flat before housing was allocated in Russia. Although it is possible to obtain this *vypiska* from the embassy of the former republic, they often charge a hefty fee and insist that applicants write a statement that they have no claims on that country. This effectively deprives Russia of the right to gain compensation from the country of exit of refugees as stipulated in bilateral agreements on responsibility for refugees and forced migrants (Gannushkina 1996b; Sokolov 1994: 38).

13 Under the auspices of the project expert interviews were conducted by the Sociological Laboratory of Ul'ianovsk State University with eight officials in institutions dealing with forced migrants and refugees in the city of Ul'ianovsk between 19 and 26 July 1995. Interviews were taped and transcribed by the Russian collaborators as the author was refused permission to conduct the interviews, but were analysed by the author. The interviews were tightly structured using standard questions for all interviewees and covered: the main areas of work performed, the structure of the organization, cooperation with other bodies, evaluations of federal and regional policy and provision in relation to refugees and forced migrants, evaluations of own and others' work, and personal opinions and attitudes to the phenomenon of forced migration. For reasons of confidentiality, interviewees, other than the head of the Territorial Migration Service, are not identified, although their role in the execution of migration policy is indicated.

14 This was the only exclusion listed in the original law.

15 Given that registration is allowed only when the whole family is in the new place of residence, this requirement makes it easier to exclude those migrants who move involuntarily but attempt to do so in an orderly fashion (one member of the family moving first, finding work and housing and then moving the rest of the family).

16 Indeed this new procedure was implemented in practice before it was included in the new law. In December 1993 the Federal Migration Service approved new regulations, drafted with the 'help' of the Ministry of Security, the Ministry of Internal Affairs, the Ministry of Foreign Affairs and the Ministry of Health which included more stringent requirements for registration for forced-migrant status, including greater documentary evidence of the grounds for the application for such status as well as a new annual re-registration requirement. Forced-migrant identification cards henceforth included a page for such re-registration stamps (Kovalev 1994: 3; Slater 1994).

17 These would exclude from status: citizens of republics of the former Soviet Union who are not Russian citizens; those who arrive in Russia illegally and fail to report to the authorities within twenty-four hours; those who have failed to use an opportunity to leave for a third country where they have close relatives; those who have committed an offence in Russia prior to being recognized as a refugee; and those denied refugee status in any of the states which are signatories to the 1951 Convention or 1967 Protocol (Korkeakivi 1996: 20–1).

18 This is an NGO closely related to the Coordinating Council for Aid to Refugees and Forced Migrants (see Chapter 4).

19 This committee included representatives of the Compatriots' Fund and the Civil Assistance Committee.

4 The institutional framework

1 The diagram represents those structures in operation in the second half of 1994, when the fieldwork was conducted. Changes to the structure since then are referred to below. International organizations are excluded from Figure 4.1 but are discussed below.

2 Already an 'enemy of the people' as far as the Duma was concerned, Yeltsin too turned on Kovalev in 1995 demoting the presidential Human Rights

Commission to a section of the presidential administration dealing with citizen correspondence as punishment for criticism of the Chechen War (Orttung 1995a). The new chair appointed on 20 May 1996 criticized his predecessor for paying more attention to violations of the human rights of Chechens than to discrimination against ethnic Russians living in Chechnia (Morvant 1996c).

3 Zatulin failed to be elected to the 1995 parliament: having switched party affiliation from the Democratic Party to the Congress of Russian Communities, the latter failed to clear the 5 per cent barrier. The chair of the CIS Affairs Committee passed to Georgii Tikhonov of the People's Power faction in the new parliament.

4 In November 1995 the Duma issued a statement expressing 'deep concern' over 'violations of the rights of ethnic Russians in Kazakhstan', calling for the release of the 'illegally arrested' Semirechie Cossack leader Nikolai Gunkin and action by President and government to protect the rights of Russians in Kazakstan (Dave 1995).

5 At the organization's Third Congress (8–9 April 1995) Iurii Skokov was elected chair of the governing body – the National Council – effectively taking over from the much younger and more radical Dmitrii Rogozin as the organization's leader and adding an established political figurehead to the Congress (Arkhangel'skaya 1995; Orttung 1995b). Skokov, a Yeltsin ally during the 1991 coup and member of the Presidential Security Council until forced out in May 1993, is a leading representative of the military-industrial complex (having headed the Russian Federation of Manufacturers after leaving government) and a strong critic of Chernomyrdin's economic policies (Arkhangel'skaya 1995; Belin 1995a). Sergei Glazev was also a defector from the Democratic Party. Until its split over the issue of whether to join the CRC's electoral bloc Glazev had been the chair of the Democratic Party of Russia faction in parliament as well as chair of the Duma's Economic Policy Committee.

6 The CRC reconstituted itself in May 1996 as the Russian People's Party and the leadership returned to the more radically nationalist Dmitrii Rogozin whose mandate to protect the Russian diaspora stems from his belief that Russia is constituted by the Russian nation not the borders of the Russian Federation. Potentially more significant is the loose cannon of Aleksandr Lebed'. Lebed', former Commander of the Russian Fourteenth Army in Moldova, effectively became king-maker in the run-off for the presidency between Yeltsin and Ziuganov in July 1996 after polling 14.5 per cent of the votes himself in the first round of voting. He was rapidly appointed to the position of Security Council Secretary on 18 June 1996 in return for which Yeltsin received his backing for the presidential run-off. However, he was equally rapidly dismissed following Yeltsin's victory but is intent on reforging his political career.

7 The three leftist parliamentary factions (the Communists, Popular Power and the Agrarians) hold a total of 221 seats, just short of an absolute majority.

8 Egor Stroev, newly appointed chair of the Federation Council – Russia's upper parliamentary chamber – was also a member of the National Council of the CRC.

9 This pressure often came from within; both Vice-President Aleksandr Rutskoi and presidential advisor Sergei Stankevich persistently took a line apparently closer to the rhetoric of parliament than that of the government (Kolstoe 1995: 271; Zevelev 1996: 276).

10 Although military involvement in Abkhaziia, Georgia and Chechnia is linked to this issue.

11 Details of these policy guidelines can be found in: 'Iz poslaniia Prezidenta Rossiiskoi Federatsii Federal'nomu Sobraniiu, 24 fevralia 1994 goda' 1994; 'Ukaz Prezidenta Rossiiskoi Federatsii "Ob osnovnikh napravleniiakh gosudarstvennoi politiki Rossiiskoi Federatsii v otnoshenii sootechestvennikov, prozhivaiushchikh za rubezhom"' 1994; Meek 1994; and Teague 1994.

12 Six such agreements have been concluded so far with Estonia, Latvia, Georgia, Tajikistan, Turkmenistan and Kyrgyzstan as has a widely applauded agreement with Kazakstan on a simplified procedure for obtaining citizenship for Russians in Kazakstan and Kazaks in the Russian Federation. However, although the Federal Council of Russia has ratified all these agreements, only Turkmenistan and Latvia have ratified them from the other side. In some cases the resistance is fundamental; Kazakstan, Uzbekistan and a number of other former republics deny altogether the existence of 'forced migration' from their countries (Regent 1996: 33).

13 The centrepiece of such agreements is the 'Agreement on aid to refugees and forced migrants' of September 1993 which makes the state of exit responsible for guaranteeing evacuation and safety of refugees and forced migrants from zones of armed and inter-ethnic conflict as well as for compensating them for housing and other property lost. The receiving country is obliged to provide help in locating temporary housing and work. Aid was to be financed via an inter-state fund. The effectiveness of the agreement has been hampered, however, by its delayed ratification and establishment of the fund to finance it.

14 Even in Kyrgyzstan, where President Akaev has, in principle, stated that he would not be against dual citizenship for the Russian population, realization is unlikely given that similar dual citizenship arrangements for the country's other ethnic minorities (such as the Uzbeks or Tajiks) would open border disputes with other post-Soviet neighbours (Rotar' 1994a).

15 Ten thousand million. Henceforth billion implies the American billion or Russian *milliard*.

16 Such a resettlement programme was announced at the beginning of June 1994 and envisaged resettling up to 11 million people from the former Soviet republics, returnees from the Far North and returning military service personnel in sparsely populated and economically underdeveloped regions of Russia.

17 This line is opposed in some government circles, however. Those informing the Ministry of Labour, for example, have suggested that in-migration presents no real threat to Russia's security (Trubin 1996).

18 Such presidential and government decrees set out the obligations of the migration service until the passing of key legislation on refugees and forced migrants in February 1993 (see Chapter 3) and six regions were instructed to make special provision for the reception of forced migrants and refugees.

19 Of these 1,805 are employed at immigration control posts.

20 See Chapter 3 for methodological details.

21 Quotations from this respondent are taken from handwritten notes of the interview since permission to record the interview was refused.

22 The list of thirty-two places best suited for compact settlement of refugees and forced migrants was included in the Russian long-term programme 'Migration' approved by the Russian government on 18 May 1992 and drawn up by the Ministry of Labour and State Economic Committee. It listed fourteen regions considered 'favourable' for concentrated settlements and a further eighteen which were 'relatively favourable' on grounds of the existence of land suitable

for housing and production, the need to preserve the existing ethnic unity of the local population and the avoidance of ecologically dangerous places, tourist resorts, protected zones, highly populated and socially tense areas.

23 According to the head of Ul'ianovsk TMS, Svaev, each district migration service is staffed by two people, but a number of employees talked about running the service on their own and the latter tallies more closely with Svaev's own total figure of thirty-three staff in Ul'ianovsk since there are twenty-two district branches in addition to the regional office.

24 It has been reported, however, that an agreement with the European Union has led to a promise on the part of the latter to finance training programmes for FMS staff (*Informatsionno-analiticheskii Biulleten'* 1995: 14).

25 It is important to note that priorities change over both time and space. District and regional migration service workers, for example, would identify their primary tasks as the simple registration of refugees and forced migrants (Objective 1) and the provision of whatever aid they could supply (Objectives 3 and 4). The FMS itself also periodically redefines its target priorities. In the most recent declaration, these were stated to be: the distribution of money allocated from the federal budget; the organization of reception and temporary settlement of refugees and forced migrants; helping forced migrants to find permanent new housing and the financial support of production enterprises created by and employing migrants; and the creation of more points of primary reception and centres of temporary settlement (Vynuzhdennie Pereselentsy v Rossii 1995: 5–6).

26 From 1 January 1994 forced migrants and refugees have been registered and dealt with separately although prior to that date they were handled together.

27 These cumulative totals run from the beginning of registration on 1 July 1992.

28 Another source suggested that in fact 43 (US) billion roubles was received (Lebedeva 1994).

29 The Russian Supreme Soviet allocated 100 million roubles for aid to refugees from Abkhaziia in the Sochi area (Schwartz 1993: 246) while regional governments under particular pressure such as Stavropol' allocated money for construction of housing for refugees and forced migrants in their areas (Baiduzhii 1993; Schwartz 1993: 246).

30 A second FMS source puts the sum received slightly higher – at 293 billion roubles, i.e. 54 per cent of allocation (*Informatsionno-analiticheskii Biulleten'* 1995: 16).

31 Totskii states that 169,000 of the 498,000 refugees and forced migrants registered by 1 January 1994 had been given one-off benefit payments (Totskii 1996: 38).

32 Kovalev has complained that it is common practice to demand payment by refugees and forced migrants for residence in temporary resettlement points including hotels and hostels directly against the demands of current legislation but made possible by the regulations on centres of temporary settlement drawn up by the FMS (Kovalev 1994: 3). He also notes that the practice of frequently moving refugees and forced migrants between places of temporary resettlement similarly contradicts their right to freedom of movement and choice of place of residence.

33 This loan is only available to forced migrants; although, prior to the 1993 legislation on forced migrants and refugees, it was available to refugees as well.

34 The figures for 1994 are cited as new flats constructed whereas the 1995 data are for housing constructed and/or purchased.

35 The 1995 amendments renew the clause saying forced migrants will be registered as unemployed regardless of how long they have been in the area.

36 What is meant by this is the absence of real state borders with the countries of the CIS which is seen to be allowing illegal migration from China, Vietnam, Africa and the Middle East into Russia.

37 Of these, seventeen are at international airports, five are at seaports and twenty-one at railway stations or on highways (*Informatsionno-analiticheskii Biulleten'* 1995: 10).

38 One of the founding members of the Civil Assistance Committee was veteran human rights campaigner Viacheslav Igrunov.

39 This is a thinly veiled criticism of the FMS which, CCARFM considers, is deliberately trying to deter forced migrants by a negative media campaign portraying the difficulties faced by migrants when they return to Russia.

40 This is the figure cited by CCARFM, other sources suggest that there are currently ninety-two compact settlements under construction (Kozlov 1994).

41 Lidiia Grafova attributes many of the problems between the FMS and CCARFM to a personal inability of Regent to forgive Grafova for her critical articles and, specifically, her 'exposure' of the use of money allocated for refugees on the instalment of a marble toilet in Regent's personal office (Grafova 1995a). For its part, the FMS rebuts criticisms of its ability to cooperate, claiming active cooperation with more than seventy social organizations dealing with problems of refugees and forced migrants.

42 There are four main refugee and forced-migrant projects in St Petersburg: a night shelter project for the homeless, a care centre mostly for Armenian refugee children, an Armenian community social assistance service, and the 'Refugee Committee' which functions largely at the political level (Schwarz 1995: 16–19).

43 Accession to the Geneva Convention is by no means supported by all Russian agencies. An official in the FMS was quoted as saying 'They (the Ministry for Foreign Affairs) want to look good to the west, without seeing that in Russia almost all of us live like refugees' (quoted from *Le Figaro*, 24 August 1993, in Slater 1994: 40).

44 An exception here is the Lawyers' Committee for Human Rights which has been conducting an active and constructive critique of Russian legislative practice in the field of refugees and forced migration.

45 The government tried to have written into the report of the CIS Conference on Refugees and Migrants in Geneva, May 1996, a paragraph stating that illegal migration from China, Vietnam, Africa and the Middle East was undermining Russian national security (Korkeakivi 1996).

46 As one commentator put it, the Russians left 'have nowhere and no one to go to and nothing to go on' (Panfilov 1994).

47 Those clauses most important to refugees and forced migrants themselves – on compensation for loss of property, cost of relocation and loss of earnings – are not implemented, while the obligation of the FMS to pursue such matters on behalf of forced migrants and refugees was removed by the 1995 legislative amendments.

48 This is explored more fully in Chapter 7.

5 Putting policy into practice

1 The full list of the twenty-five regions with the highest concentrations of forced migrants and refugees on 1 July 1995 is (in order of density): Stavropol' territory; North Osetiia; Orenburg region; Ingushetiia; Saratov region; Tatarstan; Voronezh region; Belgorod region; Rostov region; Samara region; Volgograd region; Krasnodar territory; Altai territory; Sverdlovsk region; Kemerovo region; Bashkortostan; Nizhegorod region; Novosibirsk region; Moscow; Ul'ianovsk region; Penza region; Cheliabinsk region; Kaluga region; Tambov region; and Lipetsk region (*Informatsionno-analiticheskii Biulleten'* 1995: 24). Together these regions hold more than 71 per cent of registered refugees and forced migrants.

2 This figure is made up of 20,000 Afghans, 6,000 Iraqis, 2,000 Somalis as well as Angolans, Ethiopians and Zairians.

3 Hysteria in the press focuses on illegal Chinese who are numbered at 50,000.

4 Despite the abolition of the residence permit (*propiska*), Moscow continued to employ the permit, citing the special situation of the capital city. As of 1 February 1996, however, the Moscow and Moscow region authorities no longer require residents to have a residence permit. Residents will still have to register with the authorities, though, and registration can be denied to people who do not have sufficient living space (the current norm is 18 sq metres per person) (Morvant 1996a).

5 He noted that Moscow needed 56 billion roubles to meet the needs of its refugee and forced-migrant population but had been allocated only 20 million that year.

6 The Moscow regional authorities have not declared themselves an 'exception' to normal rules for registration but the experience of one forced migrant from Uzbekistan reported in the press showed that policy was being implemented in such a way as to limit the number of forced migrants accepted (Tsykunov 1994). Only after taking her case to all the authorities possible and finally involving a central newspaper in publicizing her case did this forced migrant get the FMS to order the regional migration service to register her 'as an exception', as if normal laws did not apply to the region (ibid.).

7 There are currently 3,000 highly qualified specialists from the west, and more than 500,000 economic migrants from Ukraine, Belarus, Georgia, Vietnam and China, mostly working in construction, transport and retailing in the city.

8 Lebedeva suggests a different reason for the failure to remove the refugees, claiming that efforts by the Federal Migration Service to word the document in such a way that it would be impossible to implement its provisions were responsible (Lebedeva 1994).

9 Indeed, the high fees charged by the Moscow city government for foreign citizens wishing to reside in Moscow have now been extended to Moscow region.

10 Regions where refugees and forced migrants make up more than 1 per cent of the total population were considered to be potentially problematic (Vitkovskaia 1993: 47).

11 This decision came shortly after the renowned hard-line governor of Krasnodar territory, Nikolai Yegorov, was appointed as nationalities minister in the Russian government.

12 Luzhkov was re-elected as mayor of Moscow for a further four-year term with a majority of over 89 per cent.

13 Subsequently Yegorov was heavily defeated in regional elections for the post of governor in December 1996 and died suddenly in 1997.

14 To some extent Ul'ianovsk's policy reflects a wider and deeply conservative ideology which has cultural as well as political roots in the region (Omel'chenko 1994).

15 In fact by 1994 Ul'ianovsk was no longer distinguished by the lowest cost of living and even at the height of the 'Ul'ianovsk phenomenon' the cost of anything but those goods produced locally was generally higher than average Russian prices.

16 Of course, attitudes to the reception of forced migrants and refugees in Ul'ianovsk are not universally negative and head of the Federal Migration Service, Tat'iana Regent, actually singled out the city's university for its initiative in attracting migrants from Central Asia to posts within the university, thus helping to prevent the scattering and de-skilling of top-grade specialists (Karkavtsev 1993). Publicity has also been given to the administration's investment in developing infrastructure (roads, nursery schools, piped water and gas) in a village in the region selected for the resettlement of German migrants but subsequently financially abandoned by Moscow ('Dnevnik glavy administratsii oblasti' 1994).

17 Iudin was Yeltsin's representative in Orel region between 1993 and 1994 and, as such, Stroev's chief political opponent.

18 Given the tradition in Russia of individuals turning to newspapers to take up their complaints against the bureaucracy and help solve social problems (Lidiia Grafova's involvement in helping refugees and forced migrants is a classic example of this), this claim not to have come across the issue is surprising.

19 The Ul'ianovsk press appears particularly susceptible to the will of the local administration (Belin 1995c; Omel'chenko and Pilkington 1995).

20 This is possible because the migration commission has the right to decide whether to grant status on an individual basis for migrants from regions not automatically eligible for status.

21 These are the words of the head of the Ul'ianovsk Territorial Migration Service.

22 The head of the TMS in Ul'ianovsk justifies this policy by reference to both general and specific constraints on Ul'ianovsk, namely: the difficult housing situation; the inability of the region to 'clothe and shoe the whole of Russia from the local budget'; the high population density of the region; and the presence of a nuclear reactor in the region which prohibits the rise above a certain level of population density.

23 Those from Ukraine, Armenia or Belarus are not given status, nor is anyone who arrived before July 1992.

24 This figure is for all inward migration, not just refugees and forced migrants.

25 According to Stroev, nine districts of the region had made agreements with the FMS on the financing of unfinished housing in villages (Vachnadze 1995).

26 In 1992 3,588 people arrived and in 1993, 7,921. However, in the first nine months of 1994 only 3,066 moved into the region.

PART II SOCIAL AND CULTURAL ADAPTATION

Introduction: Into the field . . .

1 Interviewing focused on a particular housing complex in the heavily industrialized part of the city on the far side of the Volga River where refugee families from Baku had been rehoused, and on a number of hostels attached to the large automobile and aviation factories in which forced migrants lived. Networks of forced migrants from Dushanbe and of ethnic Tatars were also employed to access respondents.
2 As far as was possible key socio-demographic data (nationality, age, family status, education, profession, current employment, former place of residence, place of birth) were recorded. However, the use of interview as opposed to survey methods means that more data are 'missing' than would be desirable.
3 Of *registered* refugees and forced migrants in Ul'ianovsk 18 per cent had higher education and 32 per cent had secondary specialist education whereas among my respondents 41 per cent had higher education and 37 per cent had secondary specialist education. This reflects the contact with Ul'ianovsk State University which had employed a number of staff from the former republics. However, in Orel region education levels were, if anything, lower: 20 per cent of *registered* forced migrants and refugees had higher education and 33 per cent had secondary specialist education whereas among my respondents just 18 per cent had higher education and 36 per cent had secondary specialist education.
4 Unless otherwise stated data in charts are from the author's own study.

6 More push than pull?

1 Out-migration is particularly high from Kazakstan due to the return of migrants who had participated in the reclamation of the 'virgin lands' as part of the extensification of agricultural production under Khrushchev.
2 There are established, and working, agreements with Armenia, Belarus, Kazakstan, Kyrgyzstan, Tajikistan, Turkmenistan, Uzbekistan and Ukraine for those former Soviet citizens leaving the above countries and registering their residence in the Russian Federation to receive pensions in accordance with Russian pension legislation (Dolotin 1995).
3 Vitkovskaia found that 42 per cent of women compared to only 31 per cent of men surveyed cited such factors as the reason for migration or intended migration.
4 The high proportion of men among in-migrants – from Armenia, Azerbaijan and Tajikistan at least – might be attributed to the 'push factor' of evasion of military conscription and, thereby, of military conflict in these countries, as much as the 'pull' factor of economic opportunity in Russia, however.
5 It is quite normal for migrants to trust family members' information about migration more than, for example, migrant recruitment agencies (Fawcett 1989: 678). However, there is virtually no institutional information at all for migrants in the former Soviet Union.
6 It declined by a further 37 per cent during 1994 (*Informatsionno-analiticheskii Biulleten'* 1995: 21).

7 Significantly more nostalgia for return was shown by respondents in the Orel region than by those in Ul'ianovsk. This reflects the better living conditions and professional satisfaction for urban resettlers (see Chapter 7) and the fact that proportionately more respondents in Ul'ianovsk had directly experienced war or ethnic persecution in their former place of residence (primarily in Azerbaijan and Tajikistan).

8 It is worth noting here that the Russian migration regime encourages the permanence of migration since people may only be registered as forced migrants if the whole family has left the former republic as the presence of close family in the former place of residence suggests economic as opposed to political motivation.

9 It is interesting that the term used in Russian is the non-affective term 'population' rather than 'community'.

10 Indeed, Lebedeva's study of Russian communities in the Transcaucasus suggests that a critical mass of a particular ethnic group is central to successful settlement although the actual size of this settlement is dependent – she argues – upon the degree of cultural distance from the host nation (Lebedeva 1993).

11 See Chapter 1, note 16 for details of this survey.

12 This questionnaire was completed in interview format by Russian colleagues, Dr Natal'ia Kosmarskaia and Dr Tat'iana Sheikina and had been designed as part of ongoing research into migration between the former republics and Russia conducted by Natal'ia Kosmarskaia.

13 Respondents might have harboured suspicions about the researcher's identity for other reasons but there was no feedback to suggest a link with the state authorities. For a fuller discussion of this see Pilkington and Omel'chenko (1997).

14 There were thirty-six spontaneous references by respondents to the direct personal safety or survival of themselves or their immediate family. However, the nature of this perceived threat varied from direct persecution to a general fear that fighting would begin again, a tense situation and fear of going out at night or letting children out on their own. The latter were often for fear of criminals rather than ethnic persecution.

15 Vitkovskaia's study confirms that the Russian-speaking population felt ethnic relations had deteriorated particularly with local authorities and in public places (on public transport, in shops, schools and nurseries) (Vitkovskaia 1993: 99).

16 The precise status of Russian varies in each newly independent state but in all of the states from which my respondents had migrated Russian had been replaced as the official state language by the language of the titular nationality.

17 In Tajikistan and Uzbekistan the proportion of workers of titular nationality rose in academia from 20–30 per cent to 30–40 per cent, in health from 30–50 per cent to 50–65 per cent and in the state apparatus from 40–45 per cent to 50–60 per cent between 1977 and 1987 (Vitkovskaia 1993: 23).

18 This evidence is based on interviews with ethnic Kazaks and Russians in Almaty in April 1995.

19 'Push factors' were cited 204 times during 139 interviews while 'pull factors' were cited just 23 times. Indeed, among the latter were included statements of the kind that 'we had no alternative', or 'Russia was the only place to go' which are very weak pull factors indeed.

20 This holds true not only in the receiver but also the sender state. Thus, while the Kazak government continues to claim that Russians are leaving primarily for economic reasons, Russian community organizations claim that their sociological surveys suggest that 97 per cent of Russians would have stayed in Kazakstan if Russian had been acknowledged as the second state language (*Informatsionno-analiticheskii Biulleten'* 1995: 59).

21 This was subsequently implemented in December 1994 (Dmitriev 1996c).

22 The lower house of the Kazak parliament passed legislation on 22 November 1996 stipulating that ethnic Kazaks must know the state language by January 2001 while the Russian-speaking population had until January 2006 (Pannier 1996).

7 Surviving the drop

1 More accurately there has been a polarization of incomes creating a very rich upper stratum but keeping almost half the population around or below the poverty line.

2 Federal Migration Service data show that of those refugees and forced migrants registered in 1994 from the 'near abroad', 78 per cent had previously lived in towns and cities. However, on settling in Russia, only 64 per cent settled in towns while 36 per cent settled in rural areas (*Informatsionno-analiticheskii Biulleten'* 1995: 22).

3 Given the small-scale, qualitative nature of the study, however, relevant data from quantitative surveys and official statistics will be drawn on to support or qualify the findings.

4 The survey was conducted among 4,096 people (1,278 families) in the Altai and Stavropol' territories and Belgorod, Saratov, Kaluga, Novgorod, Pskov and Nizhegorod regions. The sample represents about 5 per cent of the total refugees and forced migrants registered by the middle of 1993. Unfortunately, no precise date for the survey is given, but it would have been conducted either at the end of 1993 or beginning of 1994.

5 The sample included only those refugees and forced migrants who had been resident in Russia for more than one year, thus it is not initial difficulties with employment which are being revealed.

6 The upper calculation of unemployment for the Russian population as a whole is 13.7 per cent; this includes the registered unemployed (the Russian government's favoured definition, which stood at 3.7 per cent in March 1996), those in the wider ILO definition (which includes all those not working, registered or not, and stands at 8.5 per cent), and those on involuntary leave and short time (Popova and Tekoniemi 1996: 34).

7 At the time of this survey – summer 1991 – the official unemployment rate was negligible.

8 In Moscow region and city the sample was 100 per cent refugees, 85 per cent of whom were Armenians. In contrast only 17 per cent of those surveyed in Orel region were refugees, among whom there were no Armenians and 72 per cent were Russian (Vitkovskaia 1993: 51–2).

9 This depends on whether you use figures for those having registered their claims to be unemployed (2.5 per cent) or those claims which have been accepted by the Federal Employment Service (1.2 per cent).

10 It should be noted here that the definition I used for 'unemployed' excluded such indicators of 'underemployment' as well as women on maternity leave or temporarily choosing not to seek waged work because it was not in their economic interests to do so.

11 The term 'de-skilling' is used here to describe a move into a job not commensurate with a respondent's qualifications and to which a lower social status is attached. It is thus distinguished from a 'sideways professional move' whereby social and professional status is retained although a significant change in occupation takes place.

12 One nurse was employed as a veterinary assistant, primarily giving injections to animals.

13 Vitkovskaia's study also finds that the proportion of respondents saying they were 'completely dissatisfied' with their work was highest in Orel region (where the sample was completely rural) and she links this to the fact that this region also had the highest proportion of respondents employed in work outside their professional area (Vitkovskaia 1993: 66).

14 It was said that one of the two main employers in the city (the aircraft builders Aviastar) simply no longer hired women at all.

15 I took this category to be those in the last ten years before retirement, thus aged 45–54 for women and 50–59 for men.

16 Of those aged 18–25 years, a third were unemployed.

17 The plaintiffs claimed that the reason it had failed was because the documentation was not available to consider the case; this documentation concerned the original financing of the house and the agreement with the occupiers, the only copies of which were held by the farm director.

18 Why women's self-esteem suffers more than men's from poor housing is explored in greater depth elsewhere (see Pilkington 1997).

19 One example which had caused much distress was the privatization of housing and building of new housing for private purchase or leasing.

20 Percentages are calculated based on eighty-three questionnaires in the Orel region and fifty-one interviews in Ul'ianovsk region.

21 Forced migrants were allowed to sign out (*vypisat'*) such essentials from the farm (at farm, not market, prices) for the initial period after their arrival.

22 Fridtjof Nansen was appointed in 1921 as the first League of Nations High Commissioner for Refugees (Widgren 1994: 43–8).

23 These are widely practised 'survival strategies' in contemporary Russia where according to Natal'ia Rimashevskaia 80 per cent of people have gardens or allotments on which they grow food and 80 per cent are involved in ancillary employment (Rimashevskaia 1996).

24 Marta Bruno found a similar gendered attitude to unemployment in her study of Moscow employees of foreign firms (Bruno 1996).

25 This individual had moved from Ukraine and while his self-definition as a forced migrant might be debatable, he was certainly a 'newcomer' (*priezhii*).

26 The Federal Migration Service survey found a much higher proportion indicating they wanted to stay put: 78.5 per cent of their sample wanted to stay in that region permanently (*Informatsionno-analiticheskii Biulleten'* 1995: 32). The difference probably reflects the higher proportion of my respondents being settled in rural areas.

8 'Us and them'

1 In Russian academic literature this is referred to as the 'psychological' problem of adaptation and is illustrated neatly by Efimova's finding from interviews with refugees and forced migrants in Ul'ianovsk that even among refugees who had solved their most pressing social-adaptation problems (who had received state housing), 25 per cent considered that they had 'lost everything' in the move. 'Loss' thus not only signifies material things but includes a wide spectrum of personal losses connected with involuntary migration (Efimova 1994).

2 In this study it was used by respondents from Abkhaziia, Armenians from Baku and a handful of people having left Tajikistan in very extreme circumstances.

3 This term was not used spontaneously by any interviewees in Ul'ianovsk, revealing its application to small communities usually only invaded by spouses from other nearby villages or towns.

4 They were present, although less common, in the talk of migrants in Orel region.

5 Other such identities were found among those from Shymkent, Sumgait, Semipalatinsk and Tashkent. Wider regional identities which identified 'us' as 'Asiatics' or 'Southerners' were also occasionally used to express the different cultural and climatic experiences and expectations of the migrants.

6 There is significant evidence, however, to suggest that this is an 'adopted' term taken from the media following the collapse of the Soviet Union.

7 During interviews it became clear that this term had almost no meaning for forced migrants and was used consistently only to differentiate the migrant community from local Russians.

8 Only those terms used by respondents in both Ul'ianovsk and Orel region are listed. In addition the following were mentioned by respondents in Orel region only: [they] help one another, settle disputes with knives, are divided into clans, put their family first, drink moderately, are very embittered, have respect for bread, have strict religious beliefs, are not clean or tidy. Ul'ianovsk respondents noted that 'they' were: sharp, crafty, stupid and fanatical.

9 Characteristics ascribed to 'there' by respondents in Orel region only included: greater respect for human rights, hard work was valued, people had large families, there was a richer culinary culture and a higher level of civilization. Characteristics mentioned only by Ul'ianovsk respondents included: easier social interaction, cleaner cities and air and more intelligentsia.

10 In addition the following characteristics were attributed by respondents in Orel region: people talk in the familiar (*na ty*), there is no rest or leisure time, feudal social relations prevail, there is a lack of culture, children are left unsupervised, everything is new/alien, there is 'nothing here', there is no respect for bread, the population is aged, wages are inadequate, 'nothing grows', there are no bath houses, there is no transport and things are thirty years behind. Ul'ianovsk respondents mentioned the following: people are inward looking, the standard of living is lower, there is widespread provincialism, people are competitive and flats are expensive.

11 In this instance the farm director.

12 There does appear to be a genuine gender difference here. Women respondents suggest that alcohol helps men integrate better into the new community since they find 'a common language' with locals over a bottle. However, some men

also expressed concern about the drinking culture of the village and admitted the difficulties in not succumbing to it (see Pilkington 1997).

13 Semi-structured interviews covered questions of: the impact of the arrival of refugees and forced migrants on the local community; the level of empathy with forced migrants; and sources of conflict or potential conflict between the two communities.

14 Interestingly, the root of this verb '*naekhat*'' is used widely in youth slang to mean 'to intimidate', 'to give grief', especially of harder subcultural groups who picked on others they perceived to be weaker than themselves.

15 Among non-Russians there were also reports of abusive remarks made about their actual nationality, especially by Armenian and Azerbaijani respondents, although also by Moldovan and Jewish respondents.

16 From a small study of refugees in the region, Ul'ianovsk social psychologist Olga Efimova found that 92 per cent of refugees were satisfied with life in Ul'ianovsk (Efimova 1994).

17 Methodological details of this survey are described in the introduction to Part II of the book.

18 It is, of course, possible that the positive picture which emerges is a result of the acceptable response factor. This is particularly the case with regard to the interviews taken with locals in one of the fieldwork bases in Orel region where it was clear from some of the responses that locals were keen to know if migrants had complained about their attitude to them and to refute any hostility. The survey data from Ul'ianovsk region are thus an important cross-check to these findings.

19 This put the issue at the bottom of respondents' priorities and it is unlikely that it would have been included spontaneously at all.

20 Rural respondents were more likely to have considered refugees and forced migrants to be a problem than urban respondents (20 per cent of rural and 13 per cent of city residents).

21 Local respondents are not identified for reasons of confidentiality.

22 The empathy of respondents with forced migrants is also evident in their response to questioning about what they would have done in the same position: 44 per cent said they would also have left the former republic either temporarily or for good while only 8 per cent answered that they would not have left under any circumstances.

23 Vitkovskaia also found that of her three survey bases, the highest proportion of migrants evaluating attitudes of the locals to them as 'unfriendly' was found in Orel region (Vitkovskaia 1993: 74).

24 The latest compact settlement to fall foul of the tax laws is the large settlement of KhOKO in Borisoglebsk, Voronezh region (see Chapter 3). Shved also reports that in Orel region accounts held by about a dozen migrant associations through the NGO Compatriots' Fund had been frozen as tax inspectors considered their activities (Shved 1996: 57).

25 The data showed that 62 per cent had lived in large cities, while there was no record of previous settlement for the remaining 12 per cent.

9 The 'other' Russians

1 Indeed, Vladimir Zhirinovskii himself grew up as a member of the Russian-speaking community in Kazakstan.

2   Such understandings of the origins of national identity focus on 'the sensitivity of human beings to the primordial facts of descent and territorial location' (Shils 1995: 100).

3   Percentages have been calculated on the basis of eighty-three questionnaires in four rural locations of Orel region. The findings are not accounted for by any 'hierarchy' of identification being activated since respondents were not restricted to one answer.

4   The notion of 'cultural hybridity' is advanced particularly in the work of Homi Bhabha and Stuart Hall. Both Bhabha and Hall dispute the totality and fixedness of 'national imagined communities' by considering the 'counter-narratives' of those who exist on the margins of nations and who disrupt or erase traditional national boundaries (Anthias and Yuval-Davis 1992: 38). Cultural hybridity suggests an identity which 'lives with and through, not despite difference' and construes national identity as a complex and constantly dynamic politics rather than an 'essence' (Hall 1990: 234).

5   In Russian the term '*rodina*' takes its root from the verb 'to be born' and thus literally means 'the place where one was born'.

6   The survey conducted among locals in Ul'ianovsk region found that even those who had not been uprooted were split on what constituted the 'native land' for Russian forced migrants. While the fact that they had not experienced the trauma of displacement meant that only 4 per cent thought forced migrants were deprived of a native land completely, the rest were split between imagining that native land to be where the forced migrants had lived the majority of their lives – 36 per cent – and where they were born – 32 per cent.

7   Russian romantic nationalism has traditionally seen the organic tie between tsar and people as the hallmark of Russianness and thus sees Russia as being bounded by the extent of the *Kulturnation* rather than politically functional state (Neumann 1996: 26, 39). Arguably this 'holy Rus'' retains a strong emotional allegiance among Russians today and is generally referred to as 'ethno-nationalism'.

10 Conclusion

1   This section draws on recommendations in published academic literature as well as observations by migration service workers and refugees and forced migrants themselves to outline areas of common concern and relevant policy recommendations.

2   The newly established system of Russian embassies in the former republics should have gone some way towards this. However, respondents interviewed in the summer and autumn of 1994 had received very little help from such institutions; one respondent (160) noted that there was a queue of 300 to 400 people to access the embassy in Tashkent, enough to deter anyone from seeking advice there.

3   A useful outline of the varied institutional and legislative provision for refugees and forced migrants in countries of the CIS and an overview of the participation of CIS states in multilateral and inter-state treaties relating to refugees and forced migrants is provided in Mukomel and Payin (1996).

4   For those born in Russia, the process might be quicker. One sympathetic passport office inspector in Ul'ianovsk said that she tried to clear such applications within a month.

5 For example, as current legislation and rights stand, in order to begin building a house you need a loan. However, to obtain a loan you must first obtain forced-migrant status. Forced-migrant status will only be granted when the whole family has moved to Russia, which means leaving the housing in the country of exit. The result is a crisis of temporary accommodation for the Russian government (Koshchueva 1994).

6 One migration service worker in Ul'ianovsk claimed there was only one telephone between six or seven staff in the regional migration service headquarters while the lack of computer equipment means that the majority of statistical and other information has to be transferred by regional migration services to Moscow by post.

Bibliography

ENGLISH LANGUAGE SOURCES

Abdulatipov, R. (1994) 'Russian minorities: The political dimension' in V. Shlapentokh, M. Sendich and E. Payin (eds) *The New Russian Diaspora: Russian Minorities in the Former Soviet Republics*, New York and London: M.E. Sharpe.

Anthias, F. and Yuval-Davis, N. (1992) *Racialized Boundaries*, London: Routledge.

Arkhangel'skaya, N. (1995) 'Congress of Russian Communities: General Lebed – False start or misalliance?', *Current Digest of the Post-Soviet Press*, 47, 15: 15.

Aukutsionek, S. and Kapelyushnikov, R. (1994) 'The Russian labor market in 1993', *RFE/RL Research Report*, 3, 29: 26–30.

Bater, J. (1996) *Russia and the Post-Soviet Scene*, London: Arnold.

Belin, L. (1995a) 'Congress of Russians living abroad opens in Moscow', *OMRI Daily Digest Part I*, 131, 7 July.

—— (1995b) 'Skokov denies rumours of his appointment as prime minister', *OMRI Daily Digest Part I*, 194, 5 October.

—— (1995c) 'Editors discuss problems of regional press', *OMRI Daily Digest Part I*, 237, 7 December.

—— (1996) 'Lebed addresses patriotic groups', *OMRI Daily Digest Part I*, 126, 28 June.

Belin, L. and Orttung, R. (1995) 'Parties proliferate on eve of elections', *Transition*, 22 September.

Bhabha, H. (1994a) *The Location of Culture*, London and New York: Routledge.

—— (1994b) 'Between identitites' (interview with Paul Thompson) in R. Benmayor and A. Skotnes *Migration and Identity*, International Yearbook of Oral History and Life Stories, Vol. III, Oxford: Oxford University Press.

Black, R. (1993) 'Geography and refugees: Current issues', in R. Black and V. Robinson (eds) *Geography and Refugees. Patterns and Processes of Change*, London and New York: Belhaven Press.

Black, R. and Robinson, V. (eds) (1993) *Geography and Refugees. Patterns and Processes of Change*, London and New York: Belhaven Press.

Boyd, M. (1989) 'Family and personal networks in international migration: Recent developments and new agendas', *International Migration Review*, 23, 3: 638–70.

Bremmer, I. (1994) 'The politics of ethnicity: Russians in the new Ukraine', *Europe–Asia Studies*, 46, 2: 261–83.

Bruno, M. (1996) 'Employment strategies and the formation of new identities in the service sector in Moscow', in H. Pilkington (ed.) *Gender, Generation and Identity in Contemporary Russia*, London and New York: Routledge.

Cherkasov, G. (1995) 'Coalition: Alliance of peoples of Russia created', *Current Digest of the Post-Soviet Press*, 47, 24: 15.

Chesnais, J.-C. (1992) 'By way of introduction', in Council of Europe, *People on the Move – New Migration Flows in Europe*, Strasbourg: Council of Europe Publishing and Documentation Service.

Chinn, J. and Kaiser, R. (1996) *Russians as the New Minority. Ethnicity and Nationalism in the Soviet Successor States*, Boulder and Oxford: Westview Press.

Chinyaeva, E. (1995) 'Russian emigres: Czechoslovak refugee policy and the development of the international refugee regime between the two world wars', *Journal of Refugee Studies*, 8, 2: 142–62.

Codagnone, C. (forthcoming) '"New" migrations in Russia in the 1990s', in H. Lutz and K. Koser (eds) *New Migration in Europe: Contradictions and Dilemmas*, London: Macmillan.

Council of Europe (1992) *People on the Move – New Migration Flows in Europe*, Strasbourg: Council of Europe Publishing and Documentation Service.

Dave, B. (1995) 'Duma expresses concern over Russians in Kazakhstan', *OMRI Daily Digest Part I*, 226, 20 November.

Demko, G., Zaionchkovskaya, Zh., Pontius, S. and Ioffe, G. (eds) (forthcoming) *Population under Duress. The Geodemography of Post-Soviet Russia*, Boulder: Westview Press.

Dmitriev, C. (1995a) 'Illegal migration threatens Russian security', *OMRI Daily Digest Part I*, 237, 12 October.

—— (1995b) 'Up to 5 million people expected to migrate to Russia', *OMRI Daily Digest Part I*, 232, 30 November.

—— (1996a) 'Federal migration service to build housing for refugees', *OMRI Daily Digest Part I*, 52, 13 March.

—— (1996b) 'New migration tests Russian immigration policy', *Transition*, 28 June: 56–7.

—— (1996c) 'Hostages of the (former) Soviet empire', *Transition*, 12 January: 18–21.

Dotsuk, E. (1993) 'Policy should be made while looking each other in the eye', *Current Digest of the Post-Soviet Press*, 45, 20: 25.

Dzhanashia, V. (1994) 'Patriots: Russian communities demand "state status for the nation"', *Current Digest of the Post-Soviet Press*, 46, 5: 8–9.

Fawcett, J. (1989) 'Networks, linkages, and migration systems', *International Migration Review*, 23, 3: 671–80.

Fielding, A. (1995) 'Migrations, institutions and politics: the evolution of European migration policies', in R. King (ed.) *The New Geography of European Migrations*, London and New York: Belhaven Press.

Gallagher, D. (1989) 'The evolution of the international refugee system', *International Migration Review*, 23, 3: 579–98.

Gannushkina, S. (1996a) 'Comments to "Some modifications and supplements to the law On Forced Migrants"', unpublished paper.

—— (1996b) 'Problems of migration in Russia', unpublished paper.

—— (1996c) 'Legal space of refugees today', unpublished paper.

Gatrell, P. (1996) '"A whole empire walking": Refugees in the Russian empire during the First World War', paper presented to the Soviet Industrialization Project Series, University of Birmingham, 11 December.

Goss, J. and Lindquist, B. (1995) 'Conceptualizing international labor migration: A structuration perspective', *International Migration Review*, 29, 2: 317–51.

Gostev, S. (1995) 'Gen. Lebed as a mirror of Russian evoluton', *Current Digest of the Post-Soviet Press*, 47, 32: 17.

Grafova, L. (1995d) 'Action programme' of CCARFM, unpublished document, Moscow 1995.

Grafova, L., Filipova, E. and Lebedeva, N. (1995) 'Compact settlement of forced migrants on the territory of Russia', unpublished report.

Grecic, V. (1993) 'Mass migration from Eastern Europe: A challenge to the west?' in R. King (ed.) *The New Geography of European Migrations*, London and New York: Belhaven Press.

Grosby, S. (1995) 'Territoriality: The transcendental, primordial feature of modern societies', *Nations and Nationalism*, 1, 2: 143–62.

Gudkov, L. (1994) 'The structure and character of migration of Russians from the former republics of the USSR', in V. Shlapentokh, M. Sendich, and E. Payin (eds) *The New Russian Diaspora: Russian Minorities in the Former Soviet Republics*, New York and London: M.E. Sharpe.

Gupta, A. and Ferguson, J. (1992) 'Beyond "culture": Space, identity, and the politics of difference', *Cultural Anthropology*, 7, 1: 6–23.

Gurak, D. and Caces, F. (1992) 'Migration networks and the shaping of migration systems' in M. Kritz, L. Lean Lim and H. Zlotnik (eds) *International Migration Systems. A Global Approach*, Oxford: Clarendon Press.

Gurushina, N. (1996) 'Moscow imposes limit on number of foreign workers', *OMRI Daily Digest Part I*, 119, 19 June.

Hall, S. (1990) 'Cultural identity and diaspora', in J. Rutherford (ed.) *Identity, Community, Culture, Difference*, London: Lawrence and Wishart.

Hamilton, K. (ed.) (1994) *Migration and the New Europe*, Washington: The Center for Strategic and International Studies.

Harris, C. (1993) 'The new Russian minorities: A statistical overview', *Post-Soviet Geography*, 34, 1: 1–27.

Helton, A. (1996) 'Lost oppportunities at the CIS Migration Conference, *Transition*, 28 June: 52–5.

Huysmans, J. (1995) 'Migrants as a security problem: Dangers of 'securitizing' societal issues', in R. Miles and D. Thranhardt (eds) *Migration and European Integration. The Dynamics of Inclusion and Exclusion*, London and Madison: Pinter Publishers and Fairleigh Dickinson University Press.

International Refugee Documentation Network Newsletter (1996), 17, 2–11 July.

Ivanov, N. (1993) 'The Ulyanovsk region: Own way in reform?', *Russian Business Monitor*, 6: 42–9.

Jessen-Petersen, S. (1994) 'International migration and security: A pragmatic response', in K. Hamilton (ed.) *Migration and the New Europe*, Washington: The Center for Strategic and International Studies.

Kamyshev, D. and Zhukov, M. (1995) 'Freedom of movement means a recognized need to restrict that freedom', *Current Digest of the Post-Soviet Press*, 47, 13: 15.

Karpov, M. (1994) 'Power: The duma and the RF foreign policy – It won't be very easy for Yeltsin and Kozyrev to continue their course', *Current Digest of the Post-Soviet Press*, 46, 3: 26.

King, R. (ed.) (1993) *The New Geography of European Migrations*, London and New York: Belhaven Press.

—— (ed.) (1995) *Mass Migration in Europe. The Legacy and the Future*, Chichester: John Wiley and Sons.

Kobishchanov, Iu. (1995) 'Who will be living in Russia in the twenty-first century?', *Current Digest of the Post-Soviet Press*, 47, 6: 1–3.

Kolstoe, P. (1995) *Russians in the Former Soviet Republics*, London: C. Hurst and Co.

Korkeakivi, A. (1996) *Commitments without Compliance. Refugees in the Russian Federation*, report of the Lawyers Committee for Human Rights, New York, May.

Kosmarskaya, N. (1995) 'Women and ethnicity in present-day Russia: Thoughts on a given theme', in N. Yuval-Davis, H. Lutz and A. Phoenix (eds) *Crossfires: Nationalism, Racism and Gender in Europe*, London: Pluto Press.

Kozyrev, A. (1994) 'Not partisan but national interests – They are what should unite diplomats and parliamentarians', *Current Digest of the Post-Soviet Press*, 46, 6: 4–5.

'Kozyrev favors military presence in neighboring states' (1994) *Current Digest of the Post-Soviet Press*, 46, 3: 26–7.

Krasnikov, E. (1994) 'Russian communities want to create a political organization', *Current Digest of the Post-Soviet Press*, 46, 5: 8.

Kritz, M. and Zlotnik, H. (1992) 'Global interactions: Migration systems, processes, and policies', in M. Kritz, L. Lean Lim and H. Zlotnik (eds) *International Migration Systems. A Global Approach*, Oxford: Clarendon Press.

Kritz, M., Lean Lim, L. and Zlotnik, H. (eds) (1992) *International Migration Systems. A Global Approach*, Oxford: Clarendon Press.

Kussbach, E. (1992) 'European challenge: East–west migration', *International Migration Review*, 26, 2: 646–67.

'Labour immigrants in Russia', (1996) *International Refugee Documentation Network*, 28, 11–21 September.

Layard, R., Blanchard, O., Dornbusch, R. and Krugman, P. (1992) *East–West Migration*, Cambridge, Mass.: The MIT Press.

'Lebed in the lead', (1995) *The Jamestown Foundation Monitor*, 1, 114, 12 October.

Lemon, A. (1995a) 'Refugee status reviewed in court', *OMRI Daily Digest Part I*, 143, 25 July.

—— (1995b) 'Labor ministry predicts migration trends', *OMRI Daily Digest Part I*, 159, 16 August.

Levin, T. (1994) 'Reimagining Central Asia', *New Formations*, 22: 13–23.

Lewis, R. and Rowland, R. (1979) *Population Redistribution in the USSR. Its Impact on Society 1897–1977*, New York: Praeger.

Livshin, S. (1991) 'Exiles in their own country', *Current Digest of the Soviet Press*, 43, 26: 6–7.

Markus, U. (1994) 'Immigrants in Ukraine', *RFE/RL Research Report*, 3, 26: 48–52.

Marnie, A. and Slater, W. (1993) 'Russia's refugees', *RFE/RL Research Report*, 2, 37, 17 September: 46–53.

Meek, J. (1994) 'Moscow draws up plans for huge migration of Russians', *Guardian*, 2 June: 11.

Melvin, N. (1994) *Forging the New Russian Nation*, discussion paper no. 50, London: Royal Institute of International Affairs.

—— (1995) *Russians beyond Russia's Borders*, London: Pinter/Royal Institute of International Affairs.
Mihalka, M. (1995) 'Yeltsin "alarmed" by status of Russian speakers', *OMRI Daily Digest Part I*, 106, 1 June.
Mikhailov, G. (1995) 'Initiative: Voronezh duma prepares law on immigration', *Current Digest of the Post-Soviet Press*, 47, 7: 16–17.
Miles, R. and Thranhardt, D. (eds) (1995) *Migration and European Integration. The Dynamics of Inclusion and Exclusion*, London and Madison: Pinter Publishers and Fairleigh Dickinson University Press.
Mitchneck, B. and Plane, D. (1995) 'Migration patterns during a period of political and economic shocks in the former Soviet Union: A case-study of Yaroslavl oblast', *The Professional Geographer*, 47, 1: 17–30.
Morozova, G. (1993) 'Current migratory phenomena. Refugees and emigrants', *Sociological Research*, 32, 2 (March–April): 86–96.
Morris, R. (1995) 'Migration problems within the CIS', unpublished paper, Fifth World Congress of Central and East European Studies, Warsaw.
Morvant, P. (1995) 'Migration trends', *OMRI Daily Digest Part I*, 183, 20 September.
—— (1996a) 'Changes to Moscow registration system mainly cosmetic', *OMRI Daily Digest Part I*, 8, 11 January.
—— (1996b) 'Kovalev quits human rights commission', *OMRI Daily Digest Part I*, 17, 24 January.
—— (1996c) 'Chairman of presidential human rights commission criticizes predecessor', *OMRI Daily Digest Part I*, 116, 14 June.
—— (1996d) 'Baltic Russians prefer Zyuganov; other ex-pats support Yeltsin', *OMRI Daily Digest Part I*, 118, 18 June.
—— (1996e) 'Police on the offensive in Moscow', *OMRI Daily Digest Part I*, 135, 15 July.
Mukomel, V. (1994) 'Demographic problems of Russian adaptation in the republics of the former Soviet Union', in V. Shlapentokh, M. Sendich and E. Payin (eds) *The New Russian Diaspora: Russian Minorities in the Former Soviet Republics*, New York and London: M.E. Sharpe.
—— (1995b) 'Some prefer the Soviet Union and some the Russian empire', *Current Digest of the Post-Soviet Press*, 47, 50: 13–14.
—— (1996) 'Forced migrants in the Commonwealth of Independent States', in J. Azrael and E. Payin (eds) *Cooperation and Conflict in the Former Soviet Union: Implications for Migration*, Santa Monica: RAND Center for Russian and Eurasian Studies/Centre for Ethnopolitical and Regional Research.
Mukomel, V. and Payin, E. (eds) (1996) *Refugees and Forced Resettlers in the CIS Countries*, Moscow: Complex Progress.
Neumann, I. (1996) *Russia and the Idea of Europe*, London and New York: Routledge.
'Nobody's a match for Lebed', (1995) *Current Digest of the Post-Soviet Press*, 47, 31: 15–16.
Oberg, S. and Boubnova, H. (1995) 'Ethnicity, nationality and migration in Eastern Europe', in R. King (ed.) *Mass Migration in Europe. The Legacy and the Future*, Chichester: John Wiley and Sons.
OECD (1995) *Trends in International Migration. Annual Report 1994*, Paris: OECD.
Omel'chenko, E. and Pilkington, H. (1995) 'Stabilization or stagnation? A regional

perspective', in P. Lentini (ed.) *Elections and Political Order in Russia*, Budapest: Central European University Press.

Open Society Institute (1995a) 'Former Soviet Union. Conference on migration', *Forced Migration Monitor*, 6.

—— (1995b) *Forced Migration Project Press Briefing*, Moscow, 20–21 July.

—— (1995c) 'Forced migrants: From policy to practice', *Forced Migration Monitor*, 7.

—— (1995d) 'Russian Federation Asylum Rule', *Forced Migration Monitor*, 8.

—— (1996a) 'Annual net migration rates per 1,000 inhabitants for Central Asia and other former Soviet states', *Forced Migration Monitor*, 10: 1.

—— (1996b) 'Update: The Russian Federation', *Forced Migration Monitor*, 10: 4.

—— (1996c) 'Displaced persons in Southern Russia', *Forced Migration Monitor*, 13: 1–3.

Orttung, R. (1995a) 'Yeltsin plans to demote Kovalev's commission', *OMRI Daily Digest Part I*, 148, 1 August.

—— (1995b) 'Lebed addresses Moscow Party Congress', *OMRI Daily Digest Part I*, 169, 30 August.

—— (1995c) 'St Petersburg DPR breaks with Glazev', *OMRI Daily Digest Part I*, 198, 11 October.

—— (1995d) 'Filatov warns of opposition victory', *OMRI Daily Digest Part I*, 202, 17 October.

—— (1995e) 'Lebed calls for military force to protect Russians abroad', *OMRI Daily Digest Part I*, 218, 8 November.

—— (1996) 'Federation council elect former politburo member as chairman', *OMRI Daily Digest Part I*, 17, 24 January.

Overbeek, H. (1995) 'Towards a new international migration regime: globalization, migration and the internationalization of the state', in R. Miles and D. Thranhardt (eds) *Migration and European Integration. The Dynamics of Inclusion and Exclusion*, London and Madison: Pinter Publishers and Fairleigh Dickinson University Press.

Owen, E. (1995a) 'Paying the high price of patriotism', *Moscow Tribune*, 12 July: 7.

—— (1995b) 'Russian migrants: No home, no future in sight', *Moscow Tribune*, 14 July: 6.

Pannier, B. (1996) 'Kazakstani lower house passes language law', *OMRI Daily Digest Part I*, 229, 26 November.

Parekh, B. (1994) 'Three theories of immigration', in S. Spencer (ed.) *Strangers and Citizens. A Positive Approach to Migrants and Refugees*, London: IPPR/Rivers Oram Press.

—— (1995a) 'The concept of national identity', *New Community*, 21, 2: 255–68

—— (1995b) 'Ethnocentricity of the nationalist discourse', *Nations and Nationalism*, 1, 1: 25–52.

Paretskaya, A. (1996) 'Duma approves new nationalities policy', *OMRI Daily Digest Part I*, 57, 20 March.

Parrish, S. (1995a) 'Kozyrev: Russians in Baltics still suffer discrimination, *OMRI Daily Digest Part I*, 115, 14 June.

—— (1995b) 'Russians abroad also turn out to vote', *OMRI Special Report: Russian Election Survey*, 15, 22 December.

Payin, E. (1994) 'The disintegration of the empire and the fate of the "imperial minority"', in V. Shlapentokh, M. Sendich and E. Payin (eds) *The New Russian*

Diaspora: Russian Minorities in the Former Soviet Republics, New York and London: M.E. Sharpe.

Pilkington, H. (1997) '"For the sake of the children . . ." Gender and migration in the former Soviet Union', in M. Buckley (ed.) *Post-Soviet Women: From the Baltics to Central Asia*, Cambridge: Cambridge University Press.

Popova, T. and Tekoniemi, M. (1996) 'Social consequences of economic reform in Russia', *Review of Economies in Transition*, 5: 27–52.

Rex, J. (1995) 'Ethnic identity and the nation state: The political sociology of multi-cultural societies', *Social Identities*, 1, 1: 21–34.

Richmond, A. (1988) 'Sociological theories of international migration: The case of refugees', *Current Sociology*, 36, 2: 7–25.

—— (1993) 'Reactive migration: Sociological perspectives on refugee movements', *Journal of Refugee Studies*, 6, 1: 7–24.

—— (1994) *Global Apartheid: Refugees, Racism and the New World Order*, Oxford: Oxford University Press.

Rotar', I. (1994a) 'Askar Akayev loves "NG" – And he's tolerant of criticism', *Current Digest of the Post-Soviet Press*, 46, 12: 23.

Rowland, R. (1993) 'Regional migration in the former Soviet Union during the 1980s: The resurgence of European regions', in R. King (ed.) *The New Geography of European Migrations*, London and New York: Belhaven Press.

Russian Economic Trends (1995) 4, 1.

Russian Independent Institute for Social and Nationality-based Problems (1994) 'Emi-graine, immi-graine, however you say it, it spells migraine', *Current Digest of the Post-Soviet Press*, 46, 20: 12–13.

Rutland, P. (1995) 'Russian border has "massive holes"', *OMRI Daily Digest Part I*, 232, 30 November.

—— (1996) 'Cold welcome for refugees', *OMRI Daily Digest Part I*, 66, 2 April.

Salt, J. (1989) 'A comparative overview of international trends and types, 1950–80', *International Migration Review*, 23, 3: 431–56.

—— (1992) 'Current and future international migration trends affecting Europe', in Council of Europe *People on the Move – New Migration Flows in Europe*, Strasbourg: Council of Europe Publishing and Documentation Service.

Schopflin, G. (1995) 'Nationhood, communism and state legitimation', *Nations and Nationalism*, 1, 1: 81–91.

Schwartz, L. (1993) 'Refugee flows and capacities for their accommodation', *Post-Soviet Geography*, 34, 4: 239–49.

Schwarz, T. (1995) 'Displaced persons in the Commonwealth of Independent States', research project at the Berlin Institute for Comparative Social Research, interim report, Berlin: Berlin Institute for Comparative Social Research.

Segbers, K. (1991) 'Migration and refugee movements from the USSR: Causes and prospects', *RFE/RL Report on the USSR*, 15 November: 6–14.

Shevtsova, L. (1992) 'Post-Soviet emigration today and tomorrow', *International Migration Review*, 26, 2: 241–57.

Shils, E. (1995) 'Nation, nationality, nationalism and civil society', *Nations and Nationalism*, 1, 1: 93–118.

Shlapentokh, V. (1989) *Public and Private Life of the Soviet People. Changing Values in Post-Stalin Russia*, Oxford: OUP.

Shlapentokh, V., Sendich, M. and Payin, E. (eds) (1994) *The New Russian Diaspora: Russian Minorities in the Former Soviet Republics*, New York and London: M.E. Sharpe.

Slater, W. (1994) 'The problem of immigration into Russia', *RFE/RL Research Report*, 3, 26: 39–44.

Smith, A. (1995) 'Gastronomy or geology? The role of nationalism in the reconstruction of nations', *Nations and Nationalism*, 1, 1: 3–23.

Susokolov, A. (1994) 'Russian refugees and migrants in Russia' in V. Shlapentokh, M. Sendich and E. Payin (eds) *The New Russian Diaspora: Russian Minorities in the Former Soviet Republics*, New York and London: M.E. Sharpe.

Teague, E. (1994) 'Plan for resettling Russian returnees', *RFE/RL Daily Report*, 104.

Trubin, V. (1996) 'Post-Soviet migration and ethno-political tension: The nature of their interaction', unpublished paper for INTAS seminar, Moscow, June.

Tunkin, G., Boguslavsky, M. and Gridin, V. (1985) *The Status of Foreigners in the USSR*, Moscow: Social Sciences Today.

Widgren, J. (1994) 'Shaping a multilateral response to future migrations', in K. Hamilton (ed.) *Migration and the New Europe*, Washington: The Center for Strategic and International Studies.

Zayonchkovskaya, Zh., Kocharyan, A. and Vitkovskaya, G. (1993) 'Forced migration and ethnic processes in the former Soviet Union', in R. Black and V. Robinson (eds) *Geography and Refugees. Patterns and Processes of Change*, London and New York: Belhaven Press.

Zevelev, I. (1996) 'Russia and the Russian diasporas', *Post-Soviet Affairs*, 12, 3: 265–84.

Zhukov, M. (1995) 'Second time around: You can live wherever you like', *Current Digest of the Post-Soviet Press*, 47, 17: 13–14.

RUSSIAN LANGUAGE SOURCES

Airapetova, N. (1996) 'Migratsiia ne dolzhna byt' begstvom', *Nezavisimaia Gazeta*, 2 April.

Anatol'ev, A. (1993) 'Prisutstvie bezhentsev nezhelatel'no', *Nezavisimaia Gazeta*, 29 April: 1.

Bai, E. (1994) 'Moskva razrabotala programmu zashchitu 30 millionov russkikh v blizhnem zarubezh'e', *Izvestiia*, 17 February: 1.

Baiduzhii, A. (1993) 'Anatolii Illarionov: "Gosudarstvo ne v sostoianii obespechit' zhil'em vsekh bezhentsev"', *Nezavisimaia Gazeta*, 5 October: 6.

Belgorodskaia, G. (1993) 'Migratsionnaia stikhiia v Rossii. Kak eiu upravliat'?', *Literaturnaia Gazeta*, 28 July: 11.

Belozertsev, S. (1994) 'Migranty znaiut, chto u nas vse kak u vsekh', *Grad Simbirsk*, 5–11 November: 4.

Blotskii, O. (1993) '"Begi mankurt, begi!"', *Literaturnaia Gazeta*, 28 July (no.30): 11.

Boikov, V. (1993) 'Nekotorie sotsial'nie posledstviia vynuzhdennoi migratsii' in Zh. Toshchenko and E. Levanov (eds) *Vynuzhdennaia Migratsiia: Prichiny, Sostoiane, Perspektivy, Migratsionnaia Politika*, Informatsionnii Biulleten' 'Politicheskaia Sotsiologiia' 3 (10), Moskva: Luch.

Boikov, V. and Levanov, E. (1993a) 'Printsipy i napravleniia migratsionnoi politiki' in Zh.Toshchenko and E. Levanov (eds) *Vynuzhdennaia Migratsiia: Prichiny, Sostoianie, Perspektivy, Migratsionnaia Politika*, Informatsionnii Biulleten' 'Politicheskaia Sotsiologiia', 3 (10), Moskva: Luch.

—— (1993b) 'Problema vynuzhdennoi migratsii: Sotsial'nie posledstviia i nekotorie puti resheniia', in *Obozrevatel': Rossiia: Problemy Natsional'nogosudarstvennoi Politiki*, Moskva: RAU Korporatsiia, 43–7.

Burkin, N. (1993) 'Ul'ianovskaia oblast': sotsial'noe partnerstvo radi cheloveka', *Chelovek i Trud*, 8: 35–7.

Chelnokov, A. (1994) '"Bezhenka? Nu i chto?" Russkie iz Sukhumi stali izgoiami v Rossii', *Izvestiia*, 16 June: 4.

Cherviakov, V., Shapiro, V., and Sheregi, F. (1991) *Mezhnatsional'nie Konflikty i Problemy Bezhentsev*, Moskva: AN SSSR Institut Sotsiologii.

Denisenko, E. (1994) 'Russkie v preddverii "chasa pik"', *Nezavisimaia Gazeta*, 16 June.

'Dnevnik glavy administratsii oblasti', (1994) *Narodnaia Gazeta*, 18 October: 1.

Dolotin, B. (1995) 'Pensiia dlia bezhentsa', *Pereselenchskaia Gazeta*, 1 (October): 5, 7.

Efimova, O. (1994) 'K probleme adaptatsii migrantov v provintsii', in V. Shkuratov (chief ed.) *Provintsial'naia Mental 'nost' Rossii v Proshlom i Nastoiashchem*, Samara: SamGPI.

Fadin, A. (1994) 'Post-SSSR kak rossiiskie Sudety', *Obshchaia Gazeta*, 14–20 October.

'Federal'naia migratsionnaia programma' (1996) *Rossiiskaia Gazeta*, 20 August: 4–8.

Gannushkina, S. (1996d) 'Somneniia vsegda v pol'zu bezhentsa', *Iuridicheskii Vestnik*, 6.

Glushko, S. (1996) 'Tat'iana Regent: "Ia zhivu mezhdu Chechnei i Minfinom"', *Rossiiskie Vesti*, 14 September: 3.

Goskomstat (1995) *Demograficheskii Ezhegodnik Rossii*, Moskva: Goskomstat.

Grafova, L. (1993) '"Molites' za nas!"', *Literaturnaia Gazeta*, 24 March: 12.

—— (1995a) Interview conducted by author, 19 July, Moscow.

—— (1995b) 'Vernulis' na rodinu, a rodiny net', *Literaturnaia Gazeta*, 5 April.

—— (1995c) 'Melkii intsident na granitse', *Literaturnaia Gazeta*, 19 July.

—— (1996) 'Gosudarstvennii reket', *Izvestiia*, 26 June.

Grudinina, I. (1994) 'V Latvii gordiatsia svoim zakonom o grazhdanstve', *Segodnia*, 25 August.

Iakovleva, E. (1994) 'Politicheskaia demonstratsiia v Orle: shchedrost' Chernomyrdina i Zaveriukhi potianula na 2.3 trilliona rublei', *Izvestiia*, 27 January: 1.

Informatsionno-analiticheskii Biulleten' (1995) 7, Moskva: FMS.

Ispolkom foruma pereselencheskikh organizatsii (1996) *Massovoe obshchestvennoe dvizhenie 'Forum pereselencheskikh organizatsii'*, Moskva-Saratov: Koordinatsionnii Sovet pomoshchi bezhentsam i vynuzhdennim pereseentsam/ Assotsiatsiia vynuzhdennikh pereselentsev 'Saratovskii istochnik'.

Iudin, N. (1995) 'Orlovskii eksperiment pokazyvaet, chto proiskhodit, kogda u vlasti kommunisty', *Izvestiia*, 8 December: 9.

'Iz poslaniia Prezidenta Rossiiskoi Federatsii Federal'nomu Sobraniiu, 24 fevralia 1994 goda' (1994) in A. Sokolov (ed.) *Kompas bezhentsa i vynuzhdennogo pereselentsa: Kratkii Spravochnik*, Moskva: Koordinatsionnii Sovet pomoshchi bezhentsam i vynuzhdennim pereselentsam.

Izvekov, V. (1994) 'Rastet migratsionnii potok', *Poisk* (Prilozhenie k 'Orlovskoi Pravde'), 30 July (7): 4.

Karkavtsev, V. (1993) 'Nuzhny li Rossii novie russkie', *Komsomol'skaia Pravda*, 4 June: 1–2.

Khutin, A. (1993) 'Novaia russkaia diaspora', *Obozrevatel': Rossiia: Problemy Natsional'no-gosudarstvennoi Politiki*, Moskva: Rai Korporatsiia, 48–52.

Kim, V. (1994) 'Propisany v Rechitse', *Orlovskaia Pravda*, 30.

Kolesnikova, I. (1994) 'Bezhentsy v Moskve chisliatsia bezrabotnimi lish' na bumage', *Izvestiia*, 4 February: 2.

Komitet po delam SNG i sviaziam s sootechestvennikami (1996) *Statisticheskie materialy po problemam migratsii*, unpublished materials for parliamentary debate, Moscow, 23 April.

Koordinatsionnii Sovet pomoshchi bezhentsam i vynuzhdenim pereselentsam (1995) 'Kompaktnie poseleniia vynuzhdennikh migrantov na territorii Rossii: Opisanie. Sravnitel'nii analiz. Vyvody. Rekomendatsii', unpublished report.

Koshchueva, A. (1994) 'Naperegonki k gosudarstvennomu koshel'ku', *Nezavisimaia Gazeta*, 1 June.

Kotov, V. (1994) 'Proshchanie slavian', *Izvestiia*, 26 October.

Kovalev, S. (1994) 'Massovie narusheniia prav cheloveka v Rossii vlasti khoteli by skryt' ot obshchestvennosti doklad Sergeia Kovaleva na etu temu', *Nezavisimaia Gazeta*, 22 July: 1, 3.

Kozlov, V. (1994) 'Nashi bezhentsy i pereselentsy', *Segodnia*, 13 October: 3.

League of Red Cross and Red Crescent Societies (1992) *Rabota s bezhentsami i Peremeshchennimi Litsami*, Moskva: Institut Problem Gumanizma i Miloserdiia.

Lebedeva, M. (1994) 'V Rossii uzhe 611220 bezhentsev. Skol'ko budet zavtra?', *Izvestiia*, 26 February: 2.

Lebedeva, N. (1993) *Sotsial'niai Psikhologiia Etnicheskikh Migratsii*, Moskva: RAN Institut Etnologii i Antropologii im. N.N. Miklukh-Maklaia.

Levanov, E. (1993) 'Perspektivy migratsionnikh protsessov, vyzvannikh obostreniem mezhnatsional'nikh otnoshenii. Rost natsional'nogo samosoznaniia kak prichina vynuzhdennoi migratsii', in Zh. Toshchenko and E. Levanov (eds) *Vynuzhdennaia Migratsiia: Prichiny, Sostoianie, Perspektivy, Migratsionnaia Politika*, Informatsionii Biulleten' 'Politicheskaia Sotsiologiia', 3 (10), Moskva: Luch.

'L'goty dlia pereselentsev' (1994) *Poisk* (supplement to *Orlovskaia Pravda*), 30 July: 4.

Michugina, A. and Rakhmaninova, M. (1996) 'Natsional'nii sostav migrantov v obmene naseleniem mezhdu rossiei i zarubezhnimi stranami', *Voprosy Statistiki*, 12: 44–8.

Migranian, A. (1994) 'Rossiia i blizhnee zarubezh'e: Vse prostranstvo byvshego SSSR iavliaetsia sferoi zhiznennikh interesov Rossii', *Nezavisimaia Gazeta*, 18 January.

'Migratsiia v Rossiiu: Problemy ostaiutsia' (1995) *Ekonomika i Zhizn'*, 21 (May): 44.

'Migratsionnii prirost uvelichilsia pochti v dva raza' (1995) *Delovoi Mir*, 18 April: 15.

Mlechin, L. (1994) ' . . . no russkomu men'shinstvu etim ne pomozhesh'', *Izvestiia*, 22 January: 4.

Mukomel', V. (1995a) Chief analyst of the Analytical Centre of the RF Presidential Apparatus. Interview conducted by author, 21 July, Moscow.

Nekrasova, M. (1994a) 'K voprosu o voprose', *Obshchaia Gazeta*, 17–23 June.

—— (1994b) ' . . . Eto – rodina moia?', *Obshchaia Gazeta*, 5–11 August.

'O bezhentsakh' (Zakon Rossiiskoi Federatsii) (1993) *Vedomosti S"ezda Narodnikh Deputatov RF i Verkhovnogo Soveta RF*, 12, (25 March), Moskva: Verkhovnii Sovet RF, 714–20.

Okulov, A. (1994) 'Bezhentsy i pereselentsy', *Posev*, 2: 8–17.

Omel'chenko, E. (1994) 'Ul'ianovskii fenomen i "sindrom provintsiala"', in V. Shkuratov (chief ed.) *Provintsial'naia Mental'nost' Rossii v Proshlom i Nastoiashchem*, Samara: SamGPI.

'O merakh po vvedeniiu immigratsionnogo kontrolia' (1993) Ukaz Prezidenta RF, 16 Dekabria, No.2145.

'O vnesenii izmeneniii i dopolnenii v zakon Rossiiskoi Federatsii "O vynuzhdennikh pereselentsakh"' (1995) *Sobranie Zakonodatel'stva*, 52, 25 December: 9317–27.

'O vynuzhdennikh pereselentsakh' (Zakon Rossiiskoi Federatsii) (1993) *Vedomosti S"ezda Narodnikh Deputatov RF i Verkhovnogo Soveta RF*, 12 (25 March), Moskva: Verkhovnii Sovet RF, 721–7.

Panfilov, O. (1994) 'Russkim ekhat' nekuda i ne na chto', *Nezavisimaia Gazeta*, 27 April: 3.

Parshutkin, V. (1994) 'O chem zhe dogovorilis' "dva mudrikh prezidenta"?', *Nezavisimaia Gazeta*, 27 August.

Pavlov, G. (1996) 'Edut rodnie – otkroite dver'!', *Literaturnaia Gazeta*, 16, 17 April: 10.

Pilkington, H. and Omel'chenko, E. (1997) '"Zachem mne vrat'?" Opyt primeneniia interviu k issledovaniiu russkoiazichnoi migratsii', *Rubezh. Al'manakh Sotsial'nikh Issledovanii*, March.

Poliakova, S. (1994) 'Dom, v kotorom my zhivem', *My i Vremia*, August–September: 5.

'Polozhenie o federal'noi migratsionnoi sluzhbe Rossii' (1994) Sovet Ministrov – Pravitel'stvo RF, 1 March.

'Poriadok predostavleniia vynuzhdennim pereselentsam dolgovremennoi besprotsentnoi vozvratnoi ssudy na stroitel'stvo ili pokupku zhil'ia' (1993) FMS Rossii, no.2341, 29 September.

Pravlenie Koordinatsionnogo Soveta (1995). Comments sent to T. Regent following preparational seminar prior to 1996 CIS meeting on refugees and forced migrants, 20 July.

Prikhodko, N. (1994) 'Russkikh shkol stanovitsia vse men'she', *Nezavisimaia Gazeta*, 21 June.

Regent, T. (1993) 'Tiazhelo nachinat' vse snachala . . . ', *Rossiiskie Vesti*, 86, 6 May: 2.

—— (1996) in *Forum Pereselencheskikh Organizatsii Rossii. Stenogramma i Dokumenty. Chast' II*, Moskva-Saratov: Koordinatsionnii Sovet pomoshchi bezhentsam i vynuzhdennim pereselentsam/Assotsiatsiia vynuzhdennikh pereselentsev 'Saratovskii istochnik'.

Rimashevskaia, N. (1996) 'Sotsial'nie posledstviia reforma v Rossii', talk at Current Affairs Seminar, Centre for Russian and East European Studies, University of Birmingham, 9 October.

Rotar', I. (1993) 'Drugie russkie: O tragedii sredneaziatskikh emigrantov', *Nezavisimaia Gazeta*, 2 June: 3.

—— (1994b) 'Russkikh pereselentsev pytaiutsia ispol'zovat' kak politiecheskuiu silu', *Nezavisimaia Gazeta*, 7 June: 3.

Safarov, R. (1994) 'Reformator Solzhenitsyn i musul'manskii vopros', *Nezavisimaia Gazeta*, 26 August.

Savin, I. (1994) 'Natsional'noe stroitel'stvo v Kazakhstane: Metamorfozy etnicheskoi politiki', *Nezavisimaia Gazeta*, 8 April.

Sergeev, A. (1995) 'Nado otdelit' politicheskikh bezhentsev ot ekonomicheskikh', *Inostranets*, 18.

Shkuratov, V. (chief ed.) (1994) *Provintsial'naia Mental'nost' Rossii v Proshlom i Nastoiashchem*, Samara: SamGPI.

Shmyganovskii, V. (1994) 'Gastarbaitery v Rossii: Prishli, chtoby ostat'sia', *Izvestiia*, 18 June.

Shved, V. (1996) in *Forum Pereselencheskikh Organizatsii Rossii. Stenogramma i Dokumenty*. *Chast' I*, Moskva-Saratov: Koordinatsionnii Sovet pomoshchi bezhentsam i vynuzhdennim pereselentsam/Assotsiatsiia vynuzhdennikh pereselentsev 'Saratovskii istochnik'.

Sobranie Zakonodatel'stva (1995), no. 52, 25 December: 9317–27.

Sokolov, A. (ed.) (1994) *Kompas bezhentsa i vynuzhdennogo pereselentsa: Kratkii Spravochnik*, Moskva: Koordinatsionnii Soviet pomoshchi bezhentsam i vynuzhdennim pereselentsam.

——— (1995) 'K proektu federal'nogo zakona "O vnesenii izmenenii i dopolnenii v Zakon RF 'O vynuzhdennikh pereselentsakh'"', *Kompas*, 27 February.

Sootechestvenniki (1996) 'Rossiiskii fond pomoshchi bezhentsam "sootechestvenniki" i obshchinnoe obustroistvo bezhentsev i vynuzhdennikh pereselentsev', unpublished report for parliamentary debate, Moscow, April.

'Status bezhentsev v stolitse budut davat' lish' rodstvennikam moskvichei' (1996) *Moskovskii Komsomolets*, 27 March: 1.

Terekhov, V. (1994) 'Bezhentsy i emigranty: Kak predotvratit' katastrofu?', *Nezavisimaia Gazeta*, 12 January: 6.

Tishkov, V., Rotar', I., Tsilevich, B. (1994) 'Slaviane novogo zarubezh'ia', *Nezavisimaia Gazeta*, 20 January: 5.

Toshchenko, Zh. (1994) 'Potentsial'no opasnie tochki', *Nezavisimaia Gazeta*, 1 March: 5.

Toshchenko, Zh. and Levanov, E. (eds) (1993) *Vynuzhdennaia Migratsiia: Prichiny, Sostoianie, Perspektivy, Migratsionnaia Politika*, Informatsionnii Biulleten' 'Politicheskaia Sotsiologiia', 3 (10), Moskva: Luch.

Totskii, N. (1996) 'Organizatsionno-pravovie problemy migratsionnoi sluzhby Rossii', *Gosudarstvo i Pravo*, 2: 35–43.

Tsykunov, I. (1994) 'Pereselentsy "v poriadke iskliucheniia"', *Obshchaia Gazeta*, 8–14 July.

'Ukaz Prezidenta Rossiiskoi Federatsii "Ob osnovnikh napravleniiakh gosudarstvennoi politiki Rossiiskoi Federatsii v otnoshenii sootechestvennikov, prozhivaiushchikh za rubezhom"' (1994) in A. Sokolov (ed.) *Kompas bezhentsa i vynuzhdennogo pereselentsa: Kratkii Spravochnik*, Moskva: Koordinatsionnii Sovet pomoshchi bezhentsam i vynuzhdenim pereselentsam.

Vachnadze, G. (1995) *Spravochnik oblastei, respublik, kraev i okrugov Rossiiskoi Federatsii*, Moskva: Kniga Ltd.

Vedomosti S"ezda Narodnikh Deputatov RF i Verkhovnogo Soveta RF (1993) no. 12, 25 March 1993, Moskva: Verkhovnii Soviet RF.

Veretennikov, A. (1994) 'Kogda starshii brat stal mladshim', *Novaia Ezhednevnaia Gazeta*, 4 August.

Vishnevskii, A. (1994) 'Neizbezhno li vozvrashchenie?', *Znamia*, 1: 177–87.

Vitkovskaia, G. (1993) *Vynuzhdennaia Migratsiia: Problemy i Perspektivy*, Moscow: Institut Narodnokhoziaistvennogo Prognozirovaniia, RAN.

——— (1995) 'Puteshestvennitsy ponevole: U zhenshchin "chemodannoe nastroenie" voznikaet chashche, chem u muzhchin', *Rossiiskoe Obozrenie*, 9, 1 March: 5.

Vladimirov, K. (1994) 'Nu net v Moskve sitsiliiskoi mafii!', *Rossiiskaia Gazeta*, 23 July: 2.

Vynuzhdennie Pereselentsy v Rossii (1995) Statisticheskii Biulleten', 5, Moskva: FMS.

Zhdakaev, S. (1994) 'Za 101-m kilometrom nachinaetsia zona osobikh interesov Rossii', *Izvestiia*, 19 February: 5.

Ziat'kov, N. (1994) 'Na Orlovshchine paniki net', *Argumenty i Fakty*, 3.

Index

Note: places referred to are *destinations* for migrants, unless otherwise specified. *Migrants, forced migrants* and *refugees* are implied throughout.